"This isn't just a richly detailed story about the hubris, corruption and incompetence that doomed Credit Suisse, it's a stark warning to all of us about what happens when we let bankers do what they like."

—Oliver Bullough, bestselling author of *Butler to the World*

"An eminently readable survey of Credit Suisse's tawdry history, and many of the industry's darker secrets."

—*The Telegraph*

"A riveting autopsy of Credit Suisse's dramatic downfall, Mavin's *Meltdown* expertly dissects decades of scandal and hubris. This meticulously researched exposé reveals how one of banking's titans gradually, then suddenly, crumbled under the weight of its own misdeeds."

—Bradley Hope, *New York Times* bestselling author of *Billion Dollar Whale* and *Blood and Oil*

"We're used by now to bankers behaving badly, yet Duncan Mavin takes it to another, shocking, anger-inducing level. Credit Suisse stood for propriety, but starting with the Holocaust and ending with the vast bank's sudden collapse, he shows this to be a total fabrication."

—Chris Blackhurst, bestselling author of *Too Big to Jail* and *The World's Biggest Cash Machine*

"*Meltdown* offers a gripping and meticulously researched account of Credit Suisse's downfall. Mavin uses vivid storytelling and deep insider knowledge to unravel the long history of scandal, hubris, and mismanagement that ultimately led to the bank's collapse. This financial thriller of a book offers a tantalising glimpse into the rot at the heart of one of the world's most powerful banks."

—Parmy Olson, bestselling author of *We Are Anonymous* and *Supremacy*

"A whistle-stop tour of Credit Suisse's litany of occasionally comical scandals. *Meltdown* is an excellent chronology."

—*Financial News*

# MELTDOWN

## GREED, SCANDAL, AND THE
## COLLAPSE OF CREDIT SUISSE

# DUNCAN MAVIN

PEGASUS BOOKS

NEW YORK LONDON

MELTDOWN

Pegasus Books, Ltd.
148 West 37th Street, 13th Floor
New York, NY 10018

ISBN: 978-1-63936-869-3

10 9 8 7 6 5 4 3 2

Printed in the United States of America
Distributed by Simon & Schuster
www.pegasusbooks.com

'How did you go bankrupt?' Bill asked.

'Two ways,' Mike said. 'Gradually and then suddenly.'

—Ernest Hemingway, Fiesta: The Sun Also Rises

# Contents

# Note on Sourcing

Piecing together a history of Credit Suisse was only possible with the guidance of those who knew the bank best. This book is based primarily on interviews with dozens of former executives of Credit Suisse, as well as reports, communications and other documentary evidence. Research for the book also involved interviews with regulators, politicians, investigators, lawyers and others whose work brought them into contact with the bank at various points in its history. Many of these sources spoke to me on condition of anonymity; for instance, because they were concerned that to be exposed would harm their future employment or standing in the industry. I'm grateful to each and every one of them for trusting me with their insight.

The book owes a great debt of gratitude to all the journalists who've worked to uncover the truth about this bank and others. I've leaned heavily on the extensive coverage of the bank in major global financial media and the Swiss domestic press. Where there were specific quotes, anecdotes or points of fact that had been unearthed by a specific journalist or publication, these are marked in the end notes. From time to time, parts of the book rely on extended biographies or works of history; these too are reflected in the notes.

The names of most banks in Switzerland changed through the course of their history, through acquisitions and mergers and other major corporate events. Credit Suisse is no different. For the sake of clarity, and to avoid messy detours into matters that don't seem all that relevant to the narrative, I've mostly referred to Credit Suisse and other banks by their most recent corporate moniker.

Some scenes described in this book are reconstructed based on information provided by a number of sources. In some cases, where there are different views, I've written a version of events that seems most plausible based on the weight of evidence. Where I came across conflicting accounts, I've tried to reflect this. I made extensive efforts to reach all the key characters in the book. Some didn't want to talk or didn't respond to my outreach. Others were more helpful. Just because someone is named in this book, readers shouldn't assume they were willing to help.

# Cast of Key Characters, in chronological order

*Alfred Escher, founder and chairman, Credit Suisse, 1856–77 and 1880–82*

Escher was nineteenth-century Switzerland's pre-eminent industrialist, politician and financier. He was also sometimes a controversial figure. In 1856, he founded Schweizerische Kreditanstalt, the forerunner to Credit Suisse, to help finance ambitious infrastructure projects that propelled Switzerland into the modern era.

*Rainer Gut, chairman, Credit Suisse, 1983–2000*

Gut was the bank's dominant leader throughout much of the late twentieth century. He rose to power in the aftermath of the Chiasso Affair and was the driving force behind Credit Suisse's push to become an international bank in the 1980s and 1990s.

*Allen Wheat, chief executive, CS First Boston, 1997–2001*

Wheat was the first high-profile American leader in the ranks. As the senior executive in charge of Credit Suisse First Boston, the firm's US investment-banking division, Wheat's strategy was to hire superstar bankers. It was an expensive experiment that sometimes pushed the bank to new heights, but often led to major bust-ups too.

*Lukas Mühlemann, CEO and chairman, Credit Suisse, 1997–2002*
Mühlemann was a former McKinsey consultant who held senior positions at Credit Suisse in a key period when the bank aimed to become a global player.

*Frank Quattrone, investment banker, CS First Boston, 1998–2003*
Quattrone was a working-class street fighter who carved out a lucrative niche serving clients in Silicon Valley during the tech boom of the late 1990s. At his peak, he reportedly earned more than $100 million a year. From 2003, Quattrone was one of the most high-profile executives caught up in lengthy legal disputes tied to the bursting of the dot.com bubble, though he was eventually cleared of wrongdoing.

*John Mack, co-CEO, Credit Suisse, 2003–4, and CEO, CS First Boston, 2001–4*
Mack was a Wall Street elder statesman, hired to bring some pizzazz and rigour to Credit Suisse's ambitions in the US. His tenure as CEO was marked by division between the American and Swiss parts of the bank.

*Oswald 'Ossie' Grübel, co-CEO, Credit Suisse, 2003–4, and CEO, Credit Suisse, 2004–7*
Grübel was a gruff, no-nonsense German trader with a keen eye for detail. Despite a directness that rubbed some Swiss executives the wrong way, he rose to the top of Credit Suisse and later went on to run UBS too.

*Brady Dougan, CEO, Credit Suisse, 2007–15*
Dougan was a quiet American who spent the majority of his career

at Credit Suisse, eventually rising to become CEO. He steered the bank through the financial crisis relatively unscathed, but his time in charge was also marked by a shift in banking regulation and the attitude of politicians toward large financial institutions.

*David Mathers, chief financial officer, Credit Suisse, 2010–22*
Mathers was a true survivor who was CFO under several of the bank's CEOs. Smart and diligent, he was sometimes accused of presenting the bank's numbers in an overly optimistic light.

*Urs Rohner, chairman, Credit Suisse, 2011–21*
Rohner was one of the longest-serving senior executives in the bank's recent history. As chief legal counsel, he missed out to rival Brady Dougan for the CEO role. When Rohner eventually became chairman, he oversaw Dougan's exit.

*Tidjane Thiam, CEO, Credit Suisse, 2015–20*
Thiam was charismatic, intellectual . . . and the ultimate outsider. As CEO, his plan was to cut costs, clean house and expand in Asia. He had few supporters in Zurich's close-knit financial establishment, and ultimately left the bank under a cloud, after an embarrassing scandal, like so many others before.

*Iqbal Khan, banker, Credit Suisse, 2013–19, and UBS, 2019–present*
Khan was an ambitious former auditor who ran the bank's wealth-management department. Seen by many as a potential CEO of the bank, his departure for bitter rival UBS set off one of the most bizarre scandals in Credit Suisse's long history.

*Patrice Lescaudron, banker, Credit Suisse, 2004–15*
Lescaudron, a French banker, served many of the bank's richest Eastern European clientele. He seemed like a dull accountant. In reality, he led a lavish lifestyle off the back of a years-long scheme to fleece his closest clients.

*Andrew Pearse, Tuna Bond banker, Credit Suisse, 2002–13*
Pearse was a high-flyer on Credit Suisse's emerging-markets desk, who had built a career lending billions to companies and governments in the developing world. He funnelled away millions of dollars after becoming involved in an elaborate plot involving Mozambiquan politicians and Gulf-based financiers.

*Thomas Gottstein, CEO, Credit Suisse, 2020–2*
Gottstein was the Swiss banking insider the board decided it needed to restore calm and credibility after a period of wild scandals. It turned out Gottstein, who also played golf for his country, was no more capable of keeping the bank out of the rough than his predecessors.

*Lara Warner, chief risk and compliance officer, Credit Suisse, 2019–21*
Warner, a dual Australian–US citizen was one of the most senior women in global banking. She was super-smart and charming too. She rose up the ranks at CS and was potentially destined for a role running one of the biggest banks in the world . . . until disaster struck. She was personally tagged in relation to both the Greensill and Archegos scandals, and ultimately lost her job because of it.

*Lex Greensill, founder, Greensill Capital, 2011–21*
Greensill, an Australian financier and entrepreneur, seemed like the ideal Credit Suisse client. But when his business collapsed amid yet another scandal, Credit Suisse's clients were left facing billions of dollars in losses.

*Bill Hwang, founder, Archegos Capital Management, 2013–21*
Sung Kook 'Bill' Hwang was a sharp-suited, super-intellectual hedge-fund manager. Credit Suisse went out of its way for Hwang's business, extending vast amounts of credit so that he could magnify his risky trades. When Hwang got it wrong, Credit Suisse lost $5.5 billion.

*António Horta-Osório, chairman, Credit Suisse, 2021–2*
Horta-Osório, a glamorous Portuguese banker, was hired from Lloyds to clean up Credit Suisse. He ruffled feathers and was ousted after he was found to have broken Covid-19 travel restrictions.

*Axel Lehmann, chairman, Credit Suisse, 2022–3*
Lehmann had spent years at UBS before decamping to Credit Suisse. He eventually became chairman, the bank's last, after Horta-Osório's surprise departure.

*Ulrich Körner, CEO, Credit Suisse, 2022–3*
Körner was the bank's mild-mannered, final CEO. Within weeks of Körner taking on the top job, a disastrous tweet sent Credit Suisse into a tailspin.

*Karin Keller-Sutter, finance minister, Switzerland, 2023–present*
Keller-Sutter landed in the Finance Ministry hotseat just as Credit Suisse's crisis deepened. Her job was to stop it becoming a global financial catastrophe.

*Colm Kelleher, chairman, UBS, 2022–present*
Kelleher was a titan of the global financial-services sector. He joined UBS after years in the trenches at Wall Street giant Morgan Stanley. When Credit Suisse began falling apart at the seams, Kelleher bailed out UBS's big rival.

*Sergio Ermotti, CEO, UBS, 2011–20 and 2023–present*
Ermotti was a charismatic banker from the Italian-speaking region of Switzerland. He took over at UBS following a costly rogue-trader scandal. He was credited with a radical overhaul of the bank. Though he retired in 2020, Ermotti returned after UBS acquired Credit Suisse in 2023.

# Prologue

Dixit Joshi was eager to get started at Credit Suisse. The new chief financial officer – a humble, well-liked actuary – had begun his career at the Swiss bank in London and New York in the 1990s, before moving to the UK's Barclays and then Germany's Deutsche Bank. His return to Swiss banking in October 2022 was a kind of homecoming and it should have been the pinnacle of his career. But in the years that Joshi had been away – almost two decades – Credit Suisse had endured a turbulent ride, and the bank's Zurich head office had witnessed one senior executive after another hastened out under the cloud of scandal.

Joshi was among a raft of new executives that landed in the space of just a few months, with a mission to get the bank back on track. There was a new chairman, Axel Lehmann, and a new chief executive officer, Ulrich 'Ueli' Körner. The bank also had a new chief risk officer and a new chief legal counsel. The head of the investment-banking division was new too, as was almost the entire senior media relations and corporate communications team.

This level of change in the executive ranks was rare at any bank, and it reflected the turmoil that had gripped Credit Suisse over the previous couple of years. The new leadership team was going to have to learn how to run the bank, clean it up and turn around its waning fortunes all at the same time. They'd have to quickly restore trust among clients, staff and the authorities that regulated the global financial system.

The urgency of their task persuaded Joshi to begin his new role early. While his family were still in London, he flew to Switzerland in the first week of October, a month or so before he was officially due to start. But he was already too late. The new CFO had barely said hello to his new colleagues when the bank was struck by another crisis – and, this time, it was potentially terminal.

Some of the executives only learned about the crisis because their kids told them that Credit Suisse was trending online. Suddenly, without warning, the bank was bleeding tens of billions of dollars, and clients were pulling their money out at lightning speed.

The trigger was a tweet by an Australian financial journalist, which simply said, 'Credible source tells me a major international investment bank is on the brink.' It didn't even mention Credit Suisse by name. But, within a few hours, the internet had decided that Credit Suisse was the bank in trouble. Social media in Asia and around the world amplified the message, panicking clients, who were switching their money into other banks at the touch of a button. The Swiss bank, which had stood for more than 160 years and whose offices spanned the globe, found itself the victim of the first-ever merciless digital bank run.

The novice crew of leaders, including Lehmann, Körner and Joshi, was perplexed. The technical data they had access to showed that the bank's balance sheet was healthy enough – at least, it had been before the Twitter storm. If the money kept flooding out, then it would become a kind of self-fulfilling death spiral. But how could you stop that?

As the bank's leaders stalled, customers continued withdrawing their funds – and the sense of panic intensified. Some of the new executives wanted to put out a statement affirming the bank was healthy and that clients' money was safe. Some thought the bank's top executives should go on television or radio to deliver a rebuttal to the digital carnage and restore confidence in the bank. Others felt that they would sound panicked and only make matters worse. Körner and Lehmann were both technocrats, intellectuals, planners and strategizers. They were smart and experienced, though neither was a natural spokesperson. Körner also said he was worried that any statement about the bank's numbers could be a breach of the rules governing ad hoc disclosures.

As CFO, Joshi was theoretically next in line – though there was no way the rookie executive could offer a convincing defence of a bank he'd only just joined. Maybe it would have been possible if he'd been with the bank for years, throughout all its recent difficulties, but he barely knew the way around the office. So, instead of speaking out, the new leaders at Credit Suisse were silent, as the meltdown gathered pace.

CREDIT SUISSE WAS one of the biggest banks in the world. It was one of only thirty firms designated as a 'Globally Systemically Important Bank' – meaning that authorities believed its failure could pose a threat to the entire international financial system. The bank was deeply embedded in the global economy. Its clients were billionaires and multinational corporations. It financed massive investments in infrastructure and provided loans to businesses and governments alike. It was too big to fail.

So how come it did just that?

The roots of its ruin stretched back decades. Credit Suisse didn't die in a day. Several themes played out across the bank's lifetime, each of which uniquely contributed to perhaps the biggest collapse in banking history.

First, the bank was a strange hybrid of American and European values. It had inherited the best and worst of both cultures, and its leaders faced a constant struggle to reconcile the two. Credit Suisse was both a hard-charging Wall Street bank, with traders and deal-makers driven by enormous bonuses, and a buttoned-up Swiss firm that serviced the financial needs of an international elite. And it was never top dog in either world, meaning that it was always striving, always taking on more risk to keep pace with competitors that were more singularly focused. The push and pull of these two cultures frequently threatened to tear the bank apart. The Swiss thought the Anglo-Saxons were gaudy, money-obsessed, egotistical and untrustworthy. The Americans and Brits thought the Swiss were aloof and constantly holding them back.

Second, throughout its history, the bank was subject to the hubris and ambition of a handful of men – and they were always men – each attempting to create and justify their own legacy. Often, this led to tension over pay and style. Frequently, it resulted in the bank whiplashing from one strategy to the next. With remarkable consistency, leaders were knifed in the back on their way out of the bank. And, with similar consistency, scandals that were sown when one man was in charge came to fruition during the reign of his successor.

It was certainly not the only bank guilty of bad conduct. Each of its rivals in New York, London, Paris, Frankfurt and Zurich has got into trouble. Most of them have been hit with billions of dollars in fines by exasperated regulators. And, in most cases, not much has changed. Bankers continue to behave badly. But Credit Suisse was the bank that most consistently courted trouble. At other firms, there were years when everything seemed to work as it should, whereas Credit Suisse's history reads like a long list of relentless wrongdoings.

Third, Credit Suisse flirted often with its biggest rival – and sometimes nemesis – UBS, the other giant Swiss-based bank. For decades, there were constant rumours the two would merge or that one would take over the other. Often, the rumours were based on truth, as clandestine meetings between chairmen and CEOs leaked into Zurich's gossip mill. The fate of the two banks were always intertwined and – as we'll come to see – ultimately, one had to win out over the other.

These themes come up time and time again, as does one overarching topic: trust. Banks depend on the trust of their customers, whose money fuels their business. They need to be trusted by their regulators and national and international authorities. They have to be able to trust their employees to act ethically. When this breaks down, when there's no more trust, there is no more bank. Credit Suisse usually had plenty of capital, but, in the end, it ran out of trust.

# PART ONE

## From Wealth We Came

# ONE

# A Child of Two Nations

The history of Credit Suisse is a tale of fortunes won and lost, of controversy and disagreement, of disputes and accusations. Sometimes, it's about profits and balance sheets and complex financial circuitry. But mostly it's about people, and it starts with the bank's trailblazing founder, Alfred Escher, the ambitious, flawed father of modern Switzerland.

Escher was born on 20 February 1819, the son of one of the most prominent dynasties in Zurich. Over the centuries, his ancestors had become rich, manufacturing and trading textiles – a business that flourished thanks to Switzerland's place at the crossroads of Europe. For hundreds of years, the Escher vom Glas family, as it was known originally, had also dominated Zurich's political scene as councillors, mayors and governors. The fortunes of the city and the family were intertwined. In the parlance of modern banking, the Eschers were systemically important.

But, from the late eighteenth century, the esteemed Escher name was tarnished by a series of moral and financial scandals. In the late 1780s, Alfred's grandfather, Hans Caspar Escher-Keller, lost a fortune speculating on financial instruments, like a modern-day rogue trader. When he was bankrupted, the whole of Zurich was brought to its knees and the family's reputation was mud.

Alfred's father, Heinrich, sought redemption – and riches – beyond Swiss borders. He studied in Paris and London, and travelled, crucially, to the nascent, freshly independent United States. There, he fell into step with a prominent Zurich-born French banker named Jean-Conrad Hottinguer. A master of finance and diplomacy, Hottinguer had wisely departed Paris during the Revolution in the early 1790s, heading to the US, where he built up a network of business and political contacts. Returning home in 1797, he became embroiled in the first major scandal of the US republic, the so-called 'X, Y, Z Affair', which erupted after French officials demanded American diplomats pay personal bribes to France's foreign minister.

Once the whiff of scandal passed, Hottinguer continued accumulating wealth and influence on both sides of the Atlantic. When he opened a banking office in the US, he turned to Heinrich Escher to run the business. There, Escher encountered exciting new ideas about liberty, trade and free markets, and rubbed shoulders with political giants like John Adams, George Washington and Thomas Jefferson.[1] Both men got rich financing projects and funnelling money between the old world and the new. Eventually, Hottinguer became a kind of founder of modern French banking, whose business legacy lasted into the twenty-first century, while Escher rebuilt his family fortune, speculating on US land deals and through trade in colonial goods such as coffee.[2] (In 2020, a study from the University of Zurich into the city's ties to slavery found that the Escher family had owned a coffee plantation in Cuba with more than eighty slaves.[3])

In 1814, Heinrich Escher returned to Zurich to get married and raise a family. A lingering bitterness over the losses incurred by his father decades earlier meant that Heinrich never reconciled with the city. He didn't repay the money his father had lost, and he declined to raise his family among the city's elites. Instead, he built a vast private estate by the lake, a few kilometres from the centre of civic life. This modern, secluded property, whose grounds were filled with exotic plants and trees from North America and beyond, later become one of Zurich's largest public parks. But, in the early 1800s, it was a kind of gilded cage on the lake, where Alfred Escher and his older sister were raised.

The boy was more closed off from Zurich society than many of his contemporaries. Tutored by Swiss academics and theologians, though under the influence of his cosmopolitan father, the young Escher was unmistakably old money, but he was also exposed to the ideas that were driving the ambitious, entrepreneurial animal spirits his father had profited from in the fast-growing independent United States. By the time Alfred Escher reached adulthood, these ideas were reshaping the world. In Switzerland – as in much of Europe – new ideas and new technologies were threatening to sweep old ways aside. Even as Escher emerged from his gilded cage, radical liberal reformers clashed with Catholic conservatives over Switzerland's future. As power swung this way and that, a short and relatively bloodless civil war saw the radicals take over, with plans to forge a cohesive, democratic Swiss nation.

Escher was a bright student who had taken a keen interest in all of this. He had studied law at the University of Zurich and spent time in Bonn and Berlin. He had also become involved in progressive student politics that urged the economic, industrial and democratic development of Switzerland. Driven by a kind of combination of patriotic loyalty to traditional Swiss values and a fervent belief in the possibilities of a more open, forward-thinking country, Escher was making moves in the country's political scene. He had grown up to be an imposing, confident workaholic with a baritone voice, whose arguments were robust and energetic. He became a rising star of radical liberal politics, with a command of detail, level of ambition and a diligence that were noted by contemporaries. At just twenty-five, he was elected to parliament, where he held a seat for the remainder of his life.

For sure, there was much work to be done. Switzerland was in danger of being left behind by its much larger neighbours on all sides. It was a small, landlocked, mountainous place, still mostly rural, and without any advantage in terms of raw materials. The country was like a 'half dilapidated barn that would have collapsed sooner or later' without a radical overhaul, according to the historian Joseph Jung.[4] The new Swiss government was far from unified about the way ahead. The politicians who dominated it were 'more of a family, or a movement like the US "Tea Party"', according to one history of Switzerland.[5] The left wing of the movement was obsessed with state-run modernization programmes and had the overt support of similarly radical political groups across Europe. Escher disavowed such notions. His view was that the future should be focused on free trade and the role of the private sector in promoting the development of Switzerland's future. This was an agenda he pushed tirelessly over the rest of his career, for good or bad.

Soon, Escher was becoming the dominant voice in Swiss politics. And one area of urgent attention was the construction of Switzerland's railway network. Other European nations had already undertaken vast building programmes, adding thousands of miles of railway, transforming them into modern, industrial economies where people, raw materials and finished goods could be moved large distances more swiftly than ever before. Switzerland lagged far, far behind, with only a few dozen miles of track laid. The extent of the Swiss railway network was just a tiny fraction of what was already in place in Germany, France and the UK.

This became Escher's great cause. He warned in parliament and in the Swiss press that the country risked becoming a forgotten backwater. Without new railways connecting the country to larger economies and trading supply lines, modernization would literally bypass Switzerland altogether. There was widespread support for Escher's view, but there was much more disagreement about how to pay for all of it. Centrist and leftist politicians supported a state construction pro- gramme funded by the government. They argued that something this important and costly couldn't be handed over to private enterprise that would become rich off the back of government largesse. But Escher had a different plan. It was best, Escher said, to 'let private activity go unhindered as long as it does not endanger the purpose of the state.'[6] His proclamation of free-market principles was a clear rejection of old European statism, and it echoed the philosophy that was driving the United States to become the most powerful economy in the world, eventually outshining much of sluggardly Europe.

It was Escher's view that won out. Within a few years, several new railway companies had sprung up – including one, Schweizerische Nordostbahn (or Swiss Northeastern Railway), founded by Escher himself. Soon, a massive track-building programme rolled across the country. Switzerland was quickly criss-crossed by railway lines that connected previously distant cities and towns and helped to deliver an industrial revolution in the second half of the century.

As this rapid development rolled out, Escher argued for more infrastructure to support his programme of industrialization and modernization. He pushed his political counterparts to develop a stronger education sector and he was a leading light in the founding of the federal technical university ETH Zurich, which produced a stream of engineers and other skilled workers. He also quickly real- ized there was a need for huge amounts of capital to fund this new Swiss economy. Initially, funding had been provided by foreign banks, but that left the Swiss railways and other industries vulnerable. The French banks in particular were demanding a say on strategy and the way the railway companies were run. This was intolerable to Escher. The interests of those banks and the interests of Switzerland were at odds, and something would have to be done about it.[7]

In 1856, Escher launched Schweizerische Kreditanstalt, a domestic bank that would lend money to fuel the growth of the railways. It was modelled on a French firm whose owners had become vastly wealthy. The bank issued shares and the people of Zurich lapped them up. Escher and his fellow founders sought an initial share capital of three million francs, but instead raised 221 million francs.[8] This early success spawned copycat financial institutions around the country, while the bank that started it all later became known as Credit Suisse.*

But not everything Escher touched was a success – far from it – and, while his reforms and ambitions had created many winners, there were losers too. The modernizing Swiss economy, open to the vagaries of the free market, began to swing more wildly than in the past. Inflation, unemployment and interest rates rose and fell sharply, and political opposition to Escher and his cohort grew. Under his watch, the bank took on greater and greater risk – and accumulated a series of losses on loans to fund failed enterprises. Many of the aggressive private railway companies that Escher had unleashed were mismanaged, missed budgets and collapsed. Escher's broad power also drew criticism. Some at the time called him by the nickname the 'Railway Baron' – an unsavoury allusion to his vast influence – while the Escher family home at Belvoir was sneered at by opponents as an unofficial federal palace.

In time, Escher was pushed from the centre of government, though his desire to be at the forefront of important decisions was undimmed. He became the leading campaigner for another expansive infrastructure project – a tunnel that would link the north and south of Europe through the Swiss mountains. This was the era of huge construction projects, such as the Suez and Panama Canals. The Swiss Gotthard Tunnel was a similarly ambitious, costly and difficult

---

* There were banks in Switzerland before Credit Suisse, but not on the same scale. It was truly the country's first modern-style bank. Though some long-lasting Italian and British banks especially predate the foundation of Credit Suisse, it nevertheless ranked as one of the oldest and most durable banks of the nineteenth and twentieth centuries. The biggest US banks were mostly launched around the same time as Credit Suisse.

undertaking. In 1871, Escher became president of the Gotthard Railway Company, which won the contract to build the tunnel. The company raised tens of millions of francs and construction began the following year. Almost immediately, Escher's firm ran into serious obstacles. The project was technically far more difficult than initially envisaged. Rockslides, accidents and gas leaks were frequent. Hundreds of workers were killed or injured. As the budget for the project escalated quickly, Escher sought ever more funding. But investors had lost faith in his powers. Escher was forced to resign.

Construction on the tunnel continued, though without Escher's involvement. When it opened in 1882, the Gotthard Tunnel was the longest on the planet – and arguably made the single biggest contribution to connecting Switzerland's economy to the outside world. It was an incredible feat of engineering and a huge achievement. Swiss dignitaries marked the moment when the two ends of the tunnel met with a triumphant ceremony. But Escher was not there. Instead, sickly and aged, and staying at a hotel in Paris, he received only a telegram notifying him of the momentous occasion.[9]

It was a fairly undignified end to Escher's career, and it was mirrored by a personal life also marked by tragedy. His wife Augusta had died young. One of his children died as a toddler. Another daughter survived Escher, though later killed herself. Escher himself died at sixty-three, essentially exiled from the centre of Swiss power.

Still, the Swiss people broadly held him in high regard. Contemporaries called him 'King Alfred', the 'King of Switzerland', the 'Tsar of Zurich'.[10] He was given what was effectively a state funeral, with the people of Zurich lining up to see his coffin carried through the streets.

A few years after his death, a bronze statue of Escher was erected outside the main train station in Zurich. Bearded, barrel-chested, the archetype of a nineteenth-century politician and industrialist, Escher still gazes down the sumptuous Bahnhofstrasse towards Paradeplatz, the heart of the city's financial district and the site of the headquarters of the bank he founded. But what would he make of the modern-day Credit Suisse? How does Escher's own complex story relate to the bank he founded?

There are several ways that Escher's biography echoes down the ages. He was the first in a long line of leaders whose personality and ambitions cast a shadow over the whole bank. He was a corporate dictator, a figurehead, strategist, politician and gambler who believed in his own exceptionalism. When decisions went against him, Escher proved inflexible, and crises often ensued. Though it was not a question at the time, later analysts disapproved of a political leader funnelling funding and directing policy to favour his own private enterprises.[11] Modern views on good corporate governance would frown upon such a clear conflict of interest. Perhaps there was something else too: Escher, in some ways, was the child of two nations, undeniably Swiss, a true patriot, but one whose ideas were shaped by American capitalism. At the bank he founded, these two forces also existed in tandem, never quite reconciled, frequently at odds, driving the bank on and tearing it apart, both at the same time.

# TWO

# Secrets and Lies

Alfred Escher's drive was what brought Credit Suisse into being, but another uniquely Swiss characteristic also shaped the bank. Neutrality was a Swiss survival technique. Enclosed on all sides by much larger nations, Switzerland had found that the best way to avoid becoming collateral damage in wars fought by other countries was to stay out of them altogether.* For Swiss banks, the flip side of neutrality was secrecy – a kind of amoral appeal to wealthy clients in neighbouring lands. In a volatile, unpredictable world, Switzerland provided a safe haven for anyone wanting to store their wealth away from the prying eyes of their enemies. It was a lucrative source of banking activity for the Swiss banks, and a controversial one too.

Some histories date the start of Swiss banking secrecy to the early eighteenth century, when the country was still a disaggregated collection of cantons at the crossroads of Europe. Others point out that the

---

* This had been Switzerland's position for hundreds of years, and it was formally confirmed by Europe's Great Powers when they drew up the rules of a post-Napoleon world at the Congress of Vienna in 1815.

idea was first loosely codified in Swiss constitutional and civil law from the mid nineteenth century, in the period when Escher and his cohort were building the foundations of the modern nation.[1] But it was undoubtedly in the first, tumultuous decades of the twentieth century that Swiss banking secrecy came to the fore.

During the Great War, the country's banks had become a go-to destination for those seeking to guard their wealth from the ravages of conflict. After the war, too, rising rates of taxation in Germany, France and elsewhere, to pay for reconstruction, fuelled the desire of wealthy individuals to funnel their money to Zurich, Basel and other Swiss cities.* Cash was flooding into Swiss bank vaults. By 1929, Switzerland had the largest bank deposit base per person of any country in the world.[2] But this flow of funds was a source of international friction and the trigger for the first great financial scandal in modern Swiss banking.

The episode began in Paris, which had become a playground for artists and writers in the decade after the First World War, a flourishing, cosmopolitan, global city. But that era was ending. The Great Depression was milder in France than elsewhere but nevertheless the economy slowed and discontent rose. By the early 1930s, left-leaning politicians were gaining influence. Rich Parisians were paranoid, and fearful of tax hikes, while the government was determined that wealthier citizens should not squirrel away their money to avoid paying their share. Authorities resolved to make sure those who helped the country's elite move their money abroad would be stopped. On Thursday, 27 October 1932, a police squad raided the Paris office of Basler Handelsbank, then one of the largest Swiss banks (which later merged into what became UBS).[3] Inside, they found a trove of documents that shed light on industrial-scale capital

---

* Some historians argue that Switzerland's neutrality, as well as the ease with which Swiss currency could be changed for French francs, Deutschmarks or sterling, were also drivers of cross-border funds into Swiss banks.

flight – the transfer of funds from France to Switzerland – much of it in the service of high-profile citizens. Further raids followed, and soon the French had composed a dossier of more than one thousand names – account holders at three suspect Swiss banks – including top politicians, generals, religious leaders, industrialists and media types. The amounts they had moved abroad were staggering. Perhaps two billion francs, equivalent to many tens of billions of euros today, had been syphoned off into Swiss bank accounts, hidden from the French tax collector.

French newspapers devoted dozens of column inches to the behaviour of their wealthy compatriots and their facilitators in the Swiss banking industry. Politicians in France erupted in anger and passed a resolution demanding the French government take 'all effective measures' to end what was seen as deliberate tax avoidance aided by Swiss banks. The issue escalated further when French authorities summoned two senior managers from Basler Handelsbank in Paris and requested access to all the bank's confidential books and records in Basel. When the managers refused, they were placed under arrest and imprisoned for two months.

In Switzerland, the tough tactics of the government in Paris were met with stiff opposition from financiers and politicians, and newspaper columnists decried 'banking espionage' and made patriotic appeals to bolster the country's banking secrecy traditions.[4]

Eventually, the affair settled down, in part because of a change in the French government, and because French clients temporarily withdrew their funds from Switzerland.[5] But the scandal had heightened a sense in Switzerland that banking secrecy was something worth fighting for.

Against this backdrop, the immediate trigger for a more defined set of banking secrecy laws occurred when one of the largest banks in Switzerland got into financial trouble. By the early 1930s, Swiss Volksbank had become the second-largest bank in the country. Hundreds of thousands of ordinary Swiss citizens had accounts there and many Swiss businesses relied on loans from the bank too. The bank, sometimes known as SVB,* had also been more aggressive than most of its rivals in expanding beyond Switzerland, especially in Germany. For a while, the strategy had bolstered profits, but when the Great Depression struck, SVB's international business was a problem. In particular, the bank was overexposed to clients in Germany, where the government was introducing strict banking rules to try to get a grip on the crisis. These measures left SVB facing massive losses. Soon, rumours began circulating in Zurich that a large Swiss bank was in trouble. Chaos ensued as nervous Swiss depositors scrambled to withdraw their money. The bank was heading for almost certain collapse, and the Swiss authorities faced a dilemma. If SVB went under, the impact on the entire domestic economy could be huge. But bailing out SVB would come at an enormous cost. It was clear that the bank would have to be restructured to avert disaster. When the Swiss government asked both Credit Suisse and a forerunner of UBS to help, neither was willing to participate in a bailout. Instead, in 1931 and again two years later, the government itself intervened to keep the bank, and the economy, afloat. In 1933 alone, the government's capital injection was equivalent to at least a quarter of the country's annual budget.[6]

Economic meltdown had been avoided, and the cost of government intervention was the demand from politicians for tighter regulation of the entire banking sector. However, when it came to writing the new rule book, the politicians left it to the experts, the bankers themselves, to navigate the fine detail.[†] The result of their efforts, the Swiss Federal Banking Act of 1934, included many new

---

* The irony that Swiss Volksbank was sometimes known as 'SVB', an early echo of the collapsed Silicon Valley Bank nine decades later and its impact on Credit Suisse, is not lost on the author.

† This pattern is repeated down the ages and across continents. When banks are bailed out following a crisis, politicians demand tough new regulations. All too frequently, those new rules are left to the bankers to determine, with

measures to tighten government control of the industry. It also beefed up the tradition of Swiss banking secrecy, making it a criminal offence to breach the confidentiality of clients. It was a historic twist. The new law meant that anyone seeking transparency from Swiss bankers – lawyers, regulators, tax authorities – would hit a brick wall. If bankers handed over information about their clients – names, addresses, the fact they were clients at all – they could end up in jail.* In practice, the lasting effect of SVB's collapse was to enshrine banking secrecy, a characteristic that was to the benefit of the banks at the expense of transparency and good governance. Indeed, over the coming decades, the secrecy laws became a veil for some of the worst wrongdoing at Swiss banks, and led to an amoral vision of banking that supported and covered up bad behaviour.

From this period on, in popular culture, Swiss bankers became synonymous with cold-bloodedness, hiding money for whomever, no questions asked. In reality, the Swiss banks lived up to their dark image too. Protected by banking secrecy, Credit Suisse, and many of its rivals, banked kleptocrats and dictators, brutal strongmen and corrupt officials.[7] For sure, Credit Suisse wasn't the only bank in

---

the result that they are watered down or include provisions that favour, rather than restrict, the banks.

* Swiss banks told a different, false version of the secrecy origin story for many years. This narrative said the rules aimed to help victims of the Nazis in Germany and the Fascists in Italy to hide their money safely. A report published by Credit Suisse in November 1966 said, 'It was . . . the intense espionage activity aimed at finding Jewish money that prompted Switzerland . . . to protect the persecuted by firming up the rules on banking secrecy, which had previously been a matter of custom rather than law . . . and to make infringement of banking secrecy a criminal act.' (Vogler, *Swiss Banking Secrecy*, 2006.) The falsehood was repeated elsewhere, as Gabriel Zucman explains in *The Hidden Wealth of Nations – The Scourge of Tax Havens*, 2015. Zucman writes that, 'In 1996, the *Economist* wrote that "many Swiss are proud of their banking secrecy law, because it . . . has admirable origins (it was passed in the 1930s to help persecuted Jews protect their savings)."'

Switzerland that took advantage, in nefarious ways, of the cover that secrecy laws provided. But it was frequently among the worst offenders. The bank hid funds from tax authorities, regulators and court officials. When these deeds were uncovered, the bank often sheltered behind its country's laws or pinned the blame on rogue employees. But the list of fraudsters and felons, and the frequency of misconduct, went on and on, spanning the globe, for years and years. This kind of activity was so common, it was more like a business model than a flaw in the system. And the fines and other punishments that stacked up against the bank were just a cost of doing the dirty work.[8]

# THREE

# The Chiasso Affair

One place that benefited greatly from Escher's Gotthard Tunnel and Switzerland's banking secrecy laws was the border town of Chiasso. Nestled just inside Switzerland, Chiasso was on an access route to the tunnel and it was one of the closest urban centres to a nearby Italian customs office. It was also a gateway for so-called black money funnelled into Switzerland, mostly from Italy.[1] Contemporaries said it was 'within suitcase-carrying distance' of the border.[2] Indeed, so much money passed through this small town that dozens of bank branches sprang up here and in the surrounding area.

Chiasso was also the centre of Credit Suisse's first major modern scandal, the location of an affair that cost the bank hundreds of millions of dollars, exposed a reckless culture that was repeated throughout the bank's history, and led to a change of leadership that would fundamentally alter the bank's trajectory for ever.

Ernst Kuhrmeier, the son of a former Credit Suisse employee, had become manager of the new Credit Suisse branch in Chiasso a few years after its opening in the late 1940s. By the 1970s, Kuhrmeier – a domineering, ill-tempered, German-speaking manager in a mostly

Italian-speaking region of Switzerland – had turned the branch into one of the highest performing offices in the entire Credit Suisse empire. Each member of staff in Chiasso generated on average three times as much profit as other Credit Suisse staff elsewhere in the organization. The source of all this income was Italy, where political and economic uncertainty was driving capital abroad – in this case, through the fifty or so kilometres of the Gotthard Tunnel. Often, Italian clients didn't even have to take the money there themselves – every Wednesday, for many years, Kuhrmeier sent one of his staff to Milan to receive currency from wealthy Italians in the private backroom of one of the local banks.

For Kuhrmeier, though, the riches this brought his way were not enough. He was frustrated by restrictions and bureaucracy imposed on his booming business by Credit Suisse's head office in Zurich; his profits were also limited by intense local competition, with banks fighting for clients; and his access to cross-border clientele was constrained by measures imposed by the Swiss government to curb inflows of foreign currency that was weighing on the Swiss franc.[3]

Kuhrmeier conjured a new plan that would supercharge his cross-border business. First, to attract more clients, his branch offered much higher interest rates than other banks. Because he was paying higher rates, Kuhrmeier also needed to generate a better return from depositors' funds. So, for the next step in his plan, he founded a holding company to invest clients' money. This holding company was set up as an *anstalt* – a kind of hybrid corporate entity that acts like a private trust and whose main benefit is murky ownership. Kuhrmeier's *anstalt* was named Texon Finanzanstalt and it was registered in Liechtenstein, a principality of just a few thousand people where business dealings were even more opaque than in Switzerland. He added an extra twist to persuade his Italian clients to part with their money: all customer funds deposited in Texon were guaranteed by Credit Suisse, which meant that they were super-safe – in theory, at least.

The problem was that this plan, including the bank guarantee, had not been cleared with Kuhrmeier's overlords in Zurich. In fact, as far as the bank was concerned, Texon was a completely separate legal entity, nothing to do with Credit Suisse at all.

Nevertheless, Kuhrmeier's plan soon started paying off as funds flooded into his bank branch, and he started investing the money in a vast empire of assets. Many of these investments, managed through Texon, were in Italy. One such company was Salumificio Milano, one of Italy's largest sausage and salami companies. The firm had been a client of the bank, but it got into financial trouble. When that happened, Texon gave the salami company a new loan to pay off its debts to Credit Suisse. When the company continued to struggle, Kuhrmeier doubled down, and eventually Texon became the salami business's largest shareholder. Kuhrmeier also directed significant chunks of Texon's investment into Italian vineyards. This started with a single loan to the widow of a Piedmontese winemaker, which was followed by more loans to major producers of Chianti and Valpolicella wines. Like the salami loans, these investments also soured. Kuhrmeier again doubled down, merging Texon's wine investments with its stake in the salami company, creating a food conglomerate run by an inexperienced Italian wine salesman, Alberto di Marchi. Under his direction, the conglomerate made further expensive investments in wineries and grocery businesses, until the company, now known as Winefood, became an enormous, bloated mess. Di Marchi continued spending deposits from the Chiasso bank. He bought a hotel in the spa town of Albano and an upmarket restaurant in Milan. He even opened a glitzy new hotel in Chiasso itself that targeted the rich clientele of Kuhrmeier's bank. So long as there was money in Texon, then Di Marchi would find a place to put it.

The Texon investments went on and on, seemingly in random directions that had little strategic meaning. Texon bought parcels of real estate, took a stake in an insolvent insurance business, acquired toy companies and dozens of small grocery-transport companies, as well as a car-parts business. It became a major investor in plastics, mostly through a Milan-based company called Ampaglas, acquired from a close friend of Kuhrmeier's. Another big Texon investment centred on the island of Albarella, a 3.5-km stretch of mostly scrubland to the south of the Venetian lagoon. Texon was to finance an exclusive new resort on the island – selling plots of land to investors who would pay a network of Chiasso-based companies to buy their own plots and build houses. When the project failed to get off the ground, Texon was left owning a selection of half-started infrastructure.

The problem with all of this was that, while some of these businesses were making a little money, many were far less successful. But that didn't matter to Kuhrmeier. So long as money kept pouring into his branch, and into the Texon *anstalt*, the whole affair would run smoothly. It was, in effect, a giant Ponzi scheme.

By the late 1970s, Texon had been running for almost two decades. Hundreds of millions of dollars in high-yielding customer deposits were theoretically matched by hundreds of millions of dollars in shady investments. And it was all mashed together in a kind of giant slush fund, with the veneer of credibility granted by Kuhrmeier's promise of a Credit Suisse guarantee to investors. Texon was a 'bank within a bank', but this was getting wildly out of hand.[4] There were even rumours of links to organized crime – which, in Italy, meant the mafia.[5]

Kuhrmeier, meanwhile, thought he was heading for greatness. He showered gifts on his colleagues – sending sumptuous hampers to fellow executives – and bought a luxurious house in one of Chiasso's most expensive suburbs, as well as a plot of land near Zurich, ahead of an anticipated promotion to head office. For years, his hubris went unpunished as Zurich failed to notice the simmering scandal, even though Texon was an increasingly open secret among Swiss bankers. A senior manager at UBS had lodged a whistle-blower complaint with Kuhrmeier's bosses. Tax officials had investigated the bank for anomalies in the branch's reported tax numbers. And a top-level UBS executive had warned his Credit Suisse counterpart to keep an eye on Kuhrmeier too.[6]

Credit Suisse's auditors had also visited the town to find out what was behind the stellar numbers Kuhrmeier was reporting to head office. Kuhrmeier, though, distracted the auditors, taking them first to visit an important client, then to a country restaurant for a heavy lunch washed down with local wine, followed not long after by dinner and more drinks at the Texon-owned Hotel Corso.[7]

It's possible the bank's control systems hadn't kept pace with its rapid growth, not just in Chiasso but internationally. According to the journalist Nicholas Faith, senior executives at Credit Suisse likely knew of Kuhrmeier's links to Texon, but tolerated it because of the money he was bringing in and because of the complexity of unravelling Texon's connections to Credit Suisse itself. The bank's chief inspector – its head internal auditor, named Joseph Muller – was conflicted because he was a friend of Kuhrmeier's and a personal client of the Chiasso bank.

From late 1976, though, everything changed. The Italian government, seeking to reverse the flow of funds out of the country, offered an amnesty to Italians who repatriated their lire. Kuhrmeier's Italian depositors began pulling their money out of his branch, which threatened to expose his whole shoddy scheme. Kuhrmeier was forced to liquidate the Texon investments to fund the client withdrawals. But the investments were worth far less than what depositors had been promised.

Around the same time, top executives in Zurich demanded further investigation of Chiasso, summoning Kuhrmeier to head office. Having turned a blind eye for fifteen years, the bank's top leaders suddenly discovered the extent of their involvement in Texon. They issued a press release explaining that the bank's internal auditors had found problems with an 'important foreign client' – a reference to Liechtenstein-registered Texon. Initially, the rumoured size of the problem was around 250 million francs, though that was later shown to be far too conservative.

Swiss prosecutors soon moved in. Kuhrmeier and two junior accomplices were questioned and then arrested. As details of the scheme emerged, the Chiasso prosecutor slammed Credit Suisse for its lax controls. The investigation became a national scandal that dragged on for two years, as headlines moved from the potential losses to the arrests, to, finally, in 1979, the court case. Kuhrmeier was eventually convicted and sentenced to four and a half years in prison – though he died of a heart attack a week after the sentencing. His chief assistant in Chiasso was also sentenced to three and a half years' jail time, while three Chiasso lawyers who had helped set up the scheme were each given suspended sentences.

By this stage, the size of the potential losses had ballooned to about $800 million – a huge sum for any bank anywhere in the world at the time, and equivalent to more than $3.5 billion today.[8] For a time, there were fears the affair could destroy the bank completely. Credit Suisse's two largest rivals, alongside the Swiss central bank, offered a billion-dollar bailout. But the bank declined and eventually the strain on its finances passed. It had survived.

In the 1970s, in the immediate aftermath, there wasn't much soul-searching at Credit Suisse. The main lesson that many Swiss financiers took away from it all was that the bank was strong enough to fend off the biggest of scandals. It was almost as though that was all that mattered. There was no shame, mostly just relief. This attitude was best exemplified by the headline on a German-language newspaper: 'Der Gigant kam nicht ins Zitern' – 'The Giant did not tremble'.[9]

But the Chiasso affair was significant for much more than the damage it did to Credit Suisse's balance sheet. It had shown up the bank's tendency to favour entrepreneurial spirit over strict controls. It had demonstrated that making profits sometimes overrode warnings about the behaviour of the bank's staff. And it had shown, very clearly, that flighty foreign money could leave the bank in a hurry – this was a lesson that the bank learned again, with far more devastating consequences, in October 2022.

The affair also brought global attention to the dangers of Swiss banking secrecy. 'The fact is,' wrote *The Washington Post*, 'nobody outside really knows where the huge amounts of capital that flow in and out of here originate. Some undoubtedly is from politicians and businessmen in countries where the future looks shaky . . . Some is from tax avoiders or evaders, some from criminal proceedings . . .'[10] The sentiment was echoed in media around the world. Swiss banks had been a cartoonish staple of Hollywood drama for years. The Chiasso affair confirmed the amoral nature of a large part of their business.

Perhaps most important of all, though, the affair led to a changing of the guard at Credit Suisse. The collapse of Texon had ended the careers of several of the bank's senior leaders. A slew of top executives were forced out for their failure to stop Kuhrmeier before his scheme got out of hand. That left the path open for one man to become CEO: an internationally focused, ambitious new leader named Rainer Gut.

# FOUR

# Gut Instincts

Rainer Gut was born in September 1932, in a village in central Switzerland. His roots were artisanal, miles away from the Zurich establishment – his grandparents had been soap makers, saddlers and seamstresses.[1] Gut's father, though, was ambitious for change and had forged a career at one of Switzerland's many smaller, regional banks. A series of promotions, inside Switzerland and abroad, culminated in his elevation to the top of the bank, and he led an expansion into other regions and sources of business.

His father's career presaged the path young Rainer would later take. As a child, though, Gut had been distracted by sports, art and music. In young adulthood, he toyed with becoming an artist himself, before abandoning this idea for a more practical pursuit. After studying in Paris and London, as well as in Zug, Switzerland, Gut followed his father into banking, starting out as a trainee at the same regional bank where his father had made his name. Early on, he also met and fell in love with a glamorous American, Josephine Lorenz – they went on to get married and have four children – and the pair moved to London in the mid-1950s. This was the beginning of a period when the City, London's financial heart, was re-establishing itself as a global banking capital following the war. Over the next decade, many foreign banks flocked to be a part of the City's rapid regrowth.

By the early 1960s, Gut was on the move again, to an even more exciting financial hub. He had joined Swiss Bank Corporation – a predecessor of UBS – and moved to the US, where he ran the bank's entire New York office.[2] Wall Street was already a buzzing banking centre, where financiers were inventing all sorts of innovative trades and transactions, and the entire culture of banking was supercharged with the promise of enormous fortunes to be made. Gut's Swiss bank was a relatively minor player, but the opportunity to learn a whole new banking language was everywhere.

At that time, SBC's position in the US was complicated because of its role in financing German industrial companies during the war. American prosecutors were going after many of these companies for their role in facilitating the war crimes of Nazi Germany, and SBC, like many others, was keen to distance itself from former clients tangled up in high-profile court trials. Gut, as the most senior SBC official in the US, played a key role as a liaison between his Swiss bosses and the Americans during their investigations. Yet, when the issues in the US were resolved, it was Gut's fellow executives in Switzerland who benefited most, promoted into more senior roles. Gut was left out in the cold.

In 1968, after seeing his colleagues richly rewarded, Gut jumped ship again.[3] This time, he became a partner in the New York investment bank Lazard Frères & Co., positioning himself close to the very top of global finance. Under the direction of Parisian banker André Meyer, Lazard had become one of the most successful and influential financial firms on Wall Street. Meyer, a keen art collector, was sometimes known as the 'Picasso of Banking', a reference to his modern tactics and dominant role in the industry. He had advised on the largest corporate transactions in the world, especially mergers and acquisitions and leveraged buyout deals, while Lazard's partners sat on the boards of mega-companies and took home multimillion-dollar compensation packages. This type of banking was a world away from the sleepy regional banks of Switzerland that focused mostly on managing customer deposits.

After a few years under Meyer's tutelage, Gut soon spied another, better opportunity. Top executives at Credit Suisse were eyeing a tentative foray into investment banking, as a way to open up a new source of revenue. But they had no idea how to go about it. Gut, Swiss-born but with global experience, was an obvious fit to lead the push. In fact, he may have been just about the only candidate with the right track record. In 1971, he was persuaded to join the Swiss bank, and became CEO of its US business. From a low starting point, he quickly drove the US division's results higher. Within a couple of years, he was appointed to the bank's executive board – the inner circle of senior officials who determined strategy and ran the entire operation.

If Gut's career had ended there, it would have been an impressive rise to the upper echelons of Swiss banking. He'd taken a circuitous route to the top table; it was perhaps the only way for someone from outside Zurich's financial establishment to get there. But his next step, to the very summit of Credit Suisse, was also in part a result of his not being from the centre of power. For, when the Chiasso affair exploded into the public domain, Gut was one of the few senior executives who could rightly claim to have had no oversight or blame for the scandal. As others were forced to step down or step aside, the path ahead cleared in Gut's favour. He was appointed as 'spokesman', in the parlance of Swiss governance at that time, effectively the chief executive officer.

This turned out to be a critical decision. Gut's vision of banking was not constrained by Swiss borders or the old ways of the country's banking industry.

His timely emergence also coincided with some handwringing

about the firm's strategic direction. The Swiss domestic banking market had long focused on managing money for wealthy individuals, Swiss or otherwise. The bank – and its main domestic rivals – had grown rapidly, in part because they were able to shuffle money through Swiss accounts around the world, and offered secrecy to those fleeing high taxes, economic uncertainty or who simply wanted to hide their money. They were famous for it. In 1964, the British politician George Brown had called Swiss bankers the 'gnomes of Zurich'.[4] But this market was becoming saturated and it was hard to keep profits growing – this was one factor behind the Chiasso affair, after all.

For Credit Suisse, the problem was particularly acute. Credit Suisse had started out as a commercial bank financing Swiss infrastructure. It then morphed into a private bank. Both these business lines were becoming exhausted. Domestically, Credit Suisse had fallen behind its two rivals, UBS and Swiss Bank Corp.* It was the third-biggest bank in Switzerland, with no obvious way to move further up the ladder. Another consequence of Chiasso was that the bank had been chastened and its reputation tarnished at home. It became the 'scandal bank' in the eyes of the Swiss public.[5] The affair had led to more banking regulations, including the demand that Credit Suisse should open no more branches in its home country.[6]

Meanwhile, a series of existential questions also lingered over the entire international banking industry. These issues included: the effect of the green shoots of globalization; the shifting fortunes of post-war global economies; technological advancements that were making banking much more international.

Gut decided that Credit Suisse would lean into these trends. His ambition was for the bank to end its reliance on simply managing money for rich people. Instead, he wanted to expand the bank's reach

---

* This dynamic only worsened when UBS and SBC merged in 1998, leaving Credit Suisse the second biggest bank, by a long way, in its home market.

within Switzerland and abroad. It would search out new clients and new businesses. It would aim big, striving to be a leading player in all areas of banking, wherever it took place around the world. Gut didn't just want to beat Credit Suisse's domestic rivals. He wanted to take on Wall Street too.

In some ways, this level of ambition seemed like a logical extension of the lessons Gut had learned from his father's career. It was also an echo of the achievements of André Meyer, Gut's old boss at Lazard. There are similarities here too with Alfred Escher – Gut was not primarily a politician, though he became an elder statesman, not just of Credit Suisse, but of the whole of Swiss industry. He played a prominent role in Swiss life beyond the bank, as a patron of the arts and sports, and as a board member at the country's most prominent companies. Perhaps in contrast to all this, he was a relatively publicity-shy leader. He rarely gave interviews – Swiss media complained he was more likely to talk to *The Wall Street Journal* than the press in his home country. Still, Gut's shadow loomed over the bank for five decades as CEO, then chairman and, finally, in an honorary role. In the end, Gut's stewardship of the bank was perhaps the most consequential period of its history, for it was his plan to grow Credit Suisse aggressively beyond Swiss borders that, ultimately, led to its demise.

# FIVE

# Shipping Up to Boston

In the latter years of the twentieth century, the global banking industry underwent a radical transformation. Though the biggest changes were in the US, few banks anywhere could avoid the impact, least of all Credit Suisse. Rainer Gut's bank had to get with the programme.

In the US, rules in place since the New Deal, which were aimed at protecting bank customers, were suddenly under threat. The Banking Act, which centralized authority with the Federal Reserve, and the Glass–Steagall Act, which separated mundane deposit-taking and lending from riskier investment banking, had provided a framework for the US banking system for decades. Though the system was piecemeal, fractured along regional lines and across business activities, few questioned this rule book, given the stability it brought to the banking industry. But that changed with the economic downturn of the 1970s, which sowed the seeds of discontent and disruption. Soon, banks were failing and deregulation was on the agenda. Over the following decades, US politicians gradually dialled back the Depression-era rules, unleashing more competition and innovation, and fostering a turbo-charged, though riskier, banking industry. Some US banks painfully fell by the wayside during this period, especially during the rolling 'savings and loans crisis' of the 1980s and early 1990s that saw more than a thousand financial firms fail. But others benefited, growing enormously from what had gone before. Smaller banks died off, while the share of assets held by just a handful of the biggest banks grew by more than 50 per cent.[1]

The coming years saw the creation of so-called 'universal banks' – giant financial-services companies that could perform pretty much any banking activity, anywhere, for any clients. The story of Citicorp and Travelers was a clear illustration of what could be achieved. From the mid-1980s, banker Sanford Weill cobbled together one of the US's fastest-growing financial conglomerates. The result was Travelers Group – an insurance and investment business put together from billions of dollars' worth of mergers and acquisitions in stockbroking, bond-trading, real estate and other related financial businesses. Then, in 1998, Weill shocked the financial world with the biggest deal yet – a $70-billion merger with US bank Citicorp. The largest corporate combination ever at the time created the world's biggest financial-services company, a 'one-stop shop' for banking and finance, its executives claimed, that operated in a hundred countries.[2]

The Citi–Travelers merger was not alone. Around this time, there were several 'supermegamergers' – mergers between financial firms that each had more than $100 billion in assets, including the coming together of Bank of America and Nations Bank, Bank One and First Chicago, and Norwest Corp. and Wells Fargo.

Wall Street investment banks boomed over this period. They issued stocks and bonds on behalf of clients keen to raise capital. They traded securities, using the firm's own money, or, often, with debt. And they managed billions of dollars in investments on behalf of millions of Americans and US institutions. This was an era of enormous pay packets and huge profits, financial innovation, risk-taking, yuppies and Gordon Gekko – the money-obsessed anti-hero of the 1987 movie *Wall Street*. Compensation soared so that, by the early 1990s, hundreds of staff at the biggest US banks were making upwards of $5 million a year, while a select few were taking home many multiples more. These were sums unheard of previously – and they were almost unconscionable for bankers elsewhere, including in Switzerland.

US banks were also expanding overseas. New technology, the ease of international travel and rising global trade all contributed to a broad and rapid increase in global flows of capital. As markets for goods and services became more global, the need for loans, trading platforms and financial advice became more international too. American commercial and investment banks – and the newly emerging universal banks that combined both activities – were tapping into clients around the world. The US banks, increasingly freed from regulation at home and with the benefit of size, having bulked up on a wave of mergers, were muscling in on foreign banks on their own turf. 'To put it plainly,' wrote Brett Fromson in *The Washington Post* in 1994, US financial firms are 'simply kicking the stuffing out of foreign competitors.'[3]

In the rest of the world, this new expansive and aggressive American banking sector was a cause for consternation. One response was that the pattern of banking deregulation in the US was echoed in other countries. In the UK, the Thatcher government's sudden deregulation of financial markets in 1986 was dubbed 'the Big Bang' because it blew up the industry, suddenly accelerating the growth of London as a financial powerhouse. From 1993, the European banking directive allowed banks on the continent to operate pretty much freely across borders, while the prospect of monetary union in the EU – the implementation of a single euro currency – also encouraged banks to think outside of their home countries.

Across much of Europe, there was a surge in domestic banking consolidation as banks beefed up by buying smaller rivals. Often they would have to stretch their capital to the limit to fund more acquisitions – a risky move because it meant the banks had less in reserve if they were to fail. Still, regulators that might otherwise have been concerned their banking industries were becoming too concentrated, or stretching themselves too thin, instead rolled over rather than have the Americans gain a foothold. Politicians across the continent often backed the idea of creating 'national champions' in banking that would support the financial needs of domestic industry.

In Zurich, Rainer Gut looked at the future of Credit Suisse and knew that it would have to respond to these global forces. Since 1962, Credit Suisse had built a relationship with the Boston-based investment bank, White Weld. The Swiss bank had bought White Weld's Zurich business, and the two banks cooperated on an investment-banking joint venture to connect their clients, in New York, Zurich and elsewhere, so that clients of Credit Suisse looking to raise money in Europe could tap investors in the US, for instance. It was widely considered a success, with CSWW, as it became known, among the leading investment banks in Europe across many categories of capital raising.[4] But, in 1978, White Weld was acquired by US bank Merrill Lynch, and the joint venture came to an end. Credit Suisse went looking for a new international partner and turned to another US investment bank.

First Boston had been created in 1932, cobbled together from bits of other investment banks. By the 1970s, it had become a major power, a so-called 'bulge bracket' bank,* and one of the big international players alongside the likes of Morgan Stanley. It was raising billions of dollars for clients every year and taking millions of dollars

---

* The term 'bulge bracket' emerged in the 1960s and 1970s. It referred to the way the names of the biggest global investment banks appeared on the 'tombstones' – printed advertisements for public share offerings. The bigger banks usually appeared at the top of the printed page, in a larger font that 'bulged' out.

in fees on each deal. It had become especially successful in the nascent and lucrative financial markets for junk bonds and derivatives.*

Gut sought a deal that would get Credit Suisse a foot in the door at Wall Street. What emerged was like the White Weld partnership on steroids. Credit Suisse and First Boston entered a joint venture – initially called Financière Crédit Suisse–First Boston and based in London – which was 60 per cent owned by the Swiss and 40 per cent by the Americans. The aim was to become a superstar of the European market for stocks and bonds. First Boston had access to American corporate clients that wanted to issue bonds outside the US, and Credit Suisse had European buyers who wanted to invest in them.

There was some strategic sense to the match-up. But the cultural fit was a potential problem. First Boston was a far more aggressive, freewheeling and exciting firm than the Swiss were used to. It was a breeding ground for major financial movers and shakers and was renowned for paying out enormous compensation packages. Among First Boston's star employees in the 1970s was Larry Fink – later the CEO of investing giant BlackRock and the most powerful man in the US economy, according to some observers – who started at First Boston as a twenty-three-year-old in 1976 and became 'something of a legend on Wall Street' over the next few years for developing a multitrillion-dollar market in mortgage-backed securities.[5] Around the same time, Joe Perella and Bruce Wasserstein were 'two corporate toreadors' who brought a high-octane approach to their work and 'a more rough-and-tumble image of opportunism and creativity' to First Boston's mergers and acquisitions division.[6] Perella was tall and slim, an intuitive thinker who trained as an accountant before coming to investment banking relatively late on in his career.

---

* Junk bonds are bonds that usually pay investors more but carry a higher risk of default. Derivatives are financial contracts whose value is tied to the value of some underlying asset.

Wasserstein was shorter, stocky, and a tough negotiator with the nickname 'Bid 'em up Bruce'.[7] They brought in many millions of dollars in fees from their role advising on landmark transactions, such as Texaco's then-record $10.1-billion acquisition of Getty Oil in 1984. Under their leadership, First Boston was called 'the archetypal deal factory', and they aimed to be involved in every major transaction in corporate America, even if they weren't invited.[8]

While these cultural differences might have caused some raised eyebrows in Zurich, Rainer Gut himself was much more used to the ways of the Americans. For the best part of a decade, the Swiss–American joint venture mostly went as planned. The partners split the globe into three hunting grounds: the Swiss looked after their small but lucrative home market; First Boston tackled North America and Australia; and, from London, the joint venture – usually referred to as the anglicized Credit Suisse First Boston or CSFB – took on Europe and the rest of the world. However, within a few years, divisions began to emerge, especially where bankers from one part of the business ran into their colleagues from another part. Global markets were becoming ever more integrated. Corporate clients and investors could pop up anywhere around the world, and the bankers who chased them found they were frequently, and unexpectedly, bumping into one another.

'First Boston executives sometimes went to Europe to urge customers to buy Treasury bonds, while Credit Suisse people pushed Swiss franc bonds, and CSFB sales people proposed innovative floating-rate notes in a variety of currencies,' wrote Steven Greenhouse in *The New York Times*.[9] First Boston's go-go M & A team, in particular, was treading on toes, turning up at the offices of CSFB clients in Europe and Japan. The overlapping patchwork of bankers was confusing for clients and bred internal tensions about how to split fees and work.

Eventually, the situation became untenable, with bankers ostensibly from the same firm competing for business against their colleagues. Some questioned whether a geographic split of the business made sense, while others asked whether two corporate cultures could coexist at all. These questions reverberated down the decades for Credit Suisse. The bank's leaders sometimes ignored the issue and let it fester. Other times, they tried to divide the bank up and made matters worse.

For now, though, there were other pressing concerns, as the shine was starting to come off at First Boston. The trading business, which had been so profitable, suddenly reversed. The rapid growth of the Euromarkets had stalled and the Black Monday stock-market crash of 19 October 1987 had wiped more than $1.5 trillion off the value of markets worldwide.* That year, First Boston's trading operations lost about $100 million after being caught out by a rise in interest rates, while the crash resulted in at least $60 million in further losses at another trading division.

While trading businesses suffered, Perella and Wasserstein's M & A division was still going gangbusters and brought in revenue of more than $350 million in 1987, more than half the total revenue for the whole firm. But the diverging results caused animosity. Perella and Wasserstein quarrelled for months with First Boston's top executives over strategy, demanding that more of the firm's resources should be given over to their dealmaking business.

'They, and Mr. Wasserstein in particular, had been arguing that First Boston needed to change course, to emphasize businesses like mergers and merchant banking over stock and bond trading,' *The Wall Street Journal* reported at the time. 'Last summer [1987],

---

* The causes of the crash have been much debated and the main arguments are too sprawling – and disputed – to go into in much depth here. Broadly, some have blamed new tax rules in the US that threatened to end the corporate dealmaking boom, while others have suggested there was a sense building in the stock market for years that shares were getting overvalued. A third possible explanation was a general weakening of confidence in the US economy.

Mr. Wasserstein heatedly contended to the management committee that First Boston's trading operation took too many risks. It
should, he said, become more of a support operation for M & A and
merchant-banking activities, rather than an independent profit
center.[10]

In 1988, Wasserstein and Perella abruptly walked out of First
Boston to set up their own firm, and took some senior colleagues and
a bunch of junior bankers with them. The marquee M & A team was
no more.

At Credit Suisse, this might have been a moment for Gut to
change course. The Swiss board and executives were schooled in running a slow-moving commercial lender and a starchy private bank.
Yet, somehow, their small bank had ended up attached to a vast and
volatile US bulge-bracket business. It was all nominally banking, but
not as the Swiss knew it. But, instead of withdrawing, Gut doubled
down. In October 1988, Credit Suisse and First Boston announced a
complicated restructuring of their relationship. They were no longer
just partners in a joint venture. The Swiss bank had taken a 44.5 per
cent stake in its US counterpart, with the rest of First Boston's shares
owned in part by its staff and in part by a Saudi Arabian investor. The
complex deal meant Credit Suisse had the biggest presence on Wall
Street of any foreign player.[11] Credit Suisse was no longer a Swiss
bank: it was a truly global bank, with a seat at the table of the fastest,
most dynamic, highest stakes banking sector on the planet.

Rainer Gut played it calm as he explained the rationale to *The New
York Times*: 'The markets have become so interconnected globally
and we were pushing in so many different directions that it was logical to bring everything under one roof.'[12] The reporter noted that Gut
'squirmed' at the suggestion Credit Suisse was growing aggressively
and preferred to think of himself as a conservative and risk-averse
CEO. It was, indeed, something of a paradox. Credit Suisse was Swiss
at heart – austere, private – but it also now had an American side,
which was fast-paced, in-your-face and daring.

The two banks were soon driven even closer together. Throughout the 1980s, First Boston had profited from financing 'leveraged buy-outs' – deals that are sometimes risky and funded with large amounts of debt. The bank would provide clients with temporary, and lucrative, 'bridge loans' to get deals over the line. These loans were then refinanced by issuing junk bonds. But, when the market for junk bonds suddenly dried up, First Boston was left holding the bag. The most infamous case was the so-called 'burning bed' deal. In 1990, First Boston made a $457-million bridging loan to a private-equity company called Gibbons, Green, van Amerongen to help fund its $1.1-billion purchase of the Ohio Mattress Company, later known as Sealy. The deal was heavily criticized. The price was way too high, and when the firm was unable to secure permanent financing through the junk-bond markets, it couldn't pay back its loan to First Boston. The bank ended up saddled with the debt, and, bizarrely, became the owner of a giant mattress company. Several years passed before the bank was able to offload this investment to another buyer at a much reduced price.[13]

In all, First Boston was suddenly stuck with about $1.2 billion in similar bridging loans tied to leveraged buyout-style takeover deals gone wrong. It was a disaster. The investment bank was in dire trouble and made a stunning loss of $500 million in 1990. This moment was yet another chance for Rainer Gut to opt out of the risky world of US bulge-bracket investment banking. Instead, he struck another deal: a $300-million bailout of First Boston that left Credit Suisse as the majority shareholder, with 60 per cent of the company. Credit Suisse also absorbed over $400 million in bad loans from its US bank. What made this an even more extraordinary turn of events was that it was technically against US banking regulations for Credit Suisse to own the investment bank. But rather than block it, US regulators simply waved the deal through, presumably weighing up that it was better for a foreign bank to plough money into First Boston than to witness its disorderly collapse. The deal was a humiliation for the US investment bankers – the rescue even saw them move locations, from a glamorous glass and steel tower in midtown Manhattan to a tired-looking, unfashionable, stone office building many blocks south.

In Zurich, Gut's hand had been forced by the failures at First Boston, but he had also exploited a moment of weakness to take full control. Credit Suisse was now the first foreign firm to take majority control of a major Wall Street bank,[14] and, in reality, it was the first truly global investment bank too.[15] Gut had become one of the biggest banking power players anywhere in the world. But though the empire he'd created was vast and rich, it was also laden with risks and riven with cultural anomalies. Yet he showed little interest in addressing such issues nor much appetite for fixing the flaws that had led to the creation of the modern Credit Suisse. 'I don't want to look back and wash dirty linen,' he told a reporter in 1989. 'I'm looking ahead. It's an exercise in futility to say what went wrong.'[16]

In truth, the bank had become a monster, a high-octane global investment bank strapped onto a relatively small, secretive Swiss firm. It was an uneasy amalgam of two potentially explosive banking cultures that, over the remainder of its existence, just kept on blowing up.

# PART TWO
## An International National Bank

# SIX

# A Swiss Reckoning

The acquisition of First Boston would eventually help drive the bank to its downfall, but it wasn't the only factor. Much of what was wrong with Credit Suisse had distinctly Swiss characteristics.

One cold afternoon in December 1995, US Senator Alfonse D'Amato returned to his office in Washington DC. He'd just had lunch in the Senate Dining Room with guests from the World Jewish Congress. Brooklyn-born D'Amato, a Republican, was known as 'Senator Pothole' – a dogged politician who got things done when others procrastinated.[1] His thirty-year-old legislative director – a kind of researcher and general runaround – was Gregg Rickman, a studious, academic type, with a masters in Russian and Middle Eastern history, who was part way through a PhD in international relations. D'Amato, a fifty-eight-year-old career politician, began to debrief Rickman on his lunch meeting.[2]

The guests had explained how, over the past three years, a coalition of Jewish organizations had worked together to expedite claims for the return of property lost in the Holocaust. They described their efforts pressuring banks – in Switzerland, in particular – to fully account for the assets of Jewish people held there since the end of the Second World War. Swiss bankers had found hundreds of dormant accounts left unclaimed since that time. They calculated the accounts were worth maybe $32 million, but the bankers were also stalling on providing further information or making any serious attempts to connect the accounts to their rightful owners. Many Jewish leaders believed the sum the Swiss banks had disclosed was far too small, and they'd need help to get the banks to go further. D'Amato agreed to help raise the profile of their efforts.

Back in his office, the senator turned to Rickman. 'You like history and digging into big issues,' he said. 'How about it?'

Rickman had more than a passing interest in the broad issues at stake. His grandfather had fled pogroms in Russia and his father-in-law was a Holocaust survivor. He also had a strong sense of right and wrong. The project, he thought, would take a couple of months, maybe a little more. That was a significant chunk of time, but worthwhile. He was in, though he was also seriously underestimating how long the hunt for the truth about Swiss banks and the Nazis would take. As it turned out, he would dedicate the next several years of his life to the project.

Rickman's starting point was to gather more information. He sent out letters requesting documents from just about any organization that might have relevant paperwork. He wrote to the US Holocaust Memorial Museum, the State Department, National Archive, CIA, Army Intelligence Archives, the Treasury Department and the embassies of several European nations. The initial response was disappointing. To get deeper, he'd need to do his own research. Already, the scale of the project was becoming clearer and Rickman knew he'd need help. A contact at the World Jewish Congress put him in touch with Willi Korte, a German-born attorney and researcher who had tracked artwork looted by the Nazis. He was also put in touch with Miriam Kleiman, a political science graduate who had previously done some work for the World Jewish Congress and who, like

Rickman, was originally from Cleveland and something of an idealist among the cynics of Washington.[3] Korte and Kleiman were hired and began digging.

An early breakthrough came when Kleiman found a US intelligence report from 1945 that listed the accounts of 182 depositors at Swiss banks, most of whom were Jewish. When Kleiman showed it to Rickman, he was dumbstruck. This single document alone seemed to show about $20 million held in Swiss banks that hadn't been repatriated. The Swiss banks' estimate of $32 million in total seemed implausible and outrageous.

Soon, Rickman, Kleiman and Korte were joined by an intern, then another and another. More archives were opened up. Crateloads of documents were retrieved from dusty storerooms. Rickman's team began laying out paper after paper, sorting them into folders by theme, or bank, or year. It was a massive, multilayered jigsaw puzzle. Rickman's small team was now joined by more researchers, journalists and even US Secret Service agents. The Holocaust Memorial Museum sent twelve college interns from Ivy League schools to help. They were awash in paper, with more documents than Rickman knew what to do with – many of them unveiling horror stories about the misbehaviour of the Swiss banks.

Meanwhile, back in Zurich, Rainer Gut was on a Swiss-centred acquisition spree, buying smaller financial businesses to beef up the Swiss side of the bank. Sometimes, these new additions came with their own problems.

One example was Bank Leu, Switzerland's oldest bank, founded in 1755. It had survived almost two and half centuries without much fanfare. That changed in the summer of 1985. Staff at the top US financial regulator, the Securities and Exchange Commission, received an anonymous tip about suspicious trading patterns at a Bank Leu branch in the Bahamas.[4] Investigators found the manager of the branch was involved in an elaborate international scheme that involved placing bets on corporate takeovers before they were announced to the public. The money trail led eventually to Dennis Levine, a former top investment banker with the US firm Drexel Burnham Lambert. Cornered by prosecutors, Levine lifted the lid on a huge insider-trading ring at the heart of Wall Street. Bank Leu's relatively obscure Bahamas office had in effect 'set off the worst scandal in Wall Street history', according to *The Washington Post*.[5] But it wasn't the only scandal at Bank Leu.

In the UK, the bank came under fire for its role in facilitating a massive share scam at the alcoholic drinks business, Guinness. The scandal grabbed headlines in London and Zurich and forced the ousting of Bank Leu's chairman and its CEO. Within a couple of years, the executive group changed again, as the bank continued to reel from its involvement in two of the biggest corporate scandals of the day. By 1990, the disgraced bank was directionless and in need of rescue. Step forward, Credit Suisse. Gut pounced. Under other circumstances, it might have been something of a coup to acquire such an ancient Swiss banking name. Instead, the country's oldest bank felt more like a distressed asset.

Another acquisition was more straightforward. In 1993, Credit Suisse bought Swiss Volksbank, then the fourth- or fifth-largest bank in Switzerland, in a deal valued at around $1.1 billion. It sent Credit Suisse higher up the domestic-banking pecking order, putting it on a more even footing with its rivals UBS and the Swiss Bank Corporation – for a while, at least. Yet, for Rainer Gut, this still wasn't enough.

In 1996, Gut attempted perhaps his most daring takeover effort yet. The result was a huge own goal. Across Zurich, Credit Suisse's rival UBS was locked in a battle with its largest shareholder. Martin Ebner, a bowtie-wearing business tycoon, had been a senior Credit Suisse executive before setting up his own investment company, the BK Vision Fund (originally named Bank Zurich). Through the late 1980s and early 1990s, Ebner's fund had built up stakes in some of Switzerland's biggest companies and often profited by agitating for changes that bumped the share price higher. By early 1996, Ebner had become critical of UBS's strategy, launched lawsuits against its top executives and was threatening to topple board members. UBS had responded by taking out newspaper ads defending its record – a highly unusual and very public step for the normally staid Swiss bankers.

UBS's chiefs were clearly rattled. Gut spotted an opportunity. A few days before Easter, he held a call with his opposite number, Nikolaus Senn, the chairman of UBS. Senn was a veteran banker, a fighter and, like Gut, an empire builder. He was not going to roll over in the face of Ebner's demands. Senn was soon to retire as chairman of the bank and was holidaying at his Florida holiday home when the call from Gut came through.[6] The Credit Suisse chairman suggested a startling way out of the mess. How about a merger of Credit Suisse and UBS?[7] The two men had known each other for years and Senn wasn't sure if the proposal was an April Fool's joke.[8] But this wasn't the first time the merger idea had been raised. The notion seemed to surface every few years. UBS and Credit Suisse – as well as Switzerland's other big bank, Swiss Bank Corp. – had produced mediocre results in recent years. There were far too many branches for too few customers in such a small country. Consultants predicted the industry would need to cut staff numbers sharply and scale back. A merger of UBS and Credit Suisse would offer the opportunity to streamline operations, while creating a banking behemoth, with assets of roughly $660 billion, the largest of any bank outside of Japan at the time. Senn agreed to take the idea to his board a few days later.

Around the same time, the investigation into Swiss banking's troubling history with Nazi Germany was gathering steam. Dozens of researchers were now sifting through historic documents. The picture that began to emerge from their work was dismal reading for bank executives – and much of it was leaking to the press on a regular basis. The Swiss banks were waking up to a massive unfolding scandal that was out of their control. In response, they hired high-priced lawyers, who sent their own squads of researchers into the archives too. The cavernous archival offices were soon crawling with teams of competing researchers fighting to get their hands on documents ahead of their rivals. Rickman, by now a full-time project manager, directed dozens of helpers to look here and there, while supplying his boss, D'Amato, with ammunition to bash the banks. What they had found fell into several different buckets.

There was clear evidence that the Swiss banks had laundered Nazi loot. When the Nazis had rolled across Europe, they'd swallowed up gold, art and money from the countries that fell, one by one. They'd also robbed their Jewish victims specifically, literally taking the gold from their teeth. But that wealth was useless in wartime if it couldn't be used to buy much-needed supplies. Some neutral countries turned their backs on the Nazis. Rickman's team of researchers found hard evidence that the Swiss banks had acted like middlemen, taking Nazi gold and other valuables without question, and then transferring it, cleansed of the Nazi taint, to accounts in banks overseas, including their own branches in the US. There was specific evidence, for instance, that Swiss banks shipped billions of dollars' worth of gold to Spain and Portugal in 1943 and 1944.

Rickman's team also found evidence that the Swiss banks, after the war, had used money in unclaimed accounts – mostly accounts owned by Jews – to pay off Swiss account holders for losses they'd incurred on loans to businesses in Eastern Europe, for instance. And they found evidence that the Swiss banks had opened accounts for known fascists – including an account at Credit Suisse containing $5,000 that belonged to none other than Benito Mussolini.[9] Another account, at Swiss Volksbank (which had just become part of Credit Suisse, remember), in Zurich, belonged to Radu Lecca, a leading Nazi officer in Romania.[10]

In all of this, Credit Suisse appeared to be among the worst offenders. Documentation showed that the bank had taken gold bars from Germany and had made financing available to the Nazis too. A

Credit Suisse branch in New York had helped Germans 'conceal the actual ownership' of their deposits. A 1945 report from the US intelligence service said that 'Credit Suisse Zurich is the most frequent violator of the Allied Code of Conduct concerning Swiss banks.'[11]

Perhaps most egregious of all was the way Swiss banks had continued to act unethically even after the war had ended. In particular, there was damning evidence about the way they responded to Jews who had tried to claim accounts in their name – or the names of their dead relatives. One case, which directly involved Credit Suisse, became a celebrated example of this. Joseph Sapir had been a Polish businessman when the spectre of Nazism began to cast its dark shadow across Europe. Sapir had travelled to Paris, London and Geneva, depositing money in accounts in banks in each of those cities in an effort to protect some of his wealth and provide for his family. Sapir had told his daughter, Estelle, how to locate the accounts should anything happen to him.

By the end of the war, Joseph had died in the Majdanek concentration camp. Estelle, who had joined the resistance, emerged from hiding and went to look for the money her father had told her about. In France and Britain, the banks quickly handed over the money that was deposited there. But, in Geneva, it was a different story. Joseph had left the money in a branch of what was to become Credit Suisse. Estelle explained her situation to a clerk, who, after some digging, confirmed that yes, her father had an account there, before insisting that, to open it, Estelle would need to provide a death certificate. In her later retelling, Estelle demanded of the bank clerk whom she should ask for a death certificate: Hitler, Himmler or Eichmann? She ran, screaming, from the bank.[12]

Eventually, in 1998, Credit Suisse agreed to pay Sapir $500,000. Though, even then, the bank made a mess of its admission of guilt – a spokesperson apologized for the mistreatment of Sapir, but also said Swiss bank secrecy laws prevented them from confirming or denying whether any of the incidents Sapir described had ever happened.[13]

This story was repeated over and over. It wasn't some mistake by an ill-informed or over-officious Credit Suisse bank clerk. This was policy. What's more, Rickman's team found that the Swiss banks had charged fees that had steadily drained the funds in inactive accounts for decades. Hundreds of thousands of accounts, perhaps more than a million, were simply closed, with the funds they held absorbed by the bank.

Armed with these stories, Rickman's boss D'Amato pushed for action. He held hearings and harangued Swiss politicians and bankers for their inactivity. Some of the most high-profile US politicians of the day were also involved, with Bill Clinton offering his support. Paul Volcker, the influential chairman of the Federal Reserve during the 1980s, was appointed to chair an Independent Committee of Eminent Persons to look into the dormant Swiss bank accounts of Jewish victims of the Holocaust. Newt Gingrich, the speaker of the House of Representatives, weighed in and slammed the banks, saying, 'a thick veil of Swiss bank secrecy has covered this entire affair for too long.'[14]

Even as the threats from the US escalated, Rainer Gut was working through the potentially huge takeover of UBS. Driving home that he was absolutely serious about the deal, Gut wrote to the UBS board outlining the rationale for his suggestion. The two banks 'would together have a chance in the medium term of making the first league of the global finance industry . . . a union between two strong partners can lead to a quantum leap forward,' he stressed, underlining his ambition for a Swiss banking champion.[15]

Gut knew a merger would be contentious in Switzerland, where influential unions would be opposed because of the prospect of layoffs, and left-wing politicians would try to block anything that would make the banks more powerful. Initially, the merger talks were kept under wraps. But, when a left-leaning Swiss newspaper broke the scoop on Gut's approach to UBS, the story caused a huge stir. Columnists lined up to bash the idea of a pooled Credit Suisse and UBS.

The merger would be bad for jobs and bad for Switzerland, according to critics in the media and politics.

UBS's board was spooked. Disturbed that the highly sensitive talks had surfaced in the press, they rejected Gut's proposal outright. In public, Senn blamed Credit Suisse for leaking the merger story to the media, and even suggested that Switzerland's other big bank, Swiss Bank Corp., would be a better merger partner for UBS. Though it might have initially sounded like no more than a dig at the bank's rival, a potential deal with Swiss Bank Corp. was now in the public domain. For Gut and Credit Suisse, this was a nightmarish outcome. For, while Gut's proposal had been tossed out the window, the vigorous debate it had stirred up had led to some serious analysis of the potential for a different bank merger in Switzerland.

Swiss Bank Corp., based in Basel, overlapped less with UBS and was smaller than its two domestic rivals, so a merger of those two would be less politically contentious. But it would still result in a bank that dwarfed Credit Suisse. Within two years of Gut's approach, that is exactly what happened. In December 1997, UBS and Swiss Bank Corp. announced that they planned to merge, creating the second-largest bank in the world and the biggest in Europe. There were some political and media challenges, but the groundwork for the deal had been laid two years earlier with the failed Credit Suisse deal.

It seemed that Gut's attempt to create a Swiss giant had backfired. The giant existed, but Credit Suisse had no part of it, and the pressures that had forced him to pursue an ever-larger bank were only intensifying. With the UBS deal gone, Credit Suisse bought the Swiss insurer Winterthur for about $9 billion, equivalent to about $17 billion today. It was a shadow of the failed UBS deal, but it was significant nonetheless, and an enormous bet that Credit Suisse would be able to cross-sell banking and insurance products to its clients. Winterthur, it was hoped, would become a cash cow supporting growth in other areas, and could provide a huge pool of funds to be deployed around the bank. It also had an enormous client list that could be used to prospect for new accounts. But that was not what played out.

Instead, there were a series of missteps. When Credit Suisse hived off Winterthur's international business and sold it to another insurance company, the deal came with some guarantees attached which cost the bank about $575 million just a few years later. The so-called bancassurance model flopped, as the bank struggled to integrate the 'high-touch' approach required of private banking with the more retail-focused insurance business. Finally, Winterthur, like much of the insurance industry, was especially hard hit by the 9/11 terror attacks in 2001. Eventually, Credit Suisse was forced to book major write-downs on the business. Winterthur began sinking fast and the bank had to inject billions of dollars of fresh capital into the company just to keep it afloat. At one point, an IPO of Winterthur was mooted, with thoughts that Credit Suisse could perhaps spin off the insurer. But there was just not enough investor interest in the flailing insurance business and the IPO never happened. Eventually, in 2006, Winterthur was sold to French insurance company Axa for a little more than Gut had paid for it almost a decade earlier.

All of that was years into the future. Back in the late nineties, Swiss banking's Nazi issues were still unresolved. The Swiss were taking a beating in the US, but, at home, the response of many of the country's bankers and politicians was denial, obfuscation and anger. Politicians and newspaper columnists insinuated that the whole affair was trumped up to undermine the rising influence of Switzerland as a financial centre. They suggested that D'Amato's interest was electioneering, to garner the support of New York's large Jewish vote. Tensions between the two countries escalated to uncomfortable levels. The Swiss ambassador to the US was forced to resign after it was leaked to the media that he'd told staff to fight a war against D'Amato and 'Jewish circles'. Rickman was defamed as 'a little filth scraper'.[16]

The banks were seen to be dragging their heels, or worse. One incident was particularly damaging. In 1997, a night security guard at UBS in Zurich found huge carts stacked with ledgers and other incriminating documents dating from the war and earlier in the bank's basement shredding room. The documents were clearly meant for destruction – a contravention of Swiss law, which forbade shredding war-era documents – but the security guard saved a handful. When he turned them over to police and the press, it caused a huge scandal within Switzerland. But the guard himself faced the loss of his job and potentially jail time for breaching Swiss bank secrecy. It seemed like the Swiss banks preferred to punish those who uncovered the truth about their bad behaviour, rather than do the right thing by their mistreated Jewish clients. In the end, the security guard fled to the US, where he was given political asylum.

The roadblocks put up by the Swiss banks were frustrating the Americans. D'Amato wrote to US Secretary of State Warren Christopher accusing the Swiss of being dishonest and obstructionist.

Eventually, in January 1997, as the drip of headlines caused fury in Switzerland and around the world, Credit Suisse was the first to blink. Gut took the lead and approached the other big banks with a suggestion that they create a fund to compensate victims of their wrongdoing. Gut was a globalist. He knew America and understood US politics too. He suggested they put $70 million into the pot – a big step up from the $32 million that had been mentioned a couple of years earlier, but still far off what Rickman and others believed was fair. D'Amato and other US critics welcomed this as a first step, but the fight was far from done. Soon, more delays, haggling and lack of transparency fuelled further resentment.

State authorities in the US began leaning on the Swiss by threatening their branches in New York and indicating that valuable business with US clients was on the line. The pressure was focused especially on UBS and Credit Suisse. State pension funds began to question whether they'd continue to work with the Swiss at all. The biggest challenge in late 1997 came from California, where the state treasurer, Matt Fong, took on the fight. Fong, who was also seeking nomination for senator the following year, announced a moratorium on investment with the Swiss banks. This amounted to the withdrawal of about $2 billion, more than half of which had been invested with Credit Suisse. A spokesperson for the bank was typically defiant, or tone-deaf, depending on which side of the argument you were on. There was no real sense of an apology; instead, the bank spokesperson said, 'We regret the announcement [from Treasurer Fong]. It is disconcerting considering all the measures that have already been taken.'[17]

Over the next few months, though Fong lifted the moratorium, the threat of further sanctions from California and elsewhere in the US hung over the banks. Yet the banks' leaders still appeared to have their heads stuck in the sand. In July 1998, Senator D'Amato held a hearing on the agreements Switzerland had made with the Allies in 1946. The CEOs of all the Swiss banks, including Rainer Gut, were invited to attend. They all declined. Instead, they continued trying to argue down the size of any ultimate settlement – by this time, their aim was to keep it below $500 million – as the potential claims swelled as a result of the work from Rickman's team and others who had piled into the investigation.

Eventually, the negative publicity and the possibility of major penalties began to take a toll at the banks. The financial performance of Credit Suisse and its Swiss peers started to fall off as clients avoided them in favour of less controversial rivals. Their share prices were hit too, given the uncertainty about any potential legal penalties. For Gut and the other bank leaders, it was time to strike a deal – and it would cost them. After years of wrangling, the banks finally agreed to a $1.2-billion settlement.

On 12 August, at 7 p.m., Rickman's boss D'Amato took to the steps of Brooklyn Court House. Surrounded by flashing cameras, reporters and his supporters, the senator announced the deal, saying, 'I am tremendously pleased and gratified to announce that we've reached an historic agreement with the Swiss banks that will bring moral and material justice to those who have suffered for so long and bring closure on these issues around the world and in Switzerland.'[18]

For Rickman, this was not quite complete justice. Even after all these years and the efforts of dozens of researchers, Rickman believed they'd only just scraped the surface of what the banks had really done to profit from the evil of the Nazis. It was far from satisfying, although he was consoled by the fact hundreds of Jews had received some kind of payment. But most frustrating of all was that the Swiss banks, including Credit Suisse, never really seemed to 'get it'. They never seemed to fully own up to the extent of their wrongdoing before and during the war, nor the cover-up that followed for decades afterwards.[19]

A joint press release from UBS and Credit Suisse to mark the final massive settlement – that came on top of their much smaller pro-posed solution – seemed to signal how the bankers really felt. The press release said: 'The aim of the additional payment by Credit Suisse Group and UBS is to avert the threat of sanctions as well as long and costly court proceedings.'[20]

Inside Switzerland, Gut took a large share of the credit for resolv-ing the long-running and embarrassing issue. But the Swiss side of the bank had been tarnished by the revelations about Nazi accounts and the treatment of victims of the Holocaust, while attempts to paper over this conduct had given historic wrongdoing a modern twist.

Meanwhile, Gut's Swiss acquisitions that aimed to rebalance the bank away from the US had failed to achieve that outcome. The attempts to grow in Switzerland had cost billions of dollars and taken up countless hours of management time. But the imbalance remained. Credit Suisse still felt lopsided. In all, it was clear by the end of the decade that Credit Suisse's problems had no simple Swiss solution.

# SEVEN

# Wheat's Crop of Stars

In the 1990s, Credit Suisse was like two different institutions. The Swiss bank was based in Zurich's Paradeplatz, a picturesque square where trams rolled slowly between centuries-old buildings. But CSFB's investment bankers in London worked out of a shiny glass and steel skyscraper in Canary Wharf,* while, in Manhattan, their home was a gargantuan art-deco tower with an enormous, vaulted lobby that covered an entire downtown block. In Switzerland, staff answered the phone, 'Credit Suisse.' In New York, it was always still, 'First Boston.'

Throughout much of this period, one man loomed over the investment bank, the portion of Credit Suisse based outside of its homeland. His name was Allen D. Wheat.

A tough, ambitious American from New Mexico, Wheat had seen

---

* The Canary Wharf development in London's former docklands was the brainchild of Michael von Clemm, a former senior executive of Credit Suisse. The bank was one of the area's first tenants, moving into the tower block at One Cabot Square in 1991.

the downside of the US banking system first hand when his father, a graduate of West Point military school, lost a fortune speculating on financial investments. (According to one profile, Wheat held a grudge against his father for years.)[1] Undeterred, Wheat financed his own way through college – first at Wharton, and then studying for an MBA at New York University.

After graduating, he ground out a career on Wall Street and in the treasury department of General Foods Corp., a predecessor to Kraft Foods. His big break had come when he joined Bankers Trust, a storied US financial firm that was going through a transformation of its own. During the 1980s, Bankers Trust got out of retail banking and focused on trading stocks and bonds and other financial instruments, especially derivatives. This was the hot new trend in finance, which involved complicated bets on contracts tied to the price of some other underlying asset, such as stocks or commodities or portfolios of real estate.

Wheat was an early expert in this burgeoning field. At that time, derivatives were still seen as some kind of dark art, little understood by most traditional bankers. But Wheat had a mind for facts and figures, and a competitive instinct that gave him the edge in what turned out to be a lucrative area of the business. He was known for his sharp brain and sharper elbows. A straight talker, Wheat was not afraid to clash with more senior executives or call them out openly if he thought they'd got something wrong. As a leader, though, he engendered loyalty among a core group of staff, who felt he had their back. High performers were well remunerated and made to feel part of a cultish inner circle.

So, in 1990, when Gut's Credit Suisse was embarking on its big adventure in investment banking, the bank turned to Allen Wheat to help accelerate its plans. He was initially hired to build a derivatives business, out of Tokyo and London, known as Credit Suisse Financial Products, or CSFP. Wheat employed similar tactics to those he'd used before – he badgered bosses and gave free rein to high-flyers on his team, many of whom had followed him from Bankers Trust, though other big shots were also lured to the bank with the promise that they would be well looked after financially, while given the freedom to run their own businesses.

It wasn't long before CSFP began replicating some of Wheat's earlier successes, generating huge profits for the bank and receiving handsome pay packets in return. Wheat personally took home tens of millions of dollars, while many of the traders who worked for him were pocketing a fortune too. Soon, Wheat was managing almost a thousand employees. Their success, he told a reporter, was because they thrived on volatility in the markets. 'Lots of volatility, lots of smiling faces around here.'[2]

Wheat's star was rising fast. By 1993, he was promoted to be president and chief operating officer of the whole investment bank. A year after that, he was given a seat on the executive board. It was impossible to ignore the successes of his parts of the bank, though Swiss colleagues were nervous about his brazen ambition, open disdain for some senior executives and obsession with personal wealth. Once, when he was asked to give a presentation to senior colleagues, they expected he would outline new ways to help clients or suggest plans to generate more revenue. Instead, Wheat mostly talked about how he could help everyone in the room to become fabulously wealthy.[3]

CSFB was seen to be innovative, at the frontier of new banking products and new markets too. The bank sold complicated investments with odd-sounding names that appealed to clients seeking an edge. The quanto, for instance, was a kind of sophisticated bet on obscure foreign exchange rates that was designed to enable investors not legally allowed to speculate on a certain currency to do so undetected.[4] Compared with rivals, the bank pushed earlier and faster into both mortgage-backed securities and emerging markets in Eastern Europe.

The firm became a fun place to work and a learning ground for a whole cohort of bankers, many of whom went on to become leading figures in global finance in the years ahead.* Staff were well paid, often taking a direct slice of the revenue they brought in. (This was always a point of contention – investment-banking bonuses drew outrage in Zurich, though Wheat's team considered their Swiss masters to be stingy and out of touch with the reality of the market.) In New York and London, the CSFB mantra was 'eat what you kill' – those who bring in the most revenue should be entitled to the highest compensation. The institution was secondary to the individual. CSFB was not the first or only bank to take this approach. But there were plenty of examples of firms that had gone this way and blown up. And that was soon the fate for Wheat's team too.

As the decade wore on, Wheat and his stable of superstars faced one problem after another. The trigger was a crisis in Asian currency markets that put the brakes on economies in the region, which in turn dried up demand for Russian oil, sparking a full-blown financial crisis in that country, starting in the summer of 1998.

Western banks had poured into Russia since the fall of the Soviet Union, making billions of dollars in loans to Russian companies and individuals that were betting on the country's rapid westernization. Credit Suisse had been at the head of the pack. It was the first foreign firm allowed to trade bonds inside Russia, the largest securities firm in the country, and its clients held about 40 per cent of all the Russian debt owned by foreigners.[5]

As the price of oil fell sharply, traders feared Russia's economy would collapse. All the positivity about Russia over the previous few years rapidly went into reverse. Inflation soared and the rouble was worth a third of what it had been days earlier. The nascent stock market crashed, and the Russian government defaulted on its own

---

* These included Bob Diamond, later the CEO of UK bank Barclays; Stephen Hester, who went on to run Royal Bank of Scotland; and Xavier Rolet, who was later the CEO of the London Stock Exchange.

debt. Western banks were sitting on massive loans to Russian companies that could no longer pay them back, or holding billions of dollars in government bonds that were worth practically nothing.

At CSFB, the focus turned to one of Wheat's wizards, a London-based Australian trader named Andrew Ipkendanz. As the bank's head of emerging markets, Ipkendanz was on a profit-sharing deal in which he was rumoured to have pocketed a fortune in the years leading up to the Russian crisis. (A 2,000-square-metre waterfront mansion he built in Sydney was later said to be the most expensive house in Australia, with an asking price of A$60 million.)[6] A typically highly numerate trader, he once told a reporter that his strategy 'is to go into the riskiest parts of the world in the least risky way.'[7] But, when the Russian market crashed, the positions Ipkendanz had put on turned negative in a flash. It was a catastrophe that threatened to cost billions of dollars.

The fallout was rippling through Wheat's bank. Another of his hotshot hires was Andy Stone, a fast-talking American real-estate banker with slicked-back black hair. He was a high-energy executive, but could be a challenging, demanding employee. 'He's the Michael Jordan of his business. But he's a Dennis Rodman management challenge,' a former colleague told the *New York Observer*.[8]

Stone had gained renown for making loans to many of the best-known, and most flamboyant, real-estate developers in Manhattan, including Donald Trump and Harry Macklowe. These loans were typically packaged up into securities and sold on to investors. His team had poured billions of dollars into commercial property, initially mostly Wall Street offices and hotels, and then a wider array of buildings, including casinos, farms and golf clubs. They'd often lend up to 95 per cent of the value of a property, much higher than rival firms. At its peak, CSFB had $14 billion tied up in real-estate investments brokered by Stone's team, for whom the work was personally lucrative – Stone's team sometimes kept 40 per cent of the profits it generated, with more than 10 per cent going to Stone himself.[9] The result was a series of huge payouts – Stone made as much as $100 million from his time at the bank. He built an enormous ten-bedroom house nestled among properties owned by titans of American industry in the Hamptons, and he jetted around the country with clients, once flying to Salt Lake City just to watch a basketball game with Donald Trump.[10]

But, when the turmoil in Russia cast a chill over the global economy, investors were suddenly more cautious on all sorts of assets, including US real estate. Demand for commercial mortgages quickly fell by almost half.[11] Credit Suisse looked to rein Stone in, demanding that he stop lending and start selling the vast quantities of real-estate loans his unit had amassed. Such a fire-sale approach inevitably meant billions of dollars in assets having to be sold into a difficult market, potentially at a significant loss.

The problems in Wheat's investment bank were mounting up at locations around the world. In December 1998, a group of London-based CSFB bankers claimed to be the most successful share traders in the world, dealing in billions of dollars of company stocks. They were said to be in line for a multimillion-dollar bonus after having delivered a stellar trading performance in what had been a volatile period in the markets. The bankers had nicknamed themselves the 'Flaming Ferraris' after their favourite rum and Grand Marnier cocktail. They even stage-managed a photoshoot of themselves in tuxedos, piling out of a ten-seater limousine and into their Christmas party at the Michelin-starred Nobu restaurant. The pictures were published in glowing profiles that touted their trading prowess.[12]

But, within a few weeks of their paparazzi-style photos having been plastered across media outlets, one of the traders was accused of wrongdoing by regulators in Sweden and the UK, while his bosses were alleged to have covered up his bad behaviour. According to authorities in Stockholm, the trader, James Archer, had attempted to manipulate shares in a Swedish paper-pulp company. Archer, who was twenty-four at the time, was the Eton- and Oxford-educated son of the controversial British novelist and politician, Lord Jeffrey Archer. The Swedish regulator said that Archer had sold shares in the pulp company at well below market price. The trades were fictitious because Archer had been both buyer and seller, in a scheme that was designed to drive down the value of the entire Swedish market.

The numbers involved were relatively small. Archer's trades stood to generate a gain of just a few hundred thousand dollars from the scheme. Swedish and UK authorities hit CSFB, Archer and his bosses with relatively modest fines and banned them from working in the City. But the colourful story gained outsized notoriety because of the flamboyant nature and outrageous lifestyles of the bankers involved. Archer and his two bosses were fired by the bank, and the UK regulator slammed their 'persistence and guile' in lying to authorities about the nature of the false trades. A spokesperson for CSFB said at the time that the incident didn't reflect wider problems and insisted that the bank was 'clear and consistent in demanding high ethical standards from our staff. There is no place in our organization for those who do not meet such requirements.'[13]

Those words rang hollow as Wheat's business was hit by yet another blow. In January 1999, investigators from Japan's financial regulator descended on Credit Suisse's offices in Tokyo. They were hunting for evidence that the derivatives unit of CSFB had been selling complex products to Japanese companies that would help them cover up losses. Acting on a tip from two of CSFB's former clients, the authorities believed the bank had helped sixty companies window-dress their accounts through dubious deals known as 'tobashi' – a kind of fraudulent, creative-accounting scheme used by some Japanese firms to shift losses around and cover them up. Instead of complying with Japan's notoriously efficient financial authorities, Shinji Yamada, the Tokyo unit's chief, tried to block their investigation. Yamada hid documents in a secret room that wasn't shown on floorplans of the office and ordered junior bankers not to talk with the investigators. Panicked staff were also ordered to parcel up documents and ship them to London. When authorities realized some papers were missing, Yamada ordered the staff to destroy them in what authorities later referred to as a 'shredding party'.[14]

Eventually, Japanese authorities fined the bank $300,000, revoked the licence of CSFB's derivatives unit and convicted the bank of criminal charges – it was the first foreign firm ever to be sanctioned this way. The Japanese judge denounced CSFB, saying, 'The obstruction of the government inspection by the defendant bank involved the whole branch and it was planned and systematic.'[15] It was a blow to Wheat personally, given his prior role in running the Japanese business.

By then, CSFB was in trouble with authorities in the US too, where Stone's compensation arrangements had come to the attention of a top banking regulator. In February 1999, officials at the Federal Reserve Bank of New York sent a letter to Wheat suggesting the arrangement was open to potential abuse. The letter said Stone's group were inappropriately front-loading loan fees, rather than having them paid over the life of the loan, to 'maximize' the amount available for the profit-sharing plan. The Fed letter criticized Wheat's hands-off approach to management. 'Senior management oversight of this business has been inadequate,' the letter read. 'The incentives of this profit-sharing arrangement, when combined with the absence of effective independent oversight . . . lead us to question whether this business is being run in a safe and sound manner.'[16]

When Wheat finally curbed the excesses of his real-estate investing wonder, the outcome was inevitable. Without the freedom to lend at will, Stone's team was always going to leave. Stone was soon on his way out, squabbling with his employer over an $80-million bonus package, as the bank was left scrambling to sell off $10 billion in real-estate loans and investments gone bad.[17]

The Russian crisis, too, was coming to a head. In March 1999, Credit Suisse announced a plan to restructure the debt, run by Ipkendanz. The details were complex and shifted some of the problem into the future, but the bank had taken a massive blow. There was even speculation that the board would consider a merger with another bank – perhaps Swiss rival UBS or Germany's Deutsche Bank.[18] Within months, Credit Suisse shockingly revealed that its exposure to Russia was more than $2 billion, by far the largest of any Western institution, and far more than investors in the bank's shares had anticipated. In all, the bank's exposure to troubled emerging markets ran into many billions of dollars. When the full extent of the problem was revealed, Credit Suisse's stock price fell sharply, by as much as 10 per cent in a day.[19]

This rolling series of crises – from London to Tokyo to New York, all via a crumbling Moscow – was a chastening, and potentially fatal, period for Wheat's leadership. His policy of hiring aggressive, entrepreneurial bankers and allowing them to run with limited direction suddenly looked very problematic.

'Russia, we got that totally wrong,' Wheat told a magazine reporter. 'We were too greedy and stupid in thinking we could keep a 30 per cent, 40 per cent or 60 per cent market share.' Managing the firm required 'a balance between control – knowing exactly what's going on – and innovation and new thought.'[20]

# EIGHT

# The Bubble

While Allen Wheat was the mastermind behind Credit Suisse's investment-banking strategy at this time, if there was one individual whose career personified its twists and turns, that was probably Frank Quattrone.

In the second half of the 1990s, there was only one place to be if you wanted to make pots of money. Silicon Valley, in Northern California, was the scene of a technology industry boom, and bankers who supported the explosion were getting rich. The flood of investment into new tech companies had begun in earnest in the middle of the decade thanks to a period of low interest rates and lasting economic growth that coincided with the widespread adoption of personal computers and the expansion of the internet. Budding entrepreneurs were hungry for capital to turn their ideas into real, multibillion-dollar businesses. Search engines, new media companies, online retailers, internet stockbrokers, telecoms businesses, home-computer and cell-phone makers – everyone needed money to fuel their ambitious growth plans. Bankers and investors supplied that funding, extracted chunky fees, and took these nascent technology companies to the public market, where their shares were sold at heady valuations. It was a kind of mania and it drove the value of technology stocks on the NASDAQ stock exchange up 800 per cent between 1995 and 2000.

Like every bank on Wall Street, CSFB wanted a piece of the action. Allen Wheat turned to his trusty playbook and set out to hire the biggest name he could find. And there was no bigger name in tech banking than Frank Quattrone, the 'Prince of Silicon Valley'.[1]

Quattrone had grown up in a working-class neighbourhood in Philadelphia. He was a smart student and won a two-year apprenticeship out of school at the blue-blooded Wall Street investment bank Morgan Stanley. He was an odd fit: confident, hard-working and bright, but a little scruffy around the edges. Still, his ambition and smarts won admirers at the firm. At the end of his apprenticeship, Quattrone could have stayed at the bank, but he chose to study for an MBA at Stanford. The tech scene was beginning to take off there and, when his studies were over, Quattrone rejoined Morgan Stanley on the condition he could remain in the Bay Area rather than move to New York.

At the time, it seemed like an odd move. The technology industry was still small, in the shadow of traditional engines of the economy, such as oil and gas, or the automotive sector. Backing established manufacturing companies, for instance, still brought in fees multiples higher than anything Silicon Valley yet offered. But Quattrone knew that tech was the future. He was building a network of personal connections, tapping the community of venture capitalists whose personal fortunes would soon fuel the explosion in tech.

Quattrone was different from the usual banker types. He had an unruly moustache and wore colourful sweaters that looked out of place on Wall Street but were less incongruous in the self-consciously casual tech world. He was also one of the toughest bankers around. Charming, funny and extremely smart, he was equally short-tempered, ruthless, and held a grudge against anyone who crossed him.[2]

Before too long, Morgan Stanley's technology business was humming. The value of tech IPOs sold by the investment bank increased from $203 million in 1990 to $5.8 billion in 1995. That year, the public listing of Netscape Communications truly fired the starting gun on the new dot.com era. Back then, Netscape was a fast-growing internet business, and it owned the world's dominant web browser. Quattrone and Morgan Stanley ran its IPO, which was a runaway success. The share price doubled on day one, and the company found itself with a $2.9-billion valuation. It was a wake-up call for the bank's greying executives back in New York, and a crowning moment for Quattrone.

Pretty soon, Quattrone was one of the biggest names in banking. His salary, just a few thousand dollars a decade earlier, reached $6 million by 1995, the highest of any investment banker in the firm.[3] He had a growing team, too, filled with young bankers who wanted in on the action. But he wanted even more. Quattrone argued for a greater share of the bank's resources and more control over key decisions. He wanted to be able to decide headcount, pay and promotions without having to consult New York. He wanted a share of the revenue his business brought to the firm, and he wanted everyone in the bank who worked on the tech sector to report to him – not just the bankers, but also the analysts and brokers. It was a highly unusual request. Typically, bankers working on deals for corporate clients reported through one line; analysts, researchers and brokers whose clients were big investors reported to someone else. This kind of separation avoided any conflict of interest, real or perceived.

Quattrone argued that his business was different. He spent all his time with tech entrepreneurs who rewrote the rules, chased their dreams and didn't need to check with anyone. These people were successful not because they toed the line, but because they were disruptive. Dealing with these clients was not the same as the old

Wall Street ways and required much more flexibility, Quattrone told his bosses. But, when he lost that argument and the bank flat-out refused his demands, Quattrone's time there was over.

In early 1996, he left for Deutsche Bank. One of Quattrone's former Morgan Stanley mentors had recently joined the German firm and promised him that he would be given the autonomy he craved. At the German bank, he would have a share of the profits he brought in and the freedom to hire his own 'dream team' of top tech-specialist bankers.[4]

Deutsche was yet another European bank trying to break into Wall Street. It didn't have the same brand name or pull with clients in the US as Morgan Stanley, and Quattrone's competitors doubted he could continue his winning run. But they were wrong. When Deutsche landed a coveted role on the Amazon.com IPO, it sent a signal that Quattrone was still the biggest player in tech banking.

The terms of the profit-sharing arrangement Quattrone had struck with his new employer meant that his team was getting rich, fast. In 1997, Quattrone's group at Deutsche Bank brought in about $150 million in profit. Half of that went to the bank and half to Quattrone to distribute to his staff. Already, though, some Deutsche executives were concerned about the scale of these compensation payments. Senior staff began grumbling that they were not paid in the same lucrative fashion and briefed anonymous stories in the media that were highly critical of Quattrone's contract.[5] A change in leadership at the bank also undermined Quattrone's position. The new chiefs talked about de-emphasizing the North American market and pushed to redraft the terms of Quattrone's pay deal, something Quattrone strongly resisted. Rumours abounded that the star tech banker was unhappy and had been shopping his group around Wall Street in search of a better offer. The stand-off was such an open secret that Quattrone even sent a letter to dozens of clients, imploring: 'We are here to stay. Please trust us.'[6]

Despite these assurances, by the middle of 1998, Quattrone and most of his team were gone, lured away to CSFB.

Wheat's bank was desperate to plant a flag in the buoyant technology sector. And hotshot Quattrone fitted the mould. He was given extraordinary latitude, freedom to manage headcount, autonomy over pay and promotions, and an enormous travel and conference budget. The bank also agreed to a lucrative compensation package.[7] On top of all that, Quattrone's team was granted about $300 million in Credit Suisse stock options as an extra incentive to get the deal done.[8]

With the tech sector turning white hot, Quattrone's business exploded. The CSFB team worked on dozens of IPOs over the next couple of years – more than all of their nearest rivals combined. They advised on mega-merger deals, like the $20-billion takeover of Ascend Communications by Lucent Technologies, which 'rained money on Quattrone and the CSFB tech group.'[9] By the end of Quattrone's first full year, 1999, CSFB was surging up the Wall Street league tables, courtesy of the work the bank was doing for technology sector clients.[10] It was a stunning climb up the investment-banking pecking order. By 1999, CSFB's tech banking team was generating as much as 20 per cent of the bank's entire revenue.[11] Early the next year, Quattrone emailed his team to say they were 'on the verge of global domination in this business.' His message projected the group's annual revenues would hit $1 billion.[12] Some reports said Quattrone personally took home $120 million that year alone.[13]

But, even then, there were creeping doubts about the methods employed at CSFB's tech unit. Critics said CSFB had a much lower threshold for taking clients public, working on IPOs for companies whose long-term revenue or profit projections seemed less viable. They also questioned CSFB's lavish pay deals and unusual reporting structure, which blurred the traditional dividing line between bankers and researchers, who were supposed to offer independent analysis on company shares. Inside the bank, there was some concern about a so-called, unofficial 'Friends of Frank' programme, whereby clients of Quattrone's team were given special treatment when it came to getting access to hot tech IPOs.[14]

By late 1999, the tech boom was at its most overhyped. Every business that could stick a '.com' suffix to its name had done so, multiplying the valuation of its shares. Many of those companies had piles of cash but were short on ideas of how to spend it constructively. Instead, it was burning a hole in their collective pockets. Stories about extravagance in the industry were commonplace. An annual conference for technology investors hosted by Quattrone's team was an illustrative example: the November 1999 conference in Arizona cost about $3 million, and featured guest appearances from comedian and actor Robin Williams and Michelin-starred chef Daniel Boulud.[15]

That conference may have marked the beginning of the end of the internet boom. Lingering concerns about the rapid rise in the valuation of dot.com stocks, and the inherent risks involved in investing in profligate businesses that had yet to turn a profit, were exacerbated when the Federal Reserve moved interest rates higher, suggesting a flood of cheap money was coming to an end.

A March 2000 article in *Barron's* magazine, headed 'Burning up: Warning: Internet companies are running out of cash – fast', turned up the heat.[16] *Barron's* was a kind of Bible to many US investors, and its cover stories could move the stock market. The article, by one of the magazine's best-known columnists, Jack Willoughby, spelled out in great detail how many dot.com businesses were unprofitable and potentially heading for bankruptcy. Willoughby showed that 74 per cent of internet companies were burning through cash quicker than they could accumulate it.

It was time to get out of tech. Share prices began to fall, and just kept tumbling. Over the next couple of years, the valuation of tech stocks lost trillions of dollars, and the tech-focused NASDAQ lost almost all the gains earned during the bubble years.

The bursting of the bubble wasn't just bad for business. It cast a shadow over the whole tech sector, including the banking industry that had facilitated its rise. Many investors were burned badly as the market fell fast, and bankers were suddenly on the radar of regulators looking to apportion blame for the crisis that ensued. Quattrone's pre-eminent position in tech banking suddenly counted against him. He was a star that shone brighter than any other, but his flameout was all the greater for it.

Initially, US regulators weren't looking at Quattrone at all. Instead, they were investigating whether CSFB brokers and some bankers had demanded kickbacks on IPOs in the form of large commissions paid on trades from unrelated activity. But, as these investigations spread, they inevitably drew in Frank.

On Sunday, 3 December 2000, CSFB's general counsel emailed Quattrone with grim news. Authorities were investigating how the bank had allocated shares on tech IPOs to clients. The bank had received federal grand jury subpoenas demanding documents and testimony from staff. Quattrone typed a response into his Blackberry: 'Are the regulators accusing us of criminal activity?' The CSFB lawyer replied, 'they are not formally accusing us . . . yet, but they are investigating because they think something bad happened . . . please do not under any circumstances discuss these facts with anyone – however innocently – because everything we say now is going to come under a microscope.'[17]

The following day, another CSFB executive sent an email to Quattrone and other senior bankers. The message said that, with the risk of litigation on 'broken tech IPOs' mounting, it was time to remind staff about document retention and 'file cleanup'. The executive signed off, 'Today it's administrative housekeeping. In January, it could be improper destruction of evidence.' Quattrone replied, 'You shouldn't make jokes like that on email.'

A couple of hours later, the executive sent a redraft of the message, which included directions to the company's documentation policies, to the entire tech-banking division, with the subject line: 'Time to clean up those files'. A day after that, Quattrone resent the email to the entire group, endorsing its message, saying, 'I strongly advise you to follow these procedures.'[18]

Hitting *send* was a fateful decision, though one Quattrone and his lawyers later said was made in the context of a busy executive dashing through dozens of emails towards the end of his working day, without too much thought. US authorities saw it differently. In their view, Quattrone had allegedly tried to stymie investigators by encouraging junior staff to destroy documents. Quattrone's empire was crumbling, and CSFB's name was dragged down too, especially in the US, where its operations were inevitably linked to broader anger over the bursting of the dot.com bubble.

In 2003, Quattrone resigned from CSFB. Days later, authorities filed a lawsuit seeking to bar him from the industry and demanding he return some of his compensation package. Then US attorney for the Southern District of New York, James Comey, also formally accused Quattrone of telling his staff to destroy evidence. Quattrone countered that he had not realized his actions could be interpreted as directing staff to interfere in an ongoing investigation. 'It never crossed my mind,' he told a court.[19] The jury rejected his argument, and, in May 2004, Quattrone was found guilty of obstruction of justice and witness tampering. Four months later, he was sentenced to eighteen months in prison. It was the first time in decades that a high-profile Wall Street figure had been convicted. But it wasn't the end of the story.

Quattrone launched an appeal – and he was successful. In 2006, his conviction was quashed on the basis that the earlier trial judge had improperly instructed the jury on the law. Quattrone was cleared of wrongdoing and free to work again.* He set up his own firm, and,

---

* In particular, the appeal judgement raised the notion of intent – whether Quattrone had known when he sent his email to staff about document retention that such an action would potentially interfere with the investigation – effectively indicating that the prior trial had not properly addressed this issue.

though his career never again reached anything like the heights of the dot.com era, it was a victory of sorts for the once high-flying banker.

For CSFB, the episode was a huge and expensive embarrassment, an indictment of Wheat's strategy. Hiring Quattrone was a reflection of Credit Suisse's desperate attempts to mimic Wall Street and compete with the biggest banks, no matter what the cost. It had certainly brought in huge amounts of revenue. But Quattrone had also been a target for critics of banking excess, and his tenure had ultimately left the bank chastened. It should have been a harsh lesson learned. Instead, it was just another step towards oblivion.

# NINE

# A Deal at the Top

By the turn of the century, the mighty Rainer Gut's time at the top was coming to an end. During his tenure, the two sides of the bank – Swiss and American – had been transformed, and endured trauma in equal measure. In mid-2000, Gut took the title 'honorary chairman'. The responsibilities that went with this made-up role were unclear, though Gut's presence continued to loom over the bank, where he had an office for many years to come.

In the US, meanwhile, Allen Wheat's stable of superstar bankers was burning to the ground. While this could have been a moment for Credit Suisse to leave US-style investment banking altogether, instead the Swiss bank doubled down on Wall Street, just as it had done time and again when Gut was in charge.

Donaldson, Lufkin & Jenrette was a US investment bank founded in 1959. DLJ was a mid-tier player, smaller than CSFB. Compared with some of its bigger, stuffier rivals, DLJ was meritocratic, and staff were encouraged to compete aggressively for financial rewards.

In an infamous 1994 email memo to staff, a senior DLJ manager decried employees who claimed to be 'too busy' to take on more work. 'The one true definition of "too busy" is being physically unable and having no more time to do more work,' the memo said. 'You are "busy" if you are working each weekday at least 16 hours and at least 16 hours on the weekend. These are working hours – not traveling, gabbing, or eating time. If these are not your hours at the office, you have the capacity to take on more work.'[1]

Bankers who could handle that ninety-six-hour work week were well remunerated. DLJ was known as one of the most open-handed Wall Street firms, paying out more of its revenue to staff than even its free-spending peers. For every dollar DLJ made in revenue, about fifty-four cents went to pay its staff, about ten cents higher than at other Wall Street firms.

One of DLJ's particular strengths was in junk bonds – bonds issued by companies with credit ratings lower than investment grade. *Barron's* magazine had given DLJ the undesirable nickname 'The New Drexel', a reference to Drexel Burnham Lambert, the junk-bond specialist that collapsed in the 1980s following accusations of illegal activity. It had been a lucrative business for many years, but, as the junk-bond market went into a drawn-out slump in the 1990s, the outlook for DLJ had dimmed. A costly and ill-conceived push into Europe, meanwhile, had resulted in DLJ hiring hundreds of expensive bankers, but without any profit to show for it.

By the turn of the millennium, the firm had a target on its back as the sector was struck by a mini wave of consolidation. Notably, UBS had bought PaineWebber, a US brokerage and investment bank, for $12 billion in the summer of 2000. That deal had leapfrogged UBS up the US banking league table and increased the pressure for other firms to bulk up too.[2]

At Credit Suisse, Wheat and the bank's new chairman Lukas Mühlemann couldn't risk being left behind. In early August 2000, Wheat met with Joe Roby, the CEO of DLJ. Over lunch, the two bankers talked mergers and discussed the challenge for smaller players like DLJ as the big banks got even bigger.

'We've been scratching our heads on these issues for a while,' Roby told a journalist later. He believed one solution was for DLJ to find its own friendly merger partner, like CSFB. Wheat 'pursued the opportunity aggressively,' Roby said.[3]

Three weeks later, Wheat and Mühlemann agreed to buy DLJ for $11.5 billion, around three times its book value – a huge premium, even in those heady days before the bursting of the dot.com bubble had taken the air out of the entire market.

Wheat said that the combined businesses would be 'a tremendous new force in the global investment-banking industry.'[4] For sure, it added some heft, including 11,000 new staff on top of the 15,000 already at CSFB. The acquisition pitched CSFB into the top tier of banks working on US stock listings, behind only Goldman Sachs and Morgan Stanley.[5] But the deal was an enormous bet on yet more star bankers and a speculative turnaround in the junk-bond markets. From the start, the deal looked like a mistake.

First, there was too much overlap between DLJ and CSFB. Credit Suisse would have to lay off thousands of the staff it had just acquired, costing hundreds of millions of dollars in redundancy payments. At the same time, many of DLJ's best bankers began heading for the exits. One of the highest-profile departures was Ken Moelis, a top DLJ dealmaker based in Southern California, who ran a team of about a hundred bankers. He had been named head of US investment banking for CSFB after the takeover, but, within just a few weeks, he left. Shockingly, Moelis joined UBS, a poke in the eye for its Swiss rival.

The point of the DLJ deal had been to bring in good people, but, with so many of them leaving, it was costing an awful lot to stop others from going too. Credit Suisse set aside more than a billion dollars for retention packages for key performers and handed out huge pay increases – as much as 50 per cent – and guaranteed bonuses. Meanwhile, several top DLJ executives were major shareholders in the firm, so, when the deal closed, they cashed in big time – a handful of key DLJ executives pocketed more than $600 million between them.[6] All of this created a bitterness among staff who were resentful of the perks and lucrative contracts of a handful of their colleagues. Many demanded better pay deals to make up the gap, and the proportion of revenue dished out in compensation headed sharply higher, towards sixty cents in every dollar.

There was anger too that the DLJ brand name had been killed off. At a party for hundreds of former DLJ staff in New York that November, a video displayed on a big screen showed a cartoon figure with the DLJ logo dancing to Gloria Gaynor's 'I Will Survive' before it was crushed by a mirror ball tagged 'Credit Suisse First Boston'.[7]

The pricey deal looked even more so as the dot.com bubble burst. Within months of the deal closing, demand for stock research, IPOs and junk bonds collapsed, and shares in financial firms tanked – making the price at which Wheat's CSFB bought DLJ seem even more expensive.

The acquisition weighed heavily on Mühlemann and Wheat. Both championed the flawed takeover which had ended up destroying value and setting CSFB on course for a prolonged series of losses. Up to this point, despite everything, Wheat's CSFB had been profitable, generally making bucketloads of money even as its staff went rogue and sometimes fell foul of the authorities. The bank's board had tolerated ethically dubious behaviour, but would they tolerate losses?

In the end, the DLJ deal had been a woefully timed investment and a colossal waste of shareholders' money that dragged the bank down for years. It drove up expenses and created more division within the ranks, while the cost of the acquisition sat on the balance sheet like an ugly reminder of a failed strategy. For the next two decades, each incoming CEO and chairman would be hampered by Wheat's legacy. It was typical that most of them simply kicked the problem further down the line.

# TEN

# Mack the Knife

The bank that Rainer Gut built was beaten up, trailing in the wake of bigger rivals and desperately in need of some sane, clear-headed leadership. Over the coming years, a series of top executives would take on the challenge. Eventually, this process would culminate in the rise of Urs Rohner, perhaps the most important chair in the bank's history. But it took some time to get to that point. Before then, there were plenty of twists and missed opportunities, and more than one misguided senior appointment.

One afternoon in the spring of 2001, John Mack took a call from an old business contact, Lionel Pincus, chairman of the private-equity firm Warburg Pincus. Mack was one of the most recognizable and renowned executives on Wall Street. He was a huge personality, a charismatic and ambitious executive who had left Morgan Stanley earlier that year after losing a power struggle with the CEO, whose job Mack had coveted. Since his exit, Mack had been working on his golf game and stewing about the circumstances of his departure from the blue-blood bank where he'd worked for almost three decades. Mack was incredibly wealthy by any measure – some reports said he left Morgan Stanley with as much as $600 million in accumulated stock and options – but he still felt like he had a point to prove.[1]

Pincus, an éminence grise of the finance world, was also fabulously rich. He was a beneficiary of Gut's expansion splurge, having sold part of his business to Credit Suisse a couple of years earlier. On the phone with Mack, he made a proposal. Pincus wanted to introduce Mack to Lukas Mühlemann. Mack agreed.

Soon after, the three met for lunch at the famed Manhattan restaurant the Four Seasons, 'a nexus of talent, money and ambition,' where being seen with other power brokers was more important than what was on the menu.[2] Mack found Mühlemann cold and formal, and wondered whether the point of the very public lunch meeting was to send a signal to Zurich that he was taking action on Credit Suisse's many problems. Mühlemann got straight to the point: 'I want you to run Credit Suisse First Boston,' he said. 'We need an eight-hundred-pound gorilla, and you're it.'[3]

For Wall Street lifers like Mack, First Boston was still a powerful brand. Yes, it was just one half of the bigger Swiss bank. And, yes, he'd be reporting to Mühlemann, who oversaw the whole bank, rather than running the show himself. But Mack spied an opportunity to return to glory, and he agreed to the offer. He was back in the game.

One person apparently caught off guard by Mühlemann's manoeuvrings was Allen Wheat. At the start of July 2001, Wheat had asked his boss outright if his job was in danger following the bank's recent run of problems. Mühlemann had assured him all was well. Yet, a week later, when Wheat was in London on a routine visit to the bank's Canary Wharf offices, he was summoned to talk with Mühlemann again. This time, Wheat was fired.[4] It was a cloak-and-dagger operation, typical of the way the bank handled the departure of top executives. Having survived numerous crises over more than a decade at the firm, there had been no direct indication to the American that this time was different, never mind that his replacement was already signed up. Credit Suisse's bare statement said simply that

Wheat was leaving 'to pursue other interests' – a Wall Street euphemism for, 'He's gone, and it wasn't his choice.'

It was an ignominious departure. The modern CSFB was Wheat's creation. But there was no loyalty at Credit Suisse, no graceful exit. Over and over, when the time came, the bank ditched its executives unceremoniously, no matter who they were. It made for whiplash-inducing changes of leadership and strategy. It also meant too many top executives just wanted to make their bonus quickly and didn't care about building for the long term. The individual came first, the firm a distant second.

For now, Mack was preparing his triumphant re-entry to the banking world, though he did get a warning about what to expect when working with the Swiss board. One trusted former colleague who'd worked in a Swiss bank told him that, to make it work, he'd have to either move to Zurich or spin off the old First Boston business into a separate company entirely.[5] Otherwise, he'd be treated just like Wheat.

Mack, a thick-skinned and outspoken executive, was not likely to be daunted. He had grown up in small-town North Carolina, the son of Lebanese immigrants. His dream, he later wrote, was to open a menswear shop, but he stumbled into financial services after taking an entry-level job in a securities firm to help pay for college. At Morgan Stanley, he was known for cultivating strong relationships with staff, walking the bank's trading floors, eating lunch with the junior bankers and playing golf with colleagues.[6] He'd also earned the predictable nickname 'Mack the Knife' – a reference to the song from the musical *The Threepenny Opera* – that reflected his reputation for a ruthless approach to cost-cutting.

In a press conference soon after taking over at CSFB, Mack signalled that he planned to attack the new role with characteristic vigour. The bank had been run like 'a big casino', he said, with staff only concerned with what they got out of the bank and not what was good for the firm or its shareholders.

Mack believed he had a licence to clean up and pinpointed two priorities. First, he would deal with the crisis in the tech team, at that stage still run by Frank Quattrone.* Mack believed Wheat hadn't engaged with the regulators, particularly in the US, and he quickly moved to bulk up CSFB's legal team, hiring experienced lawyers, including a former head of enforcement at the SEC. Within weeks of Mack's arrival, this group flew to Washington DC to meet with authorities, promising more cooperation and sending a signal that they took compliance and the ongoing investigations seriously. It was a step towards putting their relationship on a better footing. Over the next few months, Mack paid $250 million in settlements to US authorities to end their investigations.

The other big priority was to get a handle on CSFB's out-of-whack cost base and the mess left by the DLJ merger. Some bankers were treating the company like a personal piggy bank, running up enormous expense accounts. One of Mack's close lieutenants found that former DLJ executives were using a corporate pre-pay card meant for car fuel payments to fill up their private aircraft, for instance. Pay was a problem; a whole load of people were on revenue-sharing compensation schemes, which Mack despised. The merger had also left the firm with lots of bankers duplicating the work of their colleagues. 'It's like Noah's Ark,' one of Mack's allies told him. 'There are two of everything.'[7] Mack had been expecting problems, but the scale of the issues was a shock. A few months after joining the firm, he told an associate over dinner, 'I've got the biggest, most fucked-up company in the world right here.'[8]

Mack set about a plan of extensive cost-cutting and headcount

---

* Mack had known Quattrone when they both worked at Morgan Stanley. Indeed, it was Mack who'd refused Quattrone's demands for greater autonomy and more pay, leading to Quattrone's decision to leave the bank altogether. Now, Mack found himself nominally in charge of Quattrone again, at least until Quattrone was pushed out as the heat from regulators became unbearable.

reduction. Over the next year, he got rid of 6,500 jobs and reduced expenses by $3 billion.[9] He persuaded senior managers to take a 25 per cent cut in their pay and to get their staff to do the same. One department head told a reporter that, after meeting one-on-one with Mack, he spoke to his team about cutting their pay, saying, 'We can be pigs. But if the firm implodes, that isn't good for the long term. Let's think about helping John.'[10]

Mack continued squeezing out the big names that Wheat had hired, and some of the well-paid executives that had landed with the DLJ deal. He took the bank out of some of its riskier businesses and openly talked about the need for a complete ethical reset.

'The Street has the reputation of doing whatever it takes to do a deal,' he told an interviewer from *Businessweek* a few months after taking over CSFB. 'The whole money culture has skewed a lot of firms. We want people to be successful and wealthy. But not to the detriment of our clients . . . We want to be known as an ethical firm on Wall Street, and we want to be trusted.'[11]

The problem for Mack was that this effort to turn around the bank's culture coincided with a downturn in the markets following the end of the dot.com bubble and the 9/11 terror attacks, which had cast a chill over the global economy. Few corporate clients were interested in big mergers or wanted to list their shares on the stock market given the economic uncertainty. Mack said it was 'a perfect storm' – everything that could go wrong was going wrong.[12] In 2002, CSFB recorded a loss of $1.2 billion, contributing to a $2.5-billion loss at Credit Suisse, its worst set of results on record. The Swiss bank's share price was plummeting.

In Zurich, there was growing irritation with the bank's performance. A series of damning articles in the *Financial Times* had been passed around among major shareholders and board members, raising the possibility that Mühlemann could be forced out as CEO and chairman of the whole bank.

'He has lost credibility with investors completely. And inside the firm pretty much,' one anonymous bank analyst told the paper.

In the autumn of 2002, it came as little surprise that he resigned. His role as chairman was eventually taken by Walter Kielholz, who, like Mühlemann, was a graduate of St Gallen and had previously worked at the insurer Swiss Re. It was a remarkable characteristic of the bank that the board often seemed to be made up of a small group of senior Swiss businessmen whose experiences and careers were closely intertwined.

Mack, with his experience at Morgan Stanley, was the obvious candidate to take over as CEO of the whole bank. Later, he said the board had offered him the job on condition that he moved to Zurich and learned German. But he turned them down, saying he didn't have time to take language lessons. It was a clear illustration of the uncompromising cultural gulf between the two sides. It seemed that relatively petty disagreements or clashes of ego got in the way of finding the best solution.

Credit Suisse found an awkward workaround. Rather than have one chief, the bank decided to have two, and appointed Mack as co-CEO alongside Ossie Grübel, a German-born veteran of Credit Suisse. They were meant to split responsibility for the bank in half. Mack looked after the old CSFB, and Grübel ran the private bank and the Swiss business.

The relationship between the two men was awkward. Grübel was a gruff, heavy-smoking former trader, who wasn't afraid to speak his mind. He and Mack were two alpha males, forced to work in tandem. They never clashed outright. Instead, they stayed out of each other's way, only really coming together at budget meetings.

A bigger issue was the uneasy relationship between Mack and the Swiss. They gossiped behind his back that he was a hypocrite when it came to cutting back on costs, that he was too extravagant, flaunting his wealth and power. Whenever he visited Zurich, he arrived with a sweep of blacked-out cars and an entourage of American suits that irritated his Swiss colleagues. One incident at a board meeting was particularly vexing. Mack was seated at the long table in the conference room. The air was filled with tobacco smoke as usual, and Mack and the other Americans were wearing headphones so they could listen to a real-time translation of their Swiss-German-speaking colleagues. For Mack, these meetings had a single purpose. He needed to secure a big enough bonus pool to keep the troops happy. Sensing the usual reticence from his Swiss colleagues, Mack said, 'Look, I don't want this money for me. It's for my people. Quite frankly, I don't need it. I've got more money than most of you have.' Not only was this statement possibly untrue – the Swiss were good at hiding their riches – but it also confirmed the bias of many in the room who already believed that the US bankers were all cowboys: show-offs who just wanted to milk their Swiss colleagues for more money.

There was not much love lost in the other direction. Mack was frustrated that, in meetings with the Swiss regulator, for instance, they'd insist on speaking only in Swiss-German, which he couldn't understand. Another time, an American colleague and ally told him he had to stop telling the board they were stupid. 'I can't help it,' Mack replied. 'They *are* stupid.'[13] Colleagues noticed that, even years after he'd joined Credit Suisse, he continued to talk about the bank as though he was an outsider. Some felt like his heart wasn't really in it.

Mack's manner sometimes went down badly with US bankers too. Some executives took exception to his repeated calls for the bank to create an ethical culture, which implied every one of them had been unethical in the past.[14] He would badger his own staff, tell them, 'We are falling way behind Goldman and Morgan Stanley. We've got to play with the big dogs.' But then he was far less forthcoming in providing more detailed instructions. Mack confused some top executives with a vague instruction to take more risk, but not the kind that had got CSFB in trouble in the past. Some senior figures complained he didn't really make an effort to understand the CSFB business in detail. Others felt that Mack could be tone-deaf when it came to cost savings. Once, trying to demonstrate his commitment to austerity, Mack told a group of top executives that the company had bought a Gulfstream IV, rather than the more expensive Gulfstream V, to fly him from New York to Zurich. Another time, at a company party, he sang a karaoke rendition of 'Mack the Knife' that was meant to be a self-deprecating parody, but misfired given the bank was slashing headcount at the time.

Despite all of this, the bank's fortunes did appear to be turning at last, as the economy picked up steam. In 2003, a year after the bank's stunning loss, CSFB returned to profit, reporting earnings of $0.9 billion. Mack was triumphant, adding staff and confidently talking up plans to expand into new revenue streams. Even then, some board members were critical that Mack had been too slow to jump on the economic revival. Other banks had moved earlier, shifting resources into proprietary trading – in-house trading with the bank's own money – and providing capital to hedge funds and private-equity firms that were getting more active as markets picked up. Mack's CSFB had moved into these areas, but it lagged behind the likes of Goldman Sachs and Morgan Stanley.

The relationship between the co-CEO and his board was also fracturing over the long-term structural plan for Credit Suisse. Mack wanted CSFB to pursue a merger with another bank to better compete with US rivals. Some colleagues believed he was already talking with the UK's Barclays. Other European banks, including Germany's Deutsche Bank, were also mentioned in the media as potential merger partners. But Grübel and most of the board were against Mack's idea. The opponents believed a cross-border deal would be hard to get past regulators, and it would eventually become a costly distraction. They preferred the status quo. This was a major strategic question, and it would prove impossible to reconcile the different sides.

Still, there was little open sign of division as the board and senior managers gathered in Manhattan, in late June 2004, to celebrate the latest set of positive results. Mack, Grübel, Kielholz and some senior managers were clinking glasses at Per Se, the celebrated New York restaurant just off Central Park, congratulating one another on the ongoing turnaround in the bank's fortunes. As dinner rolled on into the evening, the mood was convivial, and there was no sign of a rift. And yet, early the next morning, Mack took a call from one of his allies on the board. They had decided to end his term with the bank.

He was taken totally by surprise, and his shock only deepened when he discovered the extent of the deception. The bank had set up a whole shadow operation in a different building across the street from its Manhattan office. This was complete with a duplicate communications team and press release ready to go. Mack's replacement was ready too. Grübel would become sole CEO, and the old CSFB would be run by one of Mack's senior staff, an American trader named Brady Dougan who had been with the firm for fifteen years and whose office was next door to Mack's. The two were never close, and there had been persistent rumours that Dougan was on his way out. Mack even told colleagues he'd never really trusted his fellow American.

Kielholz and the board positioned Mack's departure as an agreement between both sides not to extend his contract, which had been up for renewal. He credited Mack with 'a dramatic turnaround' of the bank and said he had enhanced its reputation by resolving regulatory issues and strengthening some areas of the business. But the chairman also said the bank had no interest in a merger, and executives briefed the media that the board had decided it no longer wanted a co-CEO structure.

Mack also said at the time that the bank needed a single CEO. But the way Credit Suisse had dispensed with him hurt. It was almost a carbon copy of the underhanded way the bank had booted out Allen Wheat just a couple of years earlier. There had been no discussion or attempt to come up with an elegant exit plan. It was clear that, if you were an executive at Credit Suisse, there was no trust. Everyone was dispensable.

In truth, Mack and the Swiss had never gelled. The former CEO and his ex-colleagues had one final dig at each other. When he'd joined the firm, the bank had agreed that, if Mack left, he could buy at cost the company jet – the Gulfstream IV the bank had acquired to zip him across the Atlantic. That was a great deal. Private jets are scarce and tend to increase in value, so the G-IV would be worth more than its cost price. Naturally, the former CEO exercised his option, winning one over on his old employer. But the Swiss couldn't let his victory pass. The agreement only mentioned the plane. In a final act of spite, they stripped the luxury aircraft of its cutlery and other items before handing it over. Any sense that Mack had left on good terms was a joke, though the banker likely had the last laugh – a year after he was ousted from Credit Suisse, Mack finally got the job he had really craved all along. In June 2005, he was named sole CEO of Morgan Stanley.

By then, though many in the banking industry didn't yet know it, another financial bubble was forming, and, when it burst, even the biggest banks would feel the pain.

# ELEVEN

# One Bank

Ossie Grübel had defaulted into becoming CEO of Credit Suisse. With Rainer Gut, Allen Wheat, Lukas Mühlemann and John Mack all gone in quick succession, he was the last man standing. For a while, he did a better job than any of them in bringing some stability to the bank.

Born in what became the old East Germany, Grübel joined Deutsche Bank as an apprentice straight out of school. He was a fast learner and showed a knack for trading securities. He joined Credit Suisse's former White Weld business and moved to London. He was a well-known figure in the City through the 1980s and early 1990s, renowned for his love of cigars and fast cars. He rose steadily and went on to run Credit Suisse's private bank, a rare achievement for a career trader, meaning he had much broader experience across the firm than most of his peers.

Still, few would have predicted Grübel's ascent to the very top of the bank. Gravel-voiced and downbeat, he was a far cry from the showmen who dominated on Wall Street. He had no university education, never mind a degree from St Gallen, the alma mater of dozens of other top Swiss banking executives. He had a dry sense of humour, and frequently upset colleagues with his blunt approach and temper. 'It is one of my faults,' he told a reporter. 'I have a very short fuse.'[1] In 2001, he had resigned from the bank after an argument with Mühlemann over strategy – but, somehow, he hung on to his office and was rehired when Mühlemann himself was pushed aside.

Grübel was certainly well respected. He was highly numerate, very analytical and had a sharp trader's instinct that got colleagues out of trouble on many occasions.[2] Grübel's view was that every manager in the bank, including the CEO, should be on top of the risks they were taking with the bank's money. He believed everyone was accountable.

Shortly after taking control of the whole bank, Grübel launched his big initiative – an effort to finally end the fiefdoms at Credit Suisse. The 'One Bank' strategy forced each division of the bank to work more closely with the others. He killed off the Credit Suisse First Boston name. From now on, that business was simply the investment-banking division. There was new branding and new reporting lines. Grübel wanted no more internal sniping and no more turf wars.

Of course, his plan drew criticism. 'The one-bank concept is coming at us from everywhere, but there is astonishingly little detail as to what it actually means,' a CSFB banker told *Forbes* magazine in 2006. 'Diluting' the First Boston culture could lead to a wave of departures, the banker said.[3]

There were certainly many bankers who lamented the demise of the First Boston name for years, clutching at their branded pens and fleece vests like treasured artefacts. But most staff fell into line with the new approach. Among Grübel's executive team, the only controversy was what shade of blue to use on the new corporate logo – the Americans dismissed a prototype that reminded them of the branding for Domino's Pizza.

Credit Suisse's management team seemed to finally be working as a single unit, an analyst who covered the bank's shares told *The Banker* magazine: 'Mr. Grübel nominated all the current executive board members. This makes it a very different place from the old, divided Credit Suisse and Credit Suisse First Boston, which were alienated from each other, didn't communicate, and were dominated by political rifts.'[4]

Meanwhile, Grübel continued cutting costs in the investment bank and expanded into faster-growing markets, especially in Asia. He also installed a reporting process that gave the senior management team a comprehensive overview of all the risks the bank faced.* And the One Bank approach meant private bankers began referring clients to their colleagues in the investment bank, and vice versa. At some other banks, this was simply the way it always had been. At Credit Suisse, Grübel's reforms offered a glimpse at a more stable type of banking.

Grübel sold the troubled Winterthur insurance business in June 2006, and he publicly stated that big acquisitions were off the table. His regime was making a clean break from the expansive empire-building of the past. And, as markets soared, Credit Suisse's results followed suit. In the three years after Grübel became CEO, profits and the share price took off.

The other big success of Grübel's tenure was that he had built a roster of senior managers committed to his plan. This included Urs Rohner, the bank's chief legal counsel; Ueli Körner, the head of the bank in Switzerland; and Brady Dougan, the investment-banking chief. In turn, each of them would get their own shot at running the bank.

Dougan in particular had a long-standing relationship with

---

* Under Grübel, Credit Suisse reduced its exposure to US sub-prime mortgage bonds in 2006, while rival banks were still piling in. It was a decision that saved the bank billions of dollars in losses within a few years when the same sub-prime mortgage bonds sparked the global financial crisis.

Grübel. The American was a trader, like Grübel, and they had worked together from time to time. Grübel found Dougan a little uninspiring – dull, even – but he was reliable and paid close attention to details. They had grown close when John Mack sent Dougan from New York to London in 2004, an attempt by Mack to exile a junior colleague he didn't trust.[5] Once Grübel became CEO, Dougan became a loyal advocate of the One Bank strategy, and a supporter of his boss's efforts to reduce costs and focus on businesses where Credit Suisse had a stronger hand than its rivals. By 2006, Dougan's investment-banking division was showing the impact of the turnaround effort as profits more than tripled to $4.9 billion.

Early the following year, Grübel shocked the bank and its investors. Out of nowhere, he announced his retirement. There were rumours that he had fallen out with the bank's chairman, Walter Kielholz. Grübel was reportedly suspicious of Kielholz's lack of banking experience, while reports suggested Kielholz had tried to push Grübel to buy the Dutch bank ABN AMRO, an idea he had flatly rejected. The German's final set of quarterly results showed record earnings, and some analysts questioned whether the arch trader was timing his exit to get out at the top.[6] Grübel simply said it was time to give someone else a go. 'Credit Suisse is in a better position than ever before and there is no need for me to hang around,' he said. 'My work here is done.'*[7]

---

* Two years after leaving Credit Suisse, Grübel was drawn out of retirement once more, this time to save UBS in the aftermath of the financial crisis. Grübel set about tightening costs, and he brought clarity to the bank's strategy. For a while, he was credited with bringing the bank back from its near-death experience, and it looked like he might be CEO for longer than expected. But that changed in 2011. A rogue trader at UBS in London had lost the bank $2.3 billion. It was an enormous amount that required a sacrifice among the bank's senior leadership. Some on UBS's board wanted Grübel to stay, but the CEO decided otherwise. 'The buck stops with me,' he said in a press conference. 'Saint Ossie', as he was dubbed in the Swiss media, felt that he had to take responsibility. Grübel was regarded as

At a dinner in Zurich to mark Grübel's retirement, the elder statesman, Rainer Gut, still lingered. In his speech, Gut lightly roasted Grübel, introducing one of the bank's most successful leaders as 'a great diamond in the rough.' Gut continued, 'I mean both of those things . . . Ossie is a big diamond, and he is seriously rough.'

Grübel stood up and unsmilingly responded: 'I'm very sorry I've been in a bad mood for the past twenty years.' It was a drily comic moment, but also a reflection of the unflashy, focused approach Grübel had brought to his role.

In later years, Grübel's reign looked like a rare period of unity, success and profitability, uninterrupted by scandals. Was he lucky? He had the benefit of a low starting point and low expectations. Certainly, the financial markets were accommodating to banks at that time too. Low interest rates and strong economies made it almost impossible not to make money. Whatever stability he brought to the bank proved to be fairly short-term, an illusion that was only temporary. Moreover, scandals that emerged in later years had been there all along. They didn't land when Grübel was CEO, but they were there, nevertheless.

In May 2007, Grübel gave his final speech as the bank's CEO at the annual general meeting in Zurich. He lauded Credit Suisse's earnings, but he also issued a series of warnings about 'fundamental forces' shaping the industry, new technologies and increasing globalization that made staff ever more independent, which increased the opportunities but also the risks. In banking, he said, there are no production facilities or patents, and preserving the trust of clients is key.

'I cannot stress how critical high ethical standards are for our sector,' he said. 'This is not just a matter of being able to distinguish

---

principled and diligent. But, like many others, he ended up leaving Swiss banking on the back of a major scandal.

between permitted and potentially illegal conduct, but also of being willing to ask critical questions and of speaking plainly."[8]

In the years that followed, these words proved enormously prescient.

# TWELVE

# The Financial Crisis

'We were partly lucky, partly smart.' That was Brady Dougan, in September 2011, explaining how Credit Suisse had somehow got through the worst financial crisis in a century in better shape than most of its peers.[1] Credit Suisse didn't just survive. It had emerged as one of the unlikely crisis winners. How on earth had that happened?

Four years earlier, when CEO Ossie Grübel surprised the bank by announcing his retirement, there were several candidates to replace him. Two executives were ahead of the pack. The first was Urs Rohner, the chief legal counsel. Though his career had been mostly in insurance, he would have represented a return to traditional Swiss leadership after the Mack and Grübel years.

Dougan was the alternative. A Credit Suisse veteran who'd worked in the bank's offices around the world, he shared Grübel's keen eye for risk, as well as his diligent, thorough and workmanlike approach. Though Dougan was from the US, his was a low-key Midwestern kind of American style, very different from that of the brash Wall Street characters that had run the bank before. Dougan drove a Toyota Prius, drank Diet Coke and was the first to leave company parties. His biggest indulgence was a morning run along the shore of Lake Zurich. Notoriously, he started work at 5 a.m. and frequently delved deep into the numbers on risky trades or complex transactions. He had mostly avoided any of the controversies that had dogged the bank, a record that earned him the nickname 'Teflon Man'.[2]

It was Dougan, then, who became CEO. The decision embittered Rohner, who made little attempt to hide his jealousy from colleagues. Within a few years, he would get his revenge.

But, in 2007, Dougan ascended to the peak of a bank in top form, supported by a tight inner circle of senior executives left behind by Grübel. Most important of these was Paul Calello, who became head of the investment bank. Calello was a particularly close counsellor who had joined Credit Suisse from Bankers Trust at the same time as Dougan in 1990. They were different characters, extroverted Calello and the more introverted Dougan, who balanced each other out. With the exception of Rohner, Brady Dougan broadly benefited from a cohesiveness among his senior staff that some of his predecessors had not enjoyed.

For the first few months, he continued where Grübel left off. He cut more costs. He pursued the One Bank strategy. Credit Suisse racked up more profitable quarters. Dougan would fly into Zurich for meetings on Tuesdays and leave for New York on Thursdays. There, he'd spend the weekend poring over numbers, line by line, before zipping back to Zurich the following Tuesday. It was a gruelling schedule.

But times were changing, and Dougan knew it. 'The markets have been quite good, but there is no doubt at some point they will turn more negative in some parts of our business and in the industry more generally', Dougan told the *Financial Times* early in his tenure.[3] Indeed, the global financial crisis was just around the corner.

For years, banks had given home loans to more and more

Americans, regardless of their ability to pay them back. Some of these loans, known as sub-prime mortgages, were packaged up in financial products that were sold to other financial firms. The inherent risks within were often masked by layers of complexity, so that investors had no idea what they'd actually bought. Dougan barely had time to decorate his new office before the whole mess started to unravel. Fissures in the US housing market led to panic in the market for sub-prime-mortgage-backed securities. Trust in the financial system evaporated.

The crisis spread quickly. In April 2007, a US sub-prime lender, New Century Financial, filed for bankruptcy. By early summer, funds that invested in sub-prime mortgages warned of massive losses. As summer turned to autumn, a handful of smaller banks in Germany and the UK collapsed. In October, UBS and Citigroup said they had each lost billions of dollars from sub-prime-related investments. In early 2008, the IMF and the Federal Reserve warned of a major slow-down. Housing and construction businesses in the US and Europe collapsed. Billions of dollars were wiped from the value of a whole range of companies as the economy tanked and the banking world went into a tailspin.

In April 2008, Credit Suisse reported a loss of $2.1 billion in the first quarter. The bank had also written off $10 billion worth of investments – a small portion of the approximately $300 billion written off by banks worldwide since the start of the crisis. The numbers were staggering, but, in the context of a broad banking catastrophe, Credit Suisse was holding up better than some of its rivals. At the bank's annual meeting for shareholders that year, Dougan said Credit Suisse had seen 'disturbing signs' in US sub-prime as early as the autumn of 2006 and had cut back its exposure even as competitors continued piling in. He lauded the bank's business model and its wise decision-making.[4]

But the crisis was worsening. US authorities stepped in to rescue Fannie Mae and Freddie Mac, America's two largest lenders. Banks desperately tried to raise new capital to stabilize their balance sheets. On a Friday afternoon in September 2008, Federal Reserve officials summoned Dougan and a dozen CEOs of the world's largest banks to an emergency summit in New York. The investment bank Lehman Brothers was about to go under. It was unthinkable. There was no last-minute rescue. What was left of it was broken up and swallowed by its competitors.[5]

More banks toppled and the end of the entire global financial system seemed plausible. Unprecedented action was needed. Over the coming weeks, authorities around the world rolled out a series of extraordinary measures to save the system. Failing banks were nationalized or forced to merge with rivals. Others were handed enormous bailouts. The US government announced a $700-billion programme to acquire toxic sub-prime mortgage debt. Around the world, governments spent more than a trillion dollars to stabilize the financial system and stop the economic disaster.

In Switzerland, UBS was on the wrong end of some of the biggest losses of the crisis. The bank's chairman and CEO resigned as it was forced to raise more than $25 billion in new capital from investors at a steep discount. At Credit Suisse, the losses were smaller but still ran to billions of dollars. Top executives at UBS considered for a moment if the two Swiss banks should merge.[6] They called Dougan to sound him out. It would have been an enormous transaction that created a true giant of the global banking industry. But the idea never took hold. Any thoughts of a merger were ditched when the Swiss government offered both banks a bailout. UBS agreed and the government invested more than $5 billion. Dougan, though, declined to take the government's money. Instead, Credit Suisse secured a private rescue package in the form of an $8.8-billion investment from a group of investors led by Qatar.

By early 2009, the scale of government largesse, especially in the US, meant the worst of the crisis was over. Credit Suisse had lost more than $8 billion the previous year, but it was already returning to profitability. It had been one of the most dysfunctional banks in the world heading into the crisis. After the carnage, Dougan said Credit Suisse was 'exceptionally well positioned to take advantage of the opportunities that exist today'.[7]

It was a high point for Credit Suisse that came during a low point for the rest of the industry. For years, Credit Suisse bankers would crow that, unlike UBS and some others, their bank hadn't needed a government bailout. In truth, the survival of the entire global banking sector was bought with government bailouts.

There were also signs, sometimes forgotten amid the chaos of the crisis, that the old Credit Suisse had never really gone away. For instance, in late 2007, a group of traders at Credit Suisse's London office were found to have deliberately mispriced investments in mortgage-backed securities to disguise their losses and record 'fictional profits', according to a filing by US authorities.[8] Their actions led the bank to write off $2.65 billion. Later, one of the traders, Kareem Serageldin, was extradited to the US and charged by authorities, including the FBI and SEC, with 'engaging in a complex scheme to fraudulently overstate the prices of $3 billion in subprime bonds during the height of the subprime credit crisis'.[9] Serageldin was eventually sentenced to thirty months in prison,[10] the only executive at any major bank to serve jail time tied to the financial crisis.[11] The judge said his conduct had been just 'a small piece of an overall evil climate within the bank and with many other banks'.

Over the coming years, a series of lawsuits, mostly in the US, showed the full extent of Credit Suisse's role in fomenting the subprime crisis. These cases showed that the bank had been an active participant in inflating the US housing bubble, and that its staff were deeply involved in repackaging sub-prime mortgages and selling them on to other unwitting financial firms. In emails published by US authorities and other litigants, Credit Suisse staff referred to some of the mortgages as 'bad loans', 'crap' and 'complete garbage'.[12] They discussed systemic failures in due diligence and wrote emails about loans that were fraudulent, unmonitored or submitted at puffed-up valuations. Senior executives couldn't pretend this was nothing to do with them. As early as 2004, a report from Credit Suisse's internal auditors – shared with senior managers, including Dougan – found that the bank's mortgage unit exposed Credit Suisse to 'a significant and unacceptable level of operational, financial or reputational risks'.[13]

Dougan and Grübel were lauded by many as smart traders who'd got out of sub-prime before it was too late. But, given the evidence that rolled out later, they also had plenty of information that potentially allowed them to see the crisis before it hit. After all, Credit Suisse had been right in the thick of it.

In the years immediately after the crisis, though, Dougan was facing a different problem. His management team, his inner circle of trusted advisers, was thinning out. He was particularly affected by the illness and death of his long-time friend and confidant, Paul Calello, who passed away of non-Hodgkin lymphoma.

Dougan was still at his desk at 5 a.m., still touring the cantons, still poring over the fine details of complex trades. But colleagues noticed that he seemed to be losing his mojo.

Dougan's navigation of the financial crisis had brought him lots of credibility – and some loyalty from among the troops. But one further development meant he was always running on borrowed time. In 2011, the board appointed Urs Rohner as the bank's new chairman. It was Rohner who was now the ultimate boss.

# PART THREE
The Great Decline

# THIRTEEN

# Sanctions Busting

For a brief moment in 2009, Credit Suisse basked in the possibility that it was one of the healthiest, best-run banks in the world. And then the moment passed. It was business as usual, with the bank's name tied to yet another episode of stunningly immoral behaviour.

The world was just beginning to emerge from the crisis. Financial markets bottomed out in the spring and began climbing steadily (and would continue to do so for a decade or so). But there was a lot of anger about the behaviour of banks that had plunged the world into chaos for the past eighteen months. Politicians were keen to seize the moment and exert some power over the banks at last. Sometimes, their actions were directly related to the origins of the crisis. At other times, authorities just wanted to use the mood to punish wrongdoing in general.

That December, the US Department of Justice blasted Credit Suisse for helping clients in sanctioned countries secretly shift their money through the US financial system. It was clear evidence that, for all the stability Dougan and Grübel had brought to the bank, fundamentally, little had changed.

The details of the Justice Department's findings were damning and showed a pattern of misconduct going back decades.[1] In the 1980s, when President Ronald Reagan had first imposed sanctions on Libya, Credit Suisse had been helping clients get around those restrictions. Soon after the Libyan sanctions were announced, Credit Suisse introduced a policy that said: 'Payment orders of Libyan banks or government organizations to third-party accounts in the United States or with US banks abroad are to be executed without stating the name of the ordering party.' The bank's staff knew that, by excluding those details, their clients' payments would evade detection in the US financial system. In the 1990s, the bank updated its policy: for sanctioned clients that didn't want to be identified, staff could replace the name with the phrase 'by order of a client'.

After the Clinton administration strengthened sanctions against Iran, Credit Suisse agreed to requests by Iranian banks to omit identifying details from payments from them too. Sometimes, bank employees stripped names and references from payment messages to avoid detection. Other times, the employees substituted client names with codewords or bland phrases such as 'one of our customers'. When payments from Credit Suisse's Iranian clients were rejected by other US institutions, the bank introduced something called 'cover payments', which shielded the Iranian client's identity by masking it with a payment from a non-sanctioned entity.

The DOJ found that Credit Suisse employees trained Iranian customers to falsify information on wire transfers. They shared images of payment orders to show clients how to avoid detection. They produced a pamphlet for Iranian clients, entitled 'How to transfer USD payments', which explained how to get around automated filters in the US banking system that flagged suspicious transactions.

The sanctions-busting business extended beyond payments. The bank had also managed investments in bonds and equities on behalf of a Libyan fund and a bank based in Sudan, both of which were under UN and US sanctions at the time. Staff working with these clients referred to them by the code names 'Wood' and 'Iron' to mask their true identity. Employees were told to prevent these clients coming into contact with the bank's legal and compliance departments. Trading in US securities on behalf of these clients was conducted through a web of accounts to provide another layer of obfuscation.

Over the years, employees of Credit Suisse disguised more than $1.6 billion in transactions from sanctioned individuals or organizations from countries including Cuba, Myanmar, Sudan, Libya and Iran. These included the Atomic Energy Organization of Iran and the Aerospace Industries Organization, both designated as proliferators of weapons of mass destruction by US authorities.[2]

These weren't the actions of rogue employees. Sanctions violations were official policy, and assisting sanctioned clients was a business model. Internal Credit Suisse client files for sanctioned Iranian banks flashed a warning: 'Do not mention the name of the Iranian bank in payment orders.' Managers emailed instructions to staff on how to alter payments to ensure they would pass through the US financial system undetected. Towards the end of the 1990s, a 'sanctioned countries' project shifted the bank's Iran business from New York and London to Zurich, to hide it from regulators.

As long as it could get away with it, the bank actively sought more of this business. The DOJ found memos, emails and other documents that showed Credit Suisse staff were in a 'continuous dialogue about evading US sanctions', with the aim of increasing business with existing and future Iranian clients. Marketing materials promised Iranian clients that all payments would be 'checked in advance by our specially designated payment team . . . [who] are most professional and aware of the special attention such payments of yours do require.' When the UK bank Lloyds stopped working with Iranian clients in

2003, Credit Suisse swooped in, picking up thousands of new customers.

'In essence,' the assistant US attorney general said, 'Credit Suisse said to sanctioned entities, "We've got a service, and that service is helping you evade US banking regulations."'

In the 2000s, the board and senior management finally started to worry that the sanctions-busting business could lead to trouble. Closer integration between the US and Swiss sides of the bank – the One Bank strategy – raised the threat of penalties against US employees. In 2005, the bank launched an internal review of its business with sanctioned entities. Its office in Tehran was closed and new policies were circulated emphasizing the need for compliance with sanctions. Over the next three years, the bank wound the business down. By then, US investigators were all over the bank.

The Americans hit Credit Suisse with a $536-million penalty and a two-year deferred prosecution agreement, meaning it could face further criminal charges if its conduct didn't improve.

Oddly, the scandal hardly seemed to register. After the massive losses of the financial crisis, a half-billion-dollar fine seemed relatively inconsequential. The bank's share price barely dipped.* But Dougan and his colleagues should have seen the punishment as a forewarning. After the crisis, the mood towards banks had shifted sharply. The excesses of the banking sector had been laid bare. The industry had crashed the entire economy and threatened global chaos. This was the era of Occupy Wall Street. In Washington, the Obama administration soon sought to crack down on wrongdoing. The US would 'hold accountable those who engage in financial misconduct,' said US Attorney General Eric Holder. The punishment

---

* Other banks were later accused of sanctions breaches too. A few years after Credit Suisse's fine, the DOJ hit France's BNP Paribas with a mammoth $8.9-billion penalty for breaking sanctions, for instance.

meted out to Credit Suisse for sanctions violations 'sends a strong message that we will not let this type of conduct stand.'

In Switzerland, too, the public and politicians took a more critical approach to the giant domestic banks. In particular, the extraordinary public bailout of UBS brought more scrutiny to the industry as a whole. There was a sense that many Swiss felt it should never happen again.

# FOURTEEN

# Tax Dodging

Pretty soon, the Americans gave yet another example of the shift in their approach to banking misconduct. This time, the implications for Credit Suisse were greater. Banking secrecy – a pillar of the Swiss financial industry – was suddenly under threat.

The episode began with a bearded banker named Bradley Birkenfeld. American-born Birkenfeld had worked briefly in private banking at Credit Suisse in the mid-1990s. He was hired by UBS in 2001 to recruit wealthy American clients. The bank sponsored art fairs and sports events, where Birkenfeld and his colleagues would schmooze their affluent targets. What they offered was the allure of Switzerland's banking secrecy law, which would give rich American clients the opportunity to hide their wealth from US tax authorities.

Over the years, Birkenfeld and his colleagues went to great lengths to satisfy these elite clients.[1] They set up sham entities to conceal their clients' wealth. They advised them to store cash in Swiss safe-deposit boxes and to purchase jewellery and artwork overseas using funds deposited in Swiss accounts. They doled out Swiss credit cards to

Americans and misrepresented funds withdrawn from Swiss accounts as loans. Once, Birkenfeld used a client's illicit money to buy diamonds and smuggled them to the US in a toothpaste tube.

Like breaking sanctions, providing tax-avoidance schemes was not an anomaly of the Swiss banking model. It was a core business. UBS helped thousands of US clients conceal their identities and the existence of about $20 billion in deposits.[2] In one year alone, UBS bankers were alleged to have travelled to the US about 3,800 times to meet with clients who had offshore accounts. Some of them even undertook training in counter-surveillance techniques to avoid detection by FBI and US customs officers.

There was important context. For years, US authorities had identified offshore tax evasion as a multitrillion-dollar problem, according to estimates from the likes of the Organisation for Economic Co-operation and Development (OECD) and the Department of State (DOS). Even before the Occupy Wall Street movement exploded, pressure was building on American politicians to do something about it, especially to help reduce the country's ballooning budget deficit. Several new pieces of legislation aimed to clamp down on tax cheats, and the US was leading an international effort to coordinate measures to restrict the use of offshore tax havens. (As with the clampdown on sanctions busting, critics of the Americans say that their action here is an example of hypocritical overreach. There may be no jurisdiction in the world that provides less transparency than is available to individuals and companies in the state of Delaware).

In May 2005, Birkenfeld's fortunes took a swift turn for the worse when the US Internal Revenue Service launched an investigation into one of his oldest, most lucrative clients. Igor Olenicoff was a Florida-based Russian real-estate billionaire, whose business was worth millions of dollars a year to Birkenfeld and UBS. After a raid by IRS investigators on Olenicoff's house, the authorities had access to years of documents fingering Birkenfeld's work. That October, he abruptly quit UBS. He said later that his exit was prompted by the discovery of an internal UBS document that appeared to disown the cross-border business. It was, he alleged, a 'sandbag job', with the bank throwing its staff under the bus to divert blame away from the institution.[3]

By 2007, both Olenicoff and Birkenfeld were cooperating with authorities. Birkenfeld flew into the US with a bagful of emails, training manuals, PowerPoint presentations and more that he would share with investigators.[4] Olenicoff pleaded guilty to tax fraud, paid a relatively small fine and received a reduced sentence in return for information about who had organized the tax fraud. The focus now turned to UBS. For the next two years, US investigators were crawling all over the bank, learning crucial details about the mechanics of its schemes to help Americans avoid declaring their wealth and paying taxes. In February 2009, the bank agreed to pay $780 million to settle criminal charges.

The US attorney for the Southern District of Florida was scathing about the bank's motivation for providing this kind of service: 'The reason was money – the business was too profitable to give up. This was not a mere compliance oversight, but rather a knowing crime motivated by greed and disrespect of the law.'[5]

The scandal played out in the most public way. Olenicoff sued UBS, unsuccessfully, alleging it had provided him with bad advice. Birkenfeld was convicted of fraud and sentenced to forty months in jail. He appeared on CBS's prime-time current-affairs show, protesting the sentence: 'I gave them the biggest tax-fraud case in the world,' he said. 'I exposed 19,000 criminals and I'm going to jail for that?'[6]

After two and a half years, Birkenfeld was released from prison. It was then his fortunes took another twist – the IRS said the information he had given them was so valuable that Birkenfeld was awarded $104 million for his whistle-blowing efforts. 'Sometimes, crime does pay,' *The New York Times* declared.[7] The landmark award – it was the biggest ever given to a tax whistle-blower – would likely encourage others to come forward to report tax fraud, Birkenfeld's lawyers said.

More significant than the fine, though, was that US authorities demanded UBS hand over names of its US account holders. The Swiss bank objected fiercely, citing Swiss bank secrecy laws. A stand-off ensued for months. Supplying client names to the Americans would break Swiss law, UBS argued. But the US authorities countered, explaining that not handing them over put UBS at much greater risk, with the promise of a criminal indictment for the bank if it failed to comply. The issue escalated to the point the US and Swiss governments were in direct talks about how to end the stalemate. Finally, in August 2009, they announced that UBS would give the names of about 4,500 account holders to Swiss authorities, who would then pass them on to their US counterparts. It was a workaround. But the under-pressure Swiss had agreed to break their sacred bank secrecy rules.

The number of account holders given up was only a relatively small portion of all the Americans on UBS's books. But the decision sent a shockwave through Switzerland's banking industry nonetheless. The government had buckled on a central pillar of the private banking sector's unique place in the global financial system. There was a political backlash in Switzerland, and years of wrangling with the Americans followed. But the settlement with the US also opened up action by other governments. The Germans and French were among several who were quick to start their own investigations into Swiss-sponsored tax evasion.

Immediately after the UBS scandal broke, US legislators turned their focus to Credit Suisse and other Swiss banks. The Senate permanent subcommittee on investigations, led by Carl Levin – a veteran Democratic Party politician renowned as the scourge of corporate America[8]– asked Credit Suisse executives whether the bank had similarly assisted tax cheats. In private, the bank's leaders admitted that it had, but promised they were already cleaning up their act.

Indeed, after UBS's massive fine, Dougan had quickly ordered an internal review to figure out the extent of Credit Suisse's exposure. Of course, his bank was at it too.

For years, Credit Suisse had been soliciting thousands of US clients and offering to hide their wealth in Switzerland.[9] Swiss bankers had been flying to the US to meet with clients, against rules that forbade them from marketing offshore banking in the US. They set up secretive meetings and recruited clients at sponsored events, such as New York's annual 'Swiss Ball' and golf tournaments in Florida. Bankers limited their written communications and routinely destroyed records, including hard copies of statements, while clients were encouraged to travel to Switzerland to do their business in person. The bank even had a branch office in Zurich airport to offer its inbound clients a full range of banking services. As at UBS, this illicit US banking business was supported by policy. At Credit Suisse, Swiss accounts opened for US clients were monitored only by Swiss bank employees, to the exclusion of US bankers who knew more about US tax requirements. The bank narrowly defined 'US persons' to deliberately exclude many US taxpayers, and assets of US clients managed through foreign offshore entities were excluded from the appropriate regulatory checks.

Dougan's post-financial-crisis glow was fading fast. In Switzerland, he had become the focus for widespread anger towards overpaid bankers. This was fuelled by a complicated deferred compensation plan that paid out big time for Dougan and a handful of other executives. The plan tied their bonuses to a comparison between Credit Suisse's stock price and those of other European banks. All the shares were in the dumps, but Credit Suisse's were relatively stronger, which earned Dougan a total pay packet of $100 million for 2010. It was a staggering amount, especially with the crisis still reverberating through the economy and the bank in the process of laying off thousands of staff. Investors were angry, politicians demanded a compensation clampdown, and Dougan's name became a lightning rod for broad anti-bank sentiment.*

Meanwhile, the bank was finally getting out of the business of helping clients avoid paying taxes. A long series of so-called 'exit projects' followed, with names like the Entities Project, Project Tom, Project Tim, Titan and Argon. These efforts focused on getting US clients to certify that they weren't subject to US taxes, with the result that the bank closed thousands of accounts containing billions of dollars over the next five years. But it wasn't enough to keep the authorities away.

A warning shot came in July 2010, when German authorities raided thirteen separate Credit Suisse locations in the country. About 150 investigators stormed the bank's offices and carted off vast quantities of data.[10] The bank eventually agreed to a fine of $150 million to settle the German investigation.

In February 2011, the tax issues went up a notch when the Department of Justice charged four Credit Suisse bankers with using secret accounts to help US citizens evade taxes.[11] The bank hadn't yet been charged with wrongdoing, but the actions of its employees, based on the DOJ's allegations, looked incriminating. The indictments talked about a conspiracy that dated back to 1953 and involved 'two generations of US tax evaders'. The suspect bankers kept thousands of secret accounts for US customers, with as much as $3 billion in them. They had accepted falsified IRS forms and advised US clients to withdraw less than $10,000 at a time to avoid raising automated alerts. Like their peers at UBS, they'd opened sham accounts and provided offshore credit cards to clients so that they could make transactions outside the US tax system.[12]

Following the indictments, Credit Suisse launched another

---

* Later, Swiss voters backed a proposal to give company shareholders a binding vote on executive pay – one of the toughest such measures anywhere in the world.

internal investigation, named Project Valentina, because it started on St Valentine's Day. Lawyers hired to conduct the probe in the US and Switzerland interviewed more than a hundred employees. They were still going through their investigation in the summer, when three more employees were indicted by the DOJ. Around the same time, the DOJ also sent a letter to the bank to say that the firm itself was now the target of a criminal investigation. The board and some senior executives were seriously spooked. Many feared they could become the target of personal legal action by US authorities. The bank stopped holding executive board meetings in the US and some Swiss executives of the bank ceased travelling to the US altogether.

By this time, Urs Rohner, who had coveted the CEO role before Dougan got it, had been appointed chairman. Rohner was a pillar of the Swiss business and social elite. He was a patron of the country's opera and theatre scene, a former hurdler for the Swiss national team and one half of a Swiss power couple – his partner, a former model, had founded the Zurich Film Festival and was a celebrated TV personality who hosted the Swiss version of *America's Next Top Model*.

Rohner was also a go-getter. He wasn't going to be a quiet chairman, passively watching in the background. Rohner wanted to determine strategy and, crucially, how the bank handled its many legal issues. For the next decade, Credit Suisse often fought regulators and other litigants rather than settling quickly. Over the years, it was a fateful approach. Issues piled up, one on top of another. In many cases, the bank suffered bigger punishments than would have been achieved with an early settlement.

Dougan, meanwhile, told colleagues the investigation was a legacy issue, held over from previous regimes. It had nothing to do with him. Some of his closest advisers argued it was a 'political hit job' by US Democratic politicians, out to bash the banks in the aftermath of the Occupy Wall Street movement.

In Washington, Senator Levin's committee was increasingly agitated by what they felt was the slow pace of Credit Suisse's clean-up, and they promptly opened a formal investigation. They found that Project Valentina had concluded without apparently getting anywhere. It hadn't figured out how many undeclared US accounts the bank operated, for instance. A few bankers had been disciplined, though none were fired. Lawyers working for the bank hadn't even produced a detailed report on their findings.

When it came to the tax-evasion issue, there was little chance of a fast resolution, and not much hope of a well-coordinated approach between the chairman and CEO, who were equally suspicious of one another. No one in a senior position at Credit Suisse was looking to admit guilt, negotiate with the US authorities, do a deal and move on. The issue lingered, damaging the bank, Rohner and Dougan too.

# FIFTEEN

# Dougan's Downfall

The financial crisis had shown that rules governing the banks were inadequate. The banks were 'too big to fail' – meaning that, unlike other businesses, governments would always feel compelled to bail them out – while the culture of banking was widely likened to that of a giant casino, with bankers gambling away other people's money on risky trading strategies.

Authorities around the world were looking to prevent this situation from ever happening again. They focused their attention on bank capital and introduced new rules that aimed to make bank balance sheets safer than they'd been in the past, while discouraging the worst kind of behaviour that led to the crisis. These new rules also posed a dilemma for Credit Suisse, whose business model was out of synch with the changes, and set up a fundamental clash between Rohner and Dougan about the future of the bank.

The view of the regulators went something like this. Banks could build up capital by selling more shares or by retaining profits. Capital was a good thing because it acted as a buffer to absorb losses. But, if you held too much capital, it acted as a kind of drag on the bank's profitability. Regulators wanted banks to hold more capital, making them less prone to failure. The more risks they took, and the more important the bank was to the whole financial system, the more capital each bank would have to hold.

Bankers everywhere complained that the new rules were too restrictive. But some banks were hurting more than others. In Europe, banks were hobbled by a secondary rolling economic crisis that stemmed from problems some governments there had in refinancing their debts. In contrast, the US economy was bouncing back, and banks there were benefiting. There were also differences in the rules applied by different national banking regulators –Swiss authorities, scarred by the near failure of UBS, had moved earlier and introduced tougher capital requirements.

Credit Suisse was in an almost uniquely difficult position. It battled with Wall Street for global investment-banking profits. That was now harder because the US banks had a much stronger domestic economy to fall back on. Within Switzerland, Credit Suisse suffered compared with UBS, which was traditionally more focused on private banking and wealth management, both areas favoured under the new rules. Still part-owned by the Swiss government, UBS also undertook a more rapid restructuring to get out of the kinds of business that no longer made sense after the global rule book had changed.

Dougan, faced with the impact that the new rules would have on the bank's business model, laid off staff and got out of some areas of investment banking that were no longer viable. His executive team considered more drastic measures. They discussed following UBS's lead with a more radical restructuring to completely exit a swathe of trading and other riskier businesses. But, in the end, Dougan decided against it. He was, after all, an investment banker, a trader at heart. The bank would stick to its traditional strengths – flaws and all – and make the most of it.

The new rules had also elevated the role of chief financial officer, the bank's top numbers whizz, who'd have to navigate the complex capital requirements. At Credit Suisse, the CFO was David Mathers. He had joined the bank in the late 1990s and gone on to run the equity research department before becoming the head of finance in the investment bank. Dougan had promoted him to CFO in 2010.

Englishman Mathers was an obsessive number cruncher like his boss. He was nerdy, ambitious and smart, a shrewd schemer with a flair for office politics. To some colleagues, he was known as 'Darth Vader' because of his cold, ruthless demeanour. Over the next few years, Mathers demonstrated a remarkable ability to manipulate Credit Suisse's accounts to show its capital position in the best light. This provided some cover for the bank as it clung to the old model.

In truth, though, the bank was struggling to adapt to the post-crisis world. Dougan seemed to switch back and forth, cutting resources in the investment bank and then adding them back, before cutting again. He bet that markets would swing in his favour, then bet the opposite. But revenue from investment banking was slumping. For the bank as a whole, profits mostly slid lower and lower, year-on-year, quarter-on-quarter.

By 2012, Rohner was losing patience. He wanted a bigger transformation. Rohner's idea was to separate the bank into four units: Asia, the Swiss bank, a US investment bank and wealth management. Asia was growing fast, with lots of entrepreneurs and quickly expanding businesses in need of banking services. In Switzerland, the Credit Suisse brand remained strong with retail customers. The investment bank would be more or less ring-fenced in the US. And more resources would be poured into wealth management, where revenue was more stable than in investment banking. Each of these pillars would operate almost independently, like separate businesses. Some executives around Dougan thought there was merit to parts of the proposal. But Dougan was reluctant. The plan was complex, and he wasn't willing to scale back the investment bank to the extent Rohner's plan demanded.

Dougan's rejection of Rohner's proposal was decisive. It would be hard to reconcile the differences between the chairman and CEO when they had such divergent views on strategy. One of them would have to go.

Meanwhile, as Credit Suisse floundered, investors were losing faith. The bank's share price was languishing and Dougan's leadership was already under fire because of his pay, the Iran sanctions revelations and the US tax-evasion investigations. Then, the CEO was dealt yet another blow. Every year, the Swiss National Bank publishes a report on financial stability. It's usually a mundane event, with the central bank trotting out vague, accepted wisdom about the direction of the global and domestic economy. But the 2012 edition contained a major surprise – a call for Credit Suisse to either cut its dividend payment to shareholders or issue new shares to bolster its balance sheet. The report warned that Credit Suisse was especially vulnerable to the ongoing Eurozone crisis, a potential housing bubble in Switzerland and weakness in the global economy. It was a stunning call. Either of the options the SNB outlined – cutting the dividend or issuing more stock – would be bad for shareholders. Credit Suisse's shares fell another 10 per cent.[1]

Dougan was completely blindsided. There had been no warning or contact from the central bank. The SNB wasn't even Credit Suisse's primary regulator – that job fell to the Swiss markets regulator, FINMA.

Dougan took to the local Swiss media to defend the bank's position. In an extraordinary interview with *SonntagsZeitung*, Dougan rebuked the head of the SNB, Thomas Jordan, who, he said, had not raised any concerns about the bank's capital position when the two had lunch ten days earlier.[2] He flat-out rejected the SNB's assertions, saying their assessment of the bank was 'difficult to comprehend'. The bank had no plan to issue new capital, he told the Swiss newspaper.

Despite Dougan's protestations, the issue gained traction. In his own weekly newspaper column, former CEO Ossie Grübel wrote that the bank would likely have to issue new shares or find some capital some other way.[3] Analysts who covered Credit Suisse's stock said that the SNB's assertion was self-fulfilling – once the regulator said more capital was needed, then the bank would surely have to find a way to find more capital, or risk a further drop in the share price. Some Credit Suisse board members began considering, again, whether the bank should merge with UBS. Combined, the banks could more easily resolve any capital concerns. In the end, the board didn't think Swiss politicians would allow it – if each bank was too big to fail, then combining them into one megabank was surely out of the question.

Within a month of the SNB report, Dougan made a humiliating about-turn. The bank would raise more capital, after all. Credit Suisse led the industry in issuing so-called CoCo bonds – contingent convertible debt securities that could be transformed into shares if the capital buffer fell below a certain level. CoCos, sometimes known as additional tier one or AT1 bonds, were expensive – they also became critical and controversial when Credit Suisse collapsed a few years later – but their magic was that they boosted capital without having to issue new shares, which was better for existing investors. Dougan announced the bank would steady its balance sheet by issuing more CoCo bonds, selling off some real estate and smaller asset-management businesses, and by cutting more costs.

The CEO's position was becoming increasingly tenuous. The American, who had made a big effort to build bridges with the Swiss, was suddenly criticized for not learning German and for spending too much time in the US.[4] Shareholders complained that Dougan only spoke in English at the annual meeting.[5] He was mocked for giving the wrong answer to a question about the workings of the Swiss government in an interview with a Swiss magazine.[6] His compensation package continued to rankle – the bank's former chairman Walter Kielholz told a Swiss television show that Dougan's latest pay award had been 'a mistake'.[7]

By 2014, the tax-evasion issue was also coming to a head. American investigators had continued their painstaking work, collecting about 100,000 documents and interviewing dozens of executives, some of whom were summoned to Washington, where they were publicly admonished and humiliated for the bank's wrongdoing. (Under questioning, Dougan claimed the airport office was for US clients who were going skiing and didn't want to visit a branch in Zurich.)

When the Senate subcommittee finally delivered its findings, the scale of the scandal mirrored what had been uncovered at UBS. At its peak, the bank had 22,000 US customers, with accounts containing as much as $12 billion. There were similarly salacious details about how its employees had conducted their illicit business. One former client described how a banker met him at the Mandarin Oriental Hotel and, over breakfast, handed him bank statements hidden inside a copy of *Sports Illustrated* magazine.

Dougan acknowledged the misconduct but downplayed it. The wrongdoing was 'centred on a small group of Swiss private bankers' and was 'unknown to our executive management,' he said. It was an aberration and never a significant source of business. He said the bank had not 'turned a blind eye to the past' and detailed its steps to fix the mess.

But the long delay in finding a resolution had irritated Senator Levin. He slammed Credit Suisse for initially 'holding back about how bad the problem was' and criticized the bank for taking five years to complete its exit projects. He complained that the Swiss had consistently thrown obstacles in the way of any proper settlement in order to preserve bank secrecy. Enforcement action had stalled and the bank had disclosed the names of only 238 account holders to the US – less than 1 per cent of the total number of potentially illicit accounts at the bank. 'The bottom line,' he said, 'is that Credit Suisse was in it as deep as UBS, aiding and abetting US tax evasion both in Switzerland and on US soil.'[8]

In Zurich, Rohner considered asking the Swiss government for a special exemption to hand over some client names to the Americans. The bank even raised the idea with the DOJ. The board thought it would potentially placate the US authorities, though they knew it would be an unpopular move in Switzerland and could put pressure on Dougan to quit. In the end, the bank decided against it.[9]

In May 2014, the bank finally pleaded guilty to charges of helping Americans cheat their taxes, and agreed to a $2.6-billion fine – the biggest-ever payment in a criminal tax case at the time. The penalty was increased because the bank had delayed cooperating with US authorities and because relevant records had been destroyed.[10] As part of the settlement, the Americans also planted a 'monitor' inside the bank to look for more examples of unreported wrongdoing. Over the next two years, about fifty US investigators continued digging through the bank's archives and interviewing staff, all at Credit Suisse's expense. Bank staff later complained that they were inundated with demands for documents and meetings resulting from the monitor's broad-ranging probe.[11]

US Attorney General Eric Holder lauded the settlement. 'The case shows that no financial institution, no matter its size or global reach, is above the law,' said Holder. 'When a bank engages in misconduct this brazen, it should expect that the Justice Department will pursue criminal prosecution to the fullest extent possible, as has happened here.'[12]

But Levin was disappointed with the outcome, especially because there was no requirement for Credit Suisse to hand over names.[13] Other US politicians complained that no senior executives had lost their jobs. A report in *Newsweek* magazine noted the bank had hired a well-connected Washington lobbying firm with close ties to President Barack Obama to help fight its corner, suggesting this had limited the scale of the punishment.[14] Dougan poured fuel on that fire when he told shareholders the $2.6 billion had no material impact on the bank's results.

In Zurich, though, the scandal had ignited yet more heated debate around the banking industry. Some politicians and media commentators were angry that the bank, in their view, had abused the secrecy laws, thereby putting Swiss law at risk of interference from US imperialists. Tax evasion, assisted by the banks, became a mainstream issue, a source of national embarrassment. The bankers were called traitors, both for setting up the tax schemes and then for conceding defeat to the Americans too. Credit Suisse may have got off lightly, but the scandal weighed heavily on public opinion, especially when it came to the reputation of senior bank executives. A Swiss newspaper poll reported that 78 per cent of readers wanted both Rohner and Dougan to step down.[15]

Both bankers dismissed that idea. It was never a consideration, Dougan told analysts on a conference call. On Swiss radio, Rohner defended himself, saying his hands were clean when it came to the tax affair, though he added, 'Whether the bank's hands have been clean over the years is another question.'[16]

It was an odd distinction. Rohner and Dougan had been at the bank, in senior roles, for years. Other bank executives elsewhere had taken the fall for misconduct, even when they weren't directly involved. At the UK's Barclays, CEO Bob Diamond resigned in 2012 after the bank admitted its staff had tried to rig interest rates. In Switzerland, Ossie Grübel, who had become CEO of UBS during the financial crisis, stepped down in 2011 after a rogue trader lost the bank billions of dollars.

At Credit Suisse, pressure was building on Dougan, on Rohner. Something would have to give. The business model was broken. The scandals were a national embarrassment. The bank's performance was mediocre at best. What made matters worse was that cross-town rival UBS was a bank transformed. From the depths a few years earlier, UBS was now hailed by some as the best-run bank in the world.[17] Under its new charismatic Swiss CEO, Sergio Ermotti, UBS had stripped back its investment bank and committed more resources to wealth management. UBS had refocused its approach to banking for a post-crisis world. It had achieved what Dougan had failed to.

By late 2014, it was an open secret that Rohner wanted Dougan out. He looked for an internal candidate, but most of the top executives were Dougan loyalists and American investment bankers who'd no more tackle the bank's structural challenges than Dougan had.[18] Instead, Rohner realized he'd have to look for an outsider. Regardless, the chairman's mind was made up. In March 2015, Dougan was out. Rohner had found a new CEO – one who would look to more radically transform the bank, for better or for worse.

# SIXTEEN

# The Man from the Prudential

Rohner's plan was to transform Credit Suisse once and for all. It had become too American, too focused on investment banking, out of touch with the post-crisis reality of the global banking industry. Fixing it might take ten years or more, and he wanted a CEO who would do whatever the chairman wanted.

He began searching for a candidate who would make big changes, who would be patient and determined. It couldn't be an investment banker. Americans were off the table. The ideal candidate would be an outsider, who wasn't tangled up in the errors of the past.

One name rose to the top of the list. Tidjane Thiam was the CEO of UK insurance company Prudential. He was a high-profile executive in an industry often run by low-key leaders. Thiam had a compelling personal story. He was born in the Ivory Coast, the youngest of seven in a prominent political family. Shortly after he was born, Thiam's father, a journalist and politician, was jailed for three years for allegedly plotting a coup. The charges were later shown to be false and, when he was released from prison, Thiam's father became a diplomat and the family moved to France.

Thiam had been a reticent student in the Ivory Coast, but he excelled at school in France. He earned a spot at the prestigious École Polytechnique in Paris, where he was awarded degrees in engineering and business. After graduating, he worked at the World Bank and for the consultancy firm McKinsey & Co. in Paris and New York. In the mid-1990s, he returned to the Ivory Coast and headed a government body that advised on infrastructure and the economy, and was later appointed minister for planning and development. Once, when he was in Paris en route to see his family in the US, he got an urgent call from one of his staff. A coup had broken out. Thiam turned back home. When he landed, gun-toting rebels roamed the streets, and Thiam was forced to live under armed guard for several weeks.[1] The country's new head of state offered him a role in government, but Thiam had no more appetite for politics at that time and chose to leave the country.

Suddenly, 'I had no job, no career, nothing at all,' Thiam told the UK radio show *Desert Island Discs*. 'If you've been in a situation where you have nothing, there's nothing much you're afraid of,' he added.

For a short while, he couldn't land a suitable role. Thiam felt that he was frequently the victim of racism, turned down for jobs because he was African. He was in Paris when he took a call from a head-hunter about a position with the UK insurance giant Aviva.

'I am very happy to interview,' he told the recruiter. 'But frankly, you need to tell them that you found someone who is black, African, Francophone and 6 ft 4.'

The recruiter concurred, and, this time, Thiam landed the job.[2] He moved to London, where he made waves as a charismatic and highly intellectual executive. He had a particular skill for explaining complex insurance issues in plain English and was tipped as a future leader of the firm. Instead, he moved to Aviva's rival, Prudential, where, in 2009, he was appointed CEO – the first African to head a

major UK company and one of the few black CEOs of a global financial firm anywhere in the world.

At the Prudential, Thiam launched an audacious $35.5-billion bid
to take over AIA, the Asian division of the giant US insurance firm
AIG, which was struggling to survive the financial crisis. The takeover proposal was an enormous bet on growth in Asia and would have
transformed the company. But some shareholders complained that it
was too expensive. A revised, lower bid was rejected, though Prudential remained on the hook for about £380 million in fees to advisers
hired to help with the deal. When AIA was later spun out of AIG as
a separate business, it thrived on the back of a rising tide of increasingly wealthy Asian clients. Thiam's plan was somewhat vindicated,
but the fact it failed looked like a missed opportunity.

Nevertheless, Prudential turned in quarter after quarter of strong
results for the next few years. Thiam became a financial celebrity in
the UK. He was a frequent guest on business television, became a
government adviser and sat alongside Kofi Annan and Bob Geldof on
the board of an African policy think tank set up by Tony Blair.

For a while, Thiam embraced life in London. He was often seen
cycling to work or watching the Arsenal football team (though he
eventually fell out with the team's French manager, Arsène Wenger,
in a disagreement over Wenger's tactics). But Thiam's relationship
with his adopted homeland soured in 2013, when the UK's financial
regulator fined Prudential £30 million and censured Thiam for the
failed AIA bid. The regulator said Thiam had not been open or coop-
erative, and complained they had first heard about the proposed
mega-deal via reports in the media. The UK's regulator was rarely so
bold. It felt like a very personal attack. In private, Thiam told associates he felt the regulator would not have taken the same action
against a white, British-born executive. It seemed only a matter of
time before Thiam would leave for another role, and he was frequently linked to jobs running big, global institutions, including the
International Monetary Fund.

At Credit Suisse, Urs Rohner wondered whether he'd be able to lure Thiam to Switzerland. They had met at the European Financial Services Round Table, an industry association for the leaders of the biggest banks and insurers in Europe. But they didn't know each other well.

Rohner turned to Kai Nargolwala, a long-time Credit Suisse board member who was also on the board at Prudential. Nargolwala knew both men, their strengths and weaknesses. He also knew the scale of the task at Credit Suisse, and he was broadly supportive of Rohner's plan to overhaul the business. Given his dual role, he wasn't allowed to be directly involved in the hiring process. But he gave Rohner some caveated encouragement. 'I don't think you'll get him,' Nargolwala told the chairman. 'But, if you do, he'll be one of the few people from outside the banking industry who would do a good job.'

Rohner sent a message to Thiam and asked for a meeting. In London, Thiam wasn't sure. The approach had come out of nowhere. He began asking his closest confidants for advice. Some of what he heard was far from complimentary. A long-time friend who ran a massive global hedge fund told him the bank had a reputation for incompetence and that it was a laughing stock in the hedge-fund industry. Another ally said the bank's brand had been badly damaged by frequent scandals, and that it was in the shadow of rival UBS.

Thiam often told junior staff to trust their instincts more. In this case, his instinct was to tell Rohner he wasn't interested. But, in truth, he was intrigued. Credit Suisse, though battered and bruised, remained a global player. It was still one of the biggest banks on Wall Street. And it had a bigger presence than most in Asia – and Thiam was a strong believer in the power of emerging markets. He agreed to meet with Rohner in London for a preliminary chat.

From the start, Thiam was very direct. He didn't have to leave Prudential and he knew Rohner wanted him. Negotiations were stacked in his favour. If he was to join, he'd need the authority to restructure the firm completely. He'd want a lot of autonomy, and he might reverse decisions of previous executives, including Rohner.

The chairman offered some assurances. The reason he wanted Thiam was precisely because he would take an entirely new approach. There would be no obstacles.

Thiam's interest was growing. He told Rohner that, if he took the job, he'd need some time to get to grips with everything. He'd never run an investment bank, so he would have to get up to speed on that. And there would be pushback for sure. Thiam knew he'd be seen as a strange choice, potentially an ill-suited one. But Rohner seemed less concerned. Insurance was complex, global, highly regulated. The differences weren't insurmountable.

Rohner was relentless. In the summer of 2014, Thiam was on holiday with his family in Miami when Rohner got in touch again. Other board members wanted to meet with their potential new CEO. Thiam agreed to talk to them. One by one, they flew out to Florida and sat down with Thiam over tea, coffee and soft drinks at the Four Seasons Hotel. One by one, they reinforced Rohner's message: the bank needed a fresh take on leadership and Thiam was their only pick.

Thiam continued to meet with members of the board. He frequently wondered aloud about his own lack of directly relevant investment-banking experience. Every time, by the end of the conversation, he felt persuaded it wouldn't be a hurdle.

Still Thiam was unsure about the role. That advice from friends about the bank's reputation nagged away in the back of his mind. But Rohner's pursuit went on. The two executives had nineteen separate meetings as the chairman tried to talk Thiam round. Twice, Thiam turned him down flat. In January 2015, Rohner and Thiam met again at the World Economic Forum at the Swiss ski resort Davos. Rohner had prepared for another tilt at persuading him to join. He reiterated that Thiam was the only candidate. They were not talking to anyone else, but he'd have to come soon. The firm was sinking, and change was urgently needed. Thiam's attitude was beginning to soften. He'd been at Prudential six years. It was time to move on. He knew Credit Suisse had problems, but it was a major, historic, global institution. With the board's backing, maybe he really could turn it around.

A few weeks later, in March 2015, Rohner announced Dougan was out and Thiam was the new CEO. Staff and analysts who covered the bank's shares were shocked. Dougan's departure had been on the cards for months, but the insurance executive was nobody's top pick to replace him. Nevertheless, the appointment was an immediate winner with investors. The share price jumped about 8 per cent in a day, while Prudential's fell sharply. Thiam's name alone was worth billions to shareholders, it seemed.

At a press conference in Zurich, Thiam switched effortlessly between German, French and English, immediately striking a sharp note of difference from his predecessor, whose stuttering attempts at German had been ridiculed in the Swiss media. It wasn't the only point of difference. Thiam was a much more comfortable public face than Dougan had ever been. He was a natural frontman.

And yet, there was also a moment that provided a glimpse of what lay ahead. Thiam appeared ruffled by a question about his credentials and his capacity for understanding the complexities of high finance. He snapped back sharply at the questioner, referencing his time at the consultants McKinsey, where he worked with big financial clients.

'I've reorganized many investment banks in my career,' he said dismissively, adding that he had run billions of dollars' worth of investments at Prudential before talking about the maths and physics he'd studied at university. 'Frankly, the maths behind derivatives are a relatively primitive version of that,' he said. 'I'm very confident that I can understand everything the investment bank does.'

It seemed overly defensive. In New York and London, some Credit Suisse employees listening to their new boss thought his answers were ignorant about their work, and arrogant. They were immediately suspicious of him.

Analysts who covered Credit Suisse fanned the flames. 'Thiam will bring some fresh air to Credit Suisse, albeit without the banking background,' one Swiss-based analyst told Bloomberg News. 'Maybe cutting the investment bank will become easier.'[3]

Years later, bankers and journalists in Switzerland, New York and London would pin the blame for Credit Suisse's eventual downfall on Thiam's root-and-branch restructuring. Their view was that Thiam was conceited, in over his head, and failed to listen to experienced bankers. His appointment and the changes that followed were the cause of the bank's demise. That analysis is flawed. It assumes the bank was in good shape when he got there, that it wasn't broken until Thiam arrived. In reality, the bank he took over was a mess, racked with scandals, riven with division and ill-equipped for success. Maybe his fix didn't work in the long run. But, when he arrived, maintaining the status quo was not an option. The chairman demanded an upheaval and that's what Thiam delivered.

Thiam officially landed in the hot seat in Zurich in the summer of 2015, surprising some executives by starting his new role a week before he was due. It had been a long courtship, and Thiam had had plenty of time to think about how he'd handle the relationship. Within just a few days, he wished he had never said yes.

# SEVENTEEN

# Capital Letters

P roblems piled up on Thiam's desk from the outset.

In the first few days, he talked to everyone on his senior management team. He'd ask, 'Tell me what's going well?' The answer was always brief. Then he'd ask, 'What do we need to do differently?' One after another, the bankers let loose with complaints, looming scandals, massive write-downs.

Romeo Cerutti, who had replaced Rohner as chief legal counsel, ran down the long list of unresolved legal issues. The big one was ongoing litigation tied to the sale of residential mortgage-backed securities (RMBS) prior to the financial crisis. Other banks had this problem and many of them had dealt with it years ago. But not Credit Suisse. Cerutti and Rohner had fought any sort of settlement for years, as was their way. The bank's public financial statements estimated that it could be fined around $1.6 billion for ongoing legal issues. But now Thiam heard that the true cost of the RMBS litigation could be several billion dollars higher than that. Maybe it would be three or four times as much as he'd previously expected. Thiam was shocked. This would be a straight hit to earnings, to his earnings, and it would put a dent in the bank's capital buffers.

Next, he delved into the accounts at the investment bank. Not only were there a handful of businesses that were barely scraping a profit, but some riskier parts of the division were seriously under-capitalized. Thiam calculated he'd need billions more to cover a gaping hole in the capital buffer from this too.

There was yet another blow. Thiam met with the bank's audit committee – the group of directors directly responsible for making sure the financial accounts were a true and fair representation of the state of the firm. The committee pointed out that the accounts still showed the ill-fated investment in Donaldson, Lufkin & Jenrette as a multibillion-dollar asset. It should have gone years ago. Thiam was told he must write it down, taking a $4-billion hit to capital. He pushed back. Why now? That balance had sat on the accounts for years. The bank could have written it down any time. Instead, the write-down would blast another hole into Thiam's accounts. It felt like sabotage, but the audit committee insisted.

There were more blows, more surprises. In all, Thiam reckoned he would have to try to raise as much as $15 billion in new capital just to keep the firm above water. This was a staggering amount. If he tried to do it in one go, shareholders would hate it.

Everything was much worse than Thiam had expected. He found the internal accounts presented to the board had been dressed up to look better, disguising the slow progress that had been made on cost savings, for instance. Mathers, the CFO, showed him how some of the business units twisted the numbers. A division of the bank might have been told to cut staff numbers, so they would present accounts that showed cuts, but omitted an offsetting increase in the cost of outsourcing.

Credit Suisse was short on capital, high on costs and addicted to investment banking that was no longer profitable. But Thiam also knew the drastic medicine required could kill the patient off altogether. Scaling back sharply and cutting costs fast risked losing too many clients. Revenue could fall faster than Thiam could generate savings. At the same time, issuing much-needed capital would signal to investors that the bank was more fragile than many realized, which would send the share price even lower. All of this would destroy morale among a staff that was already beaten up.

The new CEO surveyed the bank he had taken on and contemplated the worst. It was possible Credit Suisse couldn't be fixed. It was possible the bank could go bust.

At one board meeting early in his tenure, Thiam asked if someone could outline plan B. He'd been brought in with a fairly clear agenda to reshape the bank. But what was the plan if the restructuring he'd been asked to undertake didn't work? Most of the board members were blank-faced. They didn't seem to understand his point. Rohner replied that there was no chance the plan wouldn't work. Everything would be OK, he said.

Thiam was starting to feel like no one else understood the severity of the situation. Just weeks after joining the firm, he was already thinking about quitting. He felt he'd been set up to fail. He also knew that, if he quit, there could be no hiding the truth about the scale of the problems. The hurried departure of a brand-new CEO would almost certainly trigger a collapse in the share price. The bank would be finished for sure. He was trapped. The only option was to plough ahead.

Thiam was due to announce the details of his new strategy at the end of October 2015. He needed a team: people who knew the bank, but weren't stuck in the past. They'd need to be hungry for the chance to shape changes. They'd need to be firmly loyal to the new CEO. Thiam asked colleagues for a list of the most promising up-and-coming executives at the bank.

He pulled a group together. This included: Iqbal Khan, a former accountant and rising star who'd joined the bank a couple of years earlier; Brian Chin, a young investment banker who ran structured products, one of the better-performing areas of investment banking; and Lara Warner, a protégée of CFO Mathers, who'd risen through equity research and accounting. All three were super smart. They were a much more diverse group than the grey Swiss bankers and Wall Street types who'd managed the bank before. They were also inexperienced at the highest levels. They ended up being the core of his executive management team in the years ahead.

Thiam convened his team at a breakfast meeting. He told them, 'I want all your ideas on what works and what doesn't.' He also hired outside consultants, including McKinsey and their giant US rivals, the Boston Consultant Group. Over the next few weeks, the team sketched out a proposal for the new structure of the bank.

There were some notable exclusions from this group: a handful of top executives held over from the previous regime. Tim O'Hara, Gaël de Boissard and Jim Amine were the three most senior executives in the investment bank. Under Dougan, these three would have surely played a leading role in any major strategic planning. Thiam met with all of them, but he deliberately left them out of the task force.

In mid-October, Thiam presented his plan to the executive board, or EXB – a group of top managers, including some of the Dougan old guard. He planned to divide the business into three regionally focused divisions – Switzerland, Asia-Pacific, and international wealth management – plus two other units – global markets, and investment banking and capital markets, or IBCM. He wanted to decentralize decision-making, pushing responsibility down to the divisions.

It was an unusual approach, a hybrid matrix of regions and functions. Jim Amine, one of the company's top investment bankers, pointed out that no other successful global bank was run this way. With divisions now overlapping, staff would fight over resources, capital and clients. Thiam nodded in agreement. No other bank was run this way, he said, but then Credit Suisse was not like any other bank.

After the meeting, some of the older EXB members met privately to discuss the plan. They couldn't understand how the board would be OK with it. The new strategy was an outright rejection of the One Bank approach started by Grübel and continued under Dougan. The board had signed off on that for years. How could they now sign off on something that ripped up that playbook and went in completely the opposite direction? But, in truth, the new proposal was largely the one Rohner had pitched, way back in 2012. The chairman had bought into it years ago – it was largely his idea in the first place, and he sat at the top of the board.

At the end of the month, Credit Suisse announced the new strategy to investors. Alongside restructuring the divisions, there were several other key elements. They would sell new shares to raise about $6 billion in additional capital. Thiam said this would bolster the bank's balance sheet. In public, he said it was better to have more capital than too little – though, in private, he knew they'd need a lot more soon enough. They'd also cut costs by $2 billion over the next three years – mostly by scaling back and reducing staff numbers in the investment bank – and they would aim to hit some aggressive targets for growing the business in Asia and in wealth management.

Furthermore, the Swiss business would prepare for a possible partial IPO by 2017 that could raise several billion dollars in additional capital. Swiss media cheered – columnists said that the business was a crown jewel that deserved more credit and more autonomy. This piece of Thiam's plan was a kind of bluff. He never really intended to spin off Switzerland. The IPO plan was just meant to buy some time and show that Thiam could raise capital by selling assets if it came to that.

He also shook up the EXB. Khan and Warner from the strategy task force were added. Thomas Gottstein, an unassuming investment banker, was appointed to the group and was given the task of running the Swiss bank ahead of the IPO process. Thiam also introduced Pierre-Olivier Bouée, one of his former senior staff from Prudential, who became the bank's chief operating officer. Several Dougan appointees stood down, including de Boissard. Amine and O'Hara stayed on, as did Mathers and one or two others, but Thiam had stamped his authority on the EXB. This was now overwhelmingly his team.

Outside the bank, the new strategy left some analysts and investors confused and disappointed. The scale of cuts looked to have fallen short of what was needed. There were withering comparisons with UBS's more radical turnaround. Thiam and Rohner griped that this was unfair. UBS had effectively gone bust, bailed out by Switzerland, which meant its leaders had the benefit of starting afresh with government support. Besides, the two banks were completely different. Credit Suisse's domestic Swiss business and its wealth- and asset-management businesses were much smaller than UBS's. And the investment bank at Credit Suisse was much larger.

'The reason why this is a more complex intellectual problem is we have a really good investment bank,' Thiam told *The Wall Street Journal*. Each unit needed to be a success to support the others, he insisted. 'If your goal is really to serve the ultra-high-net-worth of this world, you better have a really good investment bank,' he said.[1]

This hid the reality that Thiam didn't like investment banking at all. He thought it was volatile, expensive and fraught with danger. But it was a necessary evil he'd have to tolerate for now.

In late December 2015, the final board meeting of the year took place at the bank's New York headquarters, as it always had done. This meeting was the one where bonuses were decided. It was always tense, a fight between the investment bankers and the Swiss. But, this time around, the tension was heightened by Thiam's barely hidden disdain for the investment bankers and his desire to cut costs back sharply. Eventually, after some wrangling, there was an agreement, and Thiam left immediately for a vacation in Florida with his family.

Shortly after he landed, he was interrupted by an urgent call. Tim

O'Hara, one of the Dougan holdovers in charge of a large slice of the investment bank, had some very bad news. The bank was sitting on a major, unexpected loss tied to some trades gone wrong. Thiam was just a few days away from closing out the year's final quarter. The numbers already looked weak. The trading losses O'Hara brought him promised to turn them nasty.

Thiam was stunned. The losses were in a part of the investment bank that trades distressed debt – loans that have gone bad. Traders had built up the problem bets from 2012, though they had quickly lost their value only in late 2015 when energy markets and interest rates had moved in the wrong direction. The cost was hundreds of millions of dollars in losses. Thiam, still in Florida, exchanged terse emails and text messages with O'Hara. Every trade would have to be discussed on a case-by-case basis, Thiam wrote.[2] He wanted more details of everything the investment bank was up to.

Within a few weeks, the distressed-debt losses had added up to almost a billion dollars. In public, Thiam said that it had come out of the blue, that he'd known nothing until was too late. 'We can't have the CEO and a CFO in a bank surprised by something like that,' he added.

Whichever way you looked at it, the situation was bad. Either Thiam had been misled, or the numbers had been deliberately hidden from him. Or else he had simply not noticed the risky trades, even though they'd been presented to him, until it was too late.

Later, in an interview with Bloomberg News, Thiam insisted the whole incident showed the need for 'cultural change' in the investment bank. The interviewer asked whether staff had deliberately withheld information. Thiam stuttered and stumbled over the answer. 'It's a very interesting question,' he eventually replied. 'The problem in the investment bank is that people have been trying to drive revenue at all costs, if I may say so.' Essentially, he was saying that, because costs were so high, the bankers had become reckless in the pursuit of revenue. The interviewer asked if he could be sure that it would never happen again. Thiam said that he was confident in the bank's processes, 'but you can never say never.'[3]

The episode set off a wave of in-fighting across the firm over who was really to blame. One view was that the losses were a result of Thiam's restructuring and that responsibility had fallen through the gaps as the bank adjusted to its complex matrix of regional and functional businesses. Some staff felt that responsibility for the losses lay with de Boissard, who had run fixed-income trading before he left. Through his lawyer, de Boissard told reporters he'd had nothing to do with those trades from the moment the restructuring was announced in October – by mid-December, he'd already left for a five-month ski trip.[4] O'Hara also took some of the blame. The losses occurred in his division, so, according to his detractors, he should have dealt with the problem or at least alerted Thiam and the CFO earlier. Other executives felt Thiam's characterization of the losses as having emerged seemingly from nowhere was misleading. All the trades were included in the 'global risk positions' regularly declared to the EXB. He should have seen them. For Thiam's critics, the episode drew a sharp contrast with the hands-on, detail-oriented approach of Dougan and Grübel. Those two previous CEOs surely would have spotted the problem and dealt with it well in advance of any major losses.

Some in the investment bank were increasingly sceptical of Thiam's leadership. Pay, as always, was a sore point. Early on, Thiam had described compensation as a 'battleground', adding that some bankers didn't accept that performance-linked bonuses could go down as well as up.[5] He planned to slash bonuses by 35 per cent in his first year, while his cost-cutting plans also meant that employee numbers in the investment bank were falling fast, putting a further dent in morale.

It wasn't just pay, though. Thiam could be brutally direct in expressing his dislike of the risk-taking culture of the past. At one meeting with a senior risk officer, Thiam had been told that they typically only looked at the average loss that might be incurred in a given scenario, rather than the worst case. He jabbed back, 'If I'm in the river and I can't swim, I don't care about the average depth of the water. I only care about its lowest point.'

It was a measure of the growing resentment that negative stories were frequently leaked to financial journalists. Some bankers were said to be considering using their shares to vote against the board at its annual meeting. Others complained that, when the new CEO was in New York, he sometimes summoned staff to meetings at his luxury hotel rather than in the office – in truth, the hotel and office shared the same midtown address, so this practice hardly seems so egregious.[6]

Thiam couldn't understand the volume of negative stories leaked to the media. In the insurance industry, where he'd spent much of his career, middle-ranking executives didn't talk to the press. In banking, it's different. Fairly junior staff have relationships with the media, often because they want to talk up their own roles on big deals, which can get them promotions, bonuses, or the attention of better-paying rivals. Those relationships could often also be an outlet for griping and score-settling. Thiam had insisted he understood the world of investment banking, but he was clearly struggling to understand the methods of investment bankers.

Outwardly, he claimed to be unaffected by the sniping. 'I'm aware that I'm not very popular right now,' he told a conference in Zurich. 'It's not my job to be popular. I'm trying to do the right thing.' But close colleagues began to notice that he seemed more insular, possibly even paranoid.

The first set of annual results Thiam announced showed the bank had lost about $3 billion in 2015 – compared with a profit of almost $2 billion the previous year. It was the first annual loss since the financial crisis and, although Thiam hadn't been there for most of the year, the results stung nonetheless. He'd looked to Rohner for support, but felt alone, facing the music with numbers that were not of his making. It already seemed a far cry from the days when the board were so desperate to recruit him and insisted he'd have their unanimous backing.

The scale of the turmoil at Credit Suisse was also under discussion across Zurich at UBS, where CEO Sergio Ermotti and a group of his lieutenants thought they spied an opportunity. They began an analysis of whether they could take over their rival. (This group included Axel Lehmann and Ueli Körner, both on UBS's executive board at that time; a few years later, they'd become the final chairman and CEO of Credit Suisse.) The team thought a takeover was compelling. Parts of Credit Suisse, such as its Asian division, would plug holes in areas where UBS's business was weaker. In the end – as had happened already many times before – they dropped the merger plan, assuming that integration would be tough and there'd be insurmountable political opposition.

When Thiam turned up to his first annual general meeting in late April 2016, the poor run of form was still continuing. The share price, which had surged when his appointment was announced, had fallen by more than a third since he'd joined the bank, and was heading lower. The meeting became angry. The chairman of a prominent shareholder advisory group, which makes recommendations to investors in major companies, said that trust in the leadership was 'shattered'.[7]

Thiam's response was to keep on slashing costs, cutting headcount and repeating the need to stick to the plan. But the negative stories just kept coming. In the summer of 2016, he gave an interview to Bloomberg in which he defended his record, pointing out that the firm he'd inherited was in terrible shape. 'The narrative in the media is "An evil person clearly came and destroyed this great bank." Sorry, that didn't happen,' Thiam said. 'Maybe [the share price has] gone down by 50 per cent since I started, but it was divided by five first – and that's over ten years. I'm here, and if I'm going to be crucified for that, so be it. But the facts are the facts, and the facts are stubborn.'[8]

By the autumn of 2016, O'Hara had left, effectively shouldering the blame for the distressed-debt losses. Thiam promoted Brian Chin, who'd been part of his strategy team, to run global markets. It was another surprise promotion. Chin hadn't previously managed a huge team with hundreds of staff. Still, Thiam thought he was smart and understood the broader turnaround plan. Perhaps more importantly, Chin was loyal to the CEO and could potentially help him quieten the unrest in the investment bank.

Thiam had consulted with other bank CEOs, including JPMorgan's Jamie Dimon, on how to handle the troops, how to get the investment bankers onside. Dimon, the longest-sitting leader on Wall Street, had told him that he needed to get to know them better, spend time with them. This was the only way to win them over. When Chin took over, he helped Thiam follow this guidance. The pair walked the trading floor, meeting with staff. Thiam felt that maybe he was finally turning a corner.

But other long-time executives saw things differently. To them, Thiam was increasingly closed off, surrounded by a group of rookies – Warner, Khan, Chin, Gottstein and Bouée. The character of the EXB had changed. Under Dougan, you turned up with an Excel spreadsheet, ready to be grilled on the maths in your bit of the business. Under Thiam, executives brought PowerPoint slides featuring buzzwords and naive growth targets, according to the CEO's critics. Thiam ordered that attendance was in person and that 75 per cent or more of the meetings had to be in Zurich rather than in London or New York, where many of the meetings had been held in the past. This also irritated some of the old-school bankers, who felt like flying to Zurich was just a waste of time.

In truth, Thiam did get a daily update on key figures sent from New York to Zurich, which he often trawled through into the early hours. This was a far less public scrutiny of the detail than had been the case under Dougan. Maybe it was a mistake – there was a performative aspect to grilling staff on their numbers in public that potentially kept everyone on their toes. Without this, many employees just assumed the CEO wasn't on top of things. Their ongoing grumbling was a reflection that many staff were resistant to outsiders and reluctant to change their ways. For Thiam, an outsider in both Zurich and New York, cracking Credit Suisse was proving to be a near impossible task.

# EIGHTEEN

# Tuna Bonds

The challenge was only made harder by a series of scandals that erupted during Thiam's reign. Many of them stemmed from misconduct that took place years earlier.

For instance, in January 2016, Credit Suisse agreed to pay $85 million to US authorities related to so-called 'dark pools' – private stock-trading platforms where clients could buy and sell shares without the usual transparency. Other banks also operated dark pools, but this was the biggest punishment dished out to any firm. Credit Suisse's dark pools had executed more than 117 million illegal trades and had 'failed to comply with numerous regulatory requirements over a multi-year period,' according to the Securities and Exchange Commission.[1]

Credit Suisse was also caught up in the sprawling multibillion-dollar embezzlement scandal that connected Hollywood, Wall Street and the Malaysian government. 1Malaysia Development Berhad, known as 1MDB, was a multibillion-dollar Malaysian government fund set up in 2009 and chaired by the country's prime minister, Najib Razak. The fund was supposed to promote development in the

Southeast Asian country. But, in 2015, documents leaked to a British journalist who ran an independent Malaysian news site, and to reporters at *The Wall Street Journal*, detailed a massive fraud. The scandal centred on a mysterious Malaysian businessman named Jho Low, who oversaw the fund. Jho Low threw lavish, star-studded parties and acquired yachts and private jets. He dated supermodels and hung out with Hollywood actors. On his thirty-first birthday, he held an outlandish event in Las Vegas, where rappers Busta Rhymes and Pharrell were among the performers, and Britney Spears jumped out of a cake.[2]

The scale of the scandal was enormous. Swiss investigators found that as much as $7 billion may have passed into the global financial system, partly with the assistance of the Swiss banking industry. After the media revealed the truth about 1MDB, Jho Low disappeared. Eventually, Najib was found guilty of corruption by a Malaysian court and sentenced to twelve years in jail. Two bankers from Goldman Sachs were found guilty of their role in the scandal, and Goldman agreed to pay $3 billion in settlements to end the investigation into its part in the affair.[3] Credit Suisse's role was relatively minor. A branch of the bank appeared to have managed money for Najib in Hong Kong. Regulators conducted probes into the bank's branches in Singapore and Switzerland, and, in both cases, found shortcomings in the bank's anti-money-laundering processes.

These incidents provided fuel to Thiam's own ongoing criticism of the bank's culture. But another scandal, also emerging from the bank's past, was especially irritating to Thiam –not least because it was perhaps one of the most reckless, most ludicrous affairs in the bank's recent history, and it was tied to his home continent, Africa.[4]

Back in 2010, Mozambique was basking in the potential riches offered by recent offshore gas discoveries that promised to transform it into one of the strongest-performing economies in Africa. The government wanted to build infrastructure to support and protect its new energy industry, especially along the country's coastline, where shipping was exposed to attack by pirates or terrorists. They decided on a series of major development projects and agreed to hire a ship-building company called Privinvest as the sole contractor to carry out the work.

Later, US prosecutors alleged Privinvest, which was owned by a French-Lebanese businessman called Iskandar Safa, had paid senior Mozambican officials to secure its role. Emails between a Mozam-bican businessman connected to the projects and a Privinvest executive named Jean Boustani shone a light on the nature of the payments. In 'democratic governments like ours, people come and go, and everyone involved will want to have his/her share of the deal while in office,' the businessman wrote. Later, he explained in barely hidden code how big the payments would need to be. 'Fine brother. I have consulted and please put 50 million chickens.' The initial price of doing business was $50 million. Over time, Privinvest paid hun-dreds of millions of dollars to Mozambicans, though Safa and Boustani always maintained that all the payments were legitimate.

Privinvest also agreed to secure financing for the projects, and so turned to Credit Suisse. The Swiss bank specialized in lending to the developing world, in part because it had found a way to make loans in risky countries appear safer – and more profitable. Credit Suisse bought insurance to cover the possibility that borrowers couldn't pay back their debts, and it sold securities backed by the loans to third parties, such as major institutional investors. This shifted the risk that the borrowers would default off the bank's balance sheet and added a layer of insurance protection for the investors. With the Mozambique loans, Credit Suisse agreed to provide financing to Privinvest but insisted the government of Mozambique write a guarantee that it would stand behind the borrowing too. The effect of all this, which became critical later, was that Mozambique was on the hook for repaying the loans.

Over the next few months, Boustani negotiated the terms of the deal with a banker named Andrew Pearse at Credit Suisse in London.

Pearse was a managing director in the global finance group, the division that made loans to clients in emerging markets. He had been quite successful but was looking for a way to leave. The atmosphere among the emerging-markets bankers was aggressive and uncooperative, with colleagues frequently pushing ethical boundaries to win clients and boost their own pay packets. Pearse felt he too had become swept up in this culture, bending the rules, hungry for money.

Pearse, who was married with three children, was having an affair with a junior colleague, a Bulgarian woman named Detelina Subeva, who was also married. They talked about quitting Credit Suisse to set up their own firm, so that they could arrange to travel together more frequently. Pretty soon, the opportunity to make this plan a reality fell into their laps.

In February 2013, Pearse flew to Maputo, the capital of Mozambique, to work on the Privinvest loans. Over drinks by his hotel swimming pool, Boustani made Pearse an offer. If he could get Credit Suisse to cut its $49-million loan fee by $11 million, then half of the savings would flow back to Pearse. The banker was shaken. No client had ever offered him a kickback. He wasn't entirely sure if Boustani was joking. Nevertheless, he agreed to cut the fee. Later, he wrote an email to Subeva and another colleague, Surjan Singh: 'He wants to reduce [the fee] by one-third. Does that work? Presume not.' Pearse asked his colleagues to rerun the numbers on the deal to get the fee down. He brought Subeva and Singh in on his conversation with Boustani too. All three would take some share of the money.

A few weeks later, Pearse and Boustani met with Privinvest owner Safa at his home in the south of France. They discussed payments Pearse would receive for securing more Credit Suisse loans for Privinvest. Safa suggested these payments should be considered fees for consultancy services. Around this time, Pearse also obtained a residency permit for the UAE, which listed his occupation as a 'tube welder' in the shipbuilding industry. He later said staff from Safa's firm helped him with the residency process and also got him a bank account – into which Privinvest would end up paying tens of millions of dollars.

Meanwhile, Credit Suisse's due-diligence process had been throwing up red flags about working with the Lebanese firm. An outside agency hired to delve into transactions with a high reputational risk had made some worrying findings, detailed in a report that was sent to Credit Suisse officials in several departments, including compliance and risk management. The report's authors described one Privinvest executive involved in the Mozambique deals as 'an expert in kickbacks, bribery and corruption'. The report said one source had said the same executive was a 'dangerous man' who would 'stop at nothing to secure a contract'.

This might have been enough to kill the Privinvest deal altogether. But some in the risk-management team wanted to push ahead. They criticized the due-diligence report. The investigators had spoken to a handful of Privinvest's fiercest rivals, who, naturally, had bad-mouthed the firm and its executives. Safa was especially high profile. His companies supplied European military organizations and he owned shipyards in Germany, Greece and Abu Dhabi. In the 1980s, he was credited with helping to release French hostages in Lebanon, though he had also spent years exiled from France following criminal charges that alleged he'd diverted cash meant to pay off the hostage takers into his own account. The charges were later dropped by French authorities.

There was no doubt that Privinvest was the target of jealous rivals. But that didn't necessarily mean the contents of the report were inaccurate. Credit Suisse's risk managers still had plenty of evidence to help them decide whether Privinvest and Mozambique was a deal worth doing. In the end, they chose to ignore the warning signs in the report the bank had commissioned and pushed ahead with the deal, lending $372 million to the Privinvest project. The Lebanese firm's fingerprints were kept off the agreement, which was signed by

Antonio Do Rosario, an official in Mozambique's state intelligence and security service, and Manuel Chang, Mozambique's finance minister.

Over the next couple of years, Credit Suisse and a Russian bank called VTB ended up lending more than $2 billion to similar Mozambican projects connected to Privinvest. The most infamous of these was called Ematum. Pearse and Boustani agreed a $500-million loan to fund a modern tuna-fishing fleet of about twenty-seven vessels. Like all the other deals, the Ematum loan, which became known as the 'tuna bond', was signed off at Credit Suisse by risk management, the European investment banking committee, and the compliance and anti-money-laundering functions.

Along the way, Mozambican officials received around $200 million in payments. Pearse, Subeva and Singh had pocketed $50 million (though Pearse took by far the lion's share). For Pearse and Subeva, there was an additional pay-off. The two had left Credit Suisse and begun working for a Privinvest subsidiary called Palomar, where Boustani was also an executive. They were free to carry on their relationship outside of the confines of their previous lives.

By the summer of 2015, as Thiam was settling into life in Zurich, the whole tuna-bond scheme was starting to unravel. Mozambique was struggling to repay the loans. The country's economy had taken a turn for the worse, the value of its currency had plummeted and the government was dealing with food shortages following a major drought. The tuna industry had been unsuccessful – by some estimates, Ematum was pulling in just 5 per cent of the fish the fleet had been projected to land.[5]

Officials from Mozambique approached Credit Suisse. They asked if the bank would restructure the Ematum debt by exchanging it for government-issued bonds. These would mature later, giving the government more time to meet its payment obligations. And they'd pay a higher rate of interest to compensate investors who'd have to wait longer to get their money. As Credit Suisse's staff delved into this plan, they became increasingly troubled.

There were rumours in Mozambique's media of corruption tied to the Privinvest deals. Senior bankers sent worried emails back and forth. For starters, they hadn't been aware of all the Russian VTB bank loans, which significantly dented Mozambique's finances and its credit rating. They were also concerned about how the Ematum loan had been spent. The bank hired independent experts to dig in. What they found was startling.

The fair market value of the tuna fleet was perhaps almost $400 million below what they were expecting, and a large chunk of the loan had been spent on military speedboats rather than fishing boats. When a Credit Suisse banker shared this assessment with Do Rosario, the Mozambican official's biggest concern was whether the outside experts had looked for evidence that any money had been diverted inappropriately to officials. The implication of the question and Do Rosario's fear was clear. But the Credit Suisse executive simply replied that the experts had only looked at the use of the loan proceeds.

Despite everything Credit Suisse's bankers had uncovered at this point, they continued with the debt-restructuring plan as though everything was fine. In March 2016, Credit Suisse arranged a 'road show' in New York and London, where Do Rosario and other Mozambican officials helped to pitch the plan to investors. Within a couple of weeks, they had enough interest to swing the deal.

Then, on 3 April, a *Wall Street Journal* story blew open details about the loans. The story described how the money intended for a tuna fleet had been diverted to military equipment, and revealed that Mozambique's government was on the hook for far more debt than had been known previously. 'Mozambique is deeper in debt, paying higher interest on the new restructured bonds and weathering a downgrade of its credit rating,' the story said. 'Investors are left with bonds that are likely worth less than they thought.'[6]

At the International Monetary Fund's Africa desk, the *Journal* story had come as a shock, revealing potential corruption and that there was as much as $1 billion in additional, undisclosed borrowing by Mozambique. In Washington, DC, Christine Lagarde, the IMF's managing director, said the agency would stop lending if it found evidence of corruption. 'We want this hanky-panky business to go away,' she added.[7]

Pretty soon, the international community turned its back on financing Mozambique. The World Bank cut off aid totalling $265 million per year. The IMF suspended $165 million in payments. Credit-rating agencies slashed their outlook on Mozambique. The impact on one of the poorest countries in Africa was devastating. Over the next three years, the episode cost Mozambique's economy billions of dollars in lost growth and may have pushed almost two million people into poverty.[8]

In time, the scandal led to recriminations and investigations in Mozambique, New York and London. Pearse, Subeva and Singh were all arrested and all pleaded guilty to charges brought by US prosecutors. In Maputo, in 2019, a new government charged twenty people with crimes related to the loans, including Ndambi Guebuza, the son of the country's former president, who was alleged to have received $33 million in payments from Privinvest. A court in the capital heard tales of lavish spending backed by the embezzled funds. Eventually, Guebuza and ten others were found guilty of charges including money laundering and bribery. Each was sentenced to more than ten years in jail. Manuel Chang, the former finance minister who signed the loan agreements, had fled the country. He was arrested in South Africa and extradited to the US in July 2023.

Privinvest became the subject of litigation in several countries. Safa and Boustani denied any wrongdoing, saying that all the payments they made were for legitimate services. They claimed that the payments covered a range of consultancy fees, investments in local businesses and campaign contributions. These payments might not have passed muster in the UK or US, but they were all lawful payments in Mozambique, lawyers asserted. As of early 2024, the government of Mozambique still had a legal claim against Privinvest to recover some of the money that was lost through the suspect loans. Boustani was indicted in the US for his role in the affair, though he was acquitted by a jury in 2019 – a verdict that was widely seen as a rebuke of the DOJ's efforts to police corruption beyond US borders. Safa also maintained his innocence right up until his death in January 2024.

At Credit Suisse, the tuna-bond scandal lingered over the remainder of Thiam's time in charge and was an ongoing issue for years. Though it predated his appointment, Thiam felt particularly angered that Credit Suisse should have stumbled so badly in Africa, given his expertise in the continent's finances.

In October 2021, the bank finally agreed to pay $275 million to the SEC and DOJ, and entered into a three-year deferred-prosecution deal, which meant there would be no criminal charges only so long as the bank stayed out of trouble. The UK's Financial Conduct Authority also fined the bank $200 million and required it to forgive $200 million in debt owed by Mozambique. A claim against Credit Suisse by the government of Mozambique was not settled until years later.

FINMA also investigated the tuna-bonds fiasco. The Swiss regulator pinpointed failings in London. The British branch of Credit Suisse was to blame. There was no fine to be paid. No punishment. FINMA's powers were limited by Swiss law. There was little it could do beyond a slap on the wrist.

At Credit Suisse, Urs Rohner repeated the sentiment he'd expressed when scandals had come to light in the past. The bank had no means of knowing about the wrongdoing emanating from its London office, he said. It was an odd view, which seemed to expose some massive flaws in governance of the bank Rohner himself headed up. It was especially odd given that the bank had literally been warned about the dangers of this business in a report that flagged the potential for kickback payments. And, if the bank had no way of knowing what was happening in London, then how would it know what its staff were up to in New York, Singapore or Hong Kong? How would it know what staff were up to in Dubai, Jakarta and Moscow?

It seemed like Rohner was in denial. Each of the scandals chipped away at any sense that Credit Suisse's top management had a grip on the behaviour of its staff. Every single misstep took the bank closer to oblivion.

# NINETEEN

# The Lescaudron Affair

One more scandal seemed to summarize much of what Tidjane Thiam had stumbled into. It connected the dots between different divisions. The details showed a disturbing tolerance for the worst behaviour, so long as the money rolled in. This scandal centred on a lone rogue banker, though his actions and the fact he got away with it for so long reflected a broken culture that encouraged employees to chase profit at all costs, and that provided few restraints when they went off the rails.

Like the tuna-bonds scandal, the Lescaudron affair predated Thiam by several years. It had nothing to do with his time in charge, except that it burst into the open when he was CEO. Nevertheless, the scandal was yet another blemish, another costly distraction that weighed on Thiam's tenure.

French-born Patrice Lescaudron looked like an auditor – the profession he'd pursued after leaving university. He had a pointed nose and thin lips, and wore wire-framed glasses, a dark suit and a beige trench coat. In the late 1990s, he embarked on a new, racier career selling and distributing cosmetics and luxury clothing in Russia to an emerging consumer class. For more than a decade, Lescaudron built a network of wealthy clients among Russia's rich elite. By 2004, he'd realized there was more money to be made in finance than in luxury goods. He joined Credit Suisse in December that year and, despite having no previous banking experience, the Swiss firm soon put him in charge of Russian 'ultra high net worth individuals', known in the banking world by the clumsy acronym UHNWIs.

Over the next eleven years, Lescaudron schmoozed some of the bank's richest clientele – typically individuals with more than $50 million of investible assets such as cash and similarly liquid holdings. He came across as experienced, knowledgeable, and able to build a good rapport with multimillionaires who could be very demanding.[1] He helped these people to open accounts and make investments, or connected them with specialist Credit Suisse bankers and advisers. At the peak of his powers, Lescaudron managed as much as $2.5 billion in client funds and generated $25 million a year in revenue. He rose steadily up the ladder and became rich, amassing several houses, a multimillion-dollar collection of watches and jewellery, and a fleet of luxury cars. He also received plaudits from his bosses, who said his work far exceeded their expectations. He was, for sure, a star performer.

And yet, there were also many serious concerns, almost from the start. In 2008, he was given a verbal warning for making an unauthorized transaction with a client's money. In 2011, he got another verbal warning for failing to disclose side accounts he had opened with several other banks, and for 'front running' – trading on valuable information on stocks or bonds ahead of his clients. In 2012, his supervisor wrote that Lescaudron's 'weak point was more on the compliance/controls side but it is improving now and should be fine by the end of the year.' In 2013, he got a written warning, this time for disregarding 'know your customer' rules – guidelines bankers follow to protect against fraud, corruption and terrorist financing.

The bank's compliance team and Lescaudron's supervisors raised red flag after red flag. He didn't attend obligatory training. He didn't fill out forms. He put too much client money into narrow investments, meaning that clients could lose it all if a single stock or trade went wrong. There were hundreds of alerts about Lescaudron's conduct. Many of these issues were investigated, documented, and elevated to more than a dozen senior executives in the bank's compliance department and among Lescaudron's supervisors. Sometimes, executives at the bank glossed over Lescaudron's violations or swept them under the carpet. The bank imposed some restrictions to curb his worst transgressions, but, on the whole, Lescaudron's bosses looked the other way as he broke the rules time and time again. When the Swiss financial regulator investigated Lescaudron's behaviour a few years later, it found that his litany of wrongdoing 'had been known to the bank since June 2011 and had also been analysed and escalated to a certain extent.'[2]

None of these concerns had much impact on his ballooning pay, either. In 2009, Lescaudron's total compensation, including bonus, was about $570,000. By 2013, it was almost $2 million. These sums are relatively small compared to the fortunes some investment bankers made at Credit Suisse – private bankers typically make far less money than their investment-banking colleagues – but Lescaudron's pay was lavish nonetheless, and out of step with his peers. His annual bonuses were sometimes ten times those of other bankers working with UNHWIs. Once, in 2012, he was docked a portion of his pay because of the warnings about his compliance failures – but he still took home around $800,000 that year, including a bonus that was about four and a half times that of bankers doing similar work.

Eventually, the Frenchman was caught out.

One of Lescaudron's most important clients was Bidzina Ivanishvili, a Georgian businessman and politician sometimes known as 'BI'. He had grown up in poverty but had scrapped his way to university in Tbilisi and Moscow. In the late 1980s and early 1990s, he turned to business and made a fortune importing and selling computers and push-button phones into Russia. BI had invested in a range of industries, from banking to mining to pharmaceuticals, becoming a multibillionaire along the way. In 2012, *Forbes* estimated his personal net worth at about $6.4 billion. His private art collection alone was said to be worth as much as $800 million. He had also built up a menagerie of exotic animals, including sharks and lemurs, and a collection of rare trees too.

BI, who was at one point a citizen of Russia, Georgia and France, has a broad grin and swept-back black hair with a dash of white in the front. He is also a liberal-leaning politician, and, in 2012, he formed the Georgian Dream party, named in reference to a rap song by his musician son. He won an election and became prime minister the following year. Critics pointed to the wealthy businessman's broad influence across the media and government agencies, which gave him a level of power that was uncomfortable for some of his European and American supporters. But he also earned friends in the West for a progressive agenda that promoted better healthcare, education, pensions and social services. He resigned after just a year, saying he wanted to focus on philanthropy, and was succeeded as prime minister by one of his own ministers.

The Georgian billionaire had become a client of Credit Suisse in 2004. From 2006 to 2015, he was personally looked after by Lescaudron, who would typically fly into Tbilisi once a year to make a big presentation to BI and his closest advisers, explaining how he was managing his vast wealth. Credit Suisse had undertaken the usual anti-money-laundering (AML) procedures and additional reviews needed for so-called 'politically exposed persons', or PEPs. The bank's AML assessment found that BI's businesses had been suspected of potential links to organized crime and money laundering, but, ultimately, the bank was satisfied there was nothing to personally implicate BI himself.

This relationship became critical both to Lescaudron's success and his downfall. Lescaudron was managing more than $1 billion of BI's money. Most of it was invested in company shares, with other stakes in hedge funds, bonds and a mixed bag of investments. Like other rich clients, BI believed Credit Suisse was managing his money smartly and responsibly. Much of it was set up in trusts in offshore locations, such as Singapore and even New Zealand. From time to time, Lescaudron would share Excel spreadsheets showing how much he was making for his biggest client – though it later turned out these spreadsheets were not official bank documents. They were just made up by Lescaudron.

In fact, for years, Lescaudron had been making up numbers to cover losses he'd suffered on behalf of clients, including BI. Unknown to his trusting clientele or to his somnambulant supervisors, he had been shuffling pots of money around, hoping that one day his luck would turn and he'd be able to plug all the gaps in the accounts he was managing. That never happened.

Instead, in October 2015, Lescaudron's work was revealed to be a fantasy. One of the stocks he had been buying for clients was a US-based company called Raptor Pharmaceuticals. When Raptor announced disappointing trial results for a new drug, its shares plunged. That was a disaster for Lescaudron. For several years prior to this revelation, Lescaudron had bought hundreds of millions of dollars of shares in Raptor, for his clients and for himself. He had bought so much Raptor stock that it occasionally popped up on the compliance alerts that senior bank executives mostly ignored. When the Raptor stock fell rapidly, the game was up. The extent of Lescaudron's misplaced investments and cumulative losses was soon apparent. He had moved money from one account to the next, hiding losses in offshore vehicles like a multibillion-dollar shell game. He had also been making money on the side based on his knowledge about the investments he was making in the name of clients.

After Lescaudron's fraud was discovered, the bank might have quickly owned up to clients and settled fast, to avoid the issue lingering. But that was never the Credit Suisse way. Instead, as in so many cases, the affair dragged on for years, playing out in the press and courtrooms, weighing on the bank's reputation and its share price.

The bank tried to position Lescaudron as a lone wolf, a rogue executive who had 'demonstrated a high degree of criminal energy violating internal controls and rules.'³ But BI and his advisers argued that the bank had allowed Lescaudron to run amok even when his misconduct was clear. The billionaire was a formidable legal foe, with plenty of firepower to use in pursuit of his claims against Credit Suisse. The Georgian and other Lescaudron clients formed a group that called themselves CS Victims. They mobilized lawyers and public-relations specialists. They took out a full-page ad in the *Financial Times* that stated Credit Suisse had worked against the victims' 'efforts to understand how the crimes were perpetrated and what happened to their assets.' They filed motions in a Swiss court to get access to a report produced by the Swiss financial regulator on what had happened. When Credit Suisse provided a version of the report that was almost entirely redacted in blacked-out ink, BI's team went to a higher court to demand more. And when Credit Suisse accidentally sent a clean copy of the report to BI's team, the bank initially took out an injunction to stop its widespread distribution. No wonder – the report detailed the bank's shameful and repeated failures to stop Lescaudron's worst behaviour.

BI's team also filed claims for damages against Credit Suisse units in Singapore, Bermuda and New Zealand, the locations of some of the offshore vehicles set up by Lescaudron to manage BI's money. In court, Credit Suisse tried to suggest BI and Lescaudron had been very close, so the Georgian surely should have been aware of what the banker was up to. A lawyer for the bank pointed to phone records showing that, on a single day, Lescaudron and BI had spoken by phone for 240 minutes – except the phone records actually showed they spoke for just 240 seconds. 'I don't even talk to my wife on the phone that long,' BI had joked in court.

The Georgian argued that the whole point of entrusting his

money to Credit Suisse – more than $1 billion – was that the bank had systems, processes and safeguards. 'If someone from the bank sends me a document to sign, then I sign it,' he said.

In December 2022, the judge in Bermuda found that Credit Suisse had 'turned a "blind eye"' to Lescaudron's behaviour, because the bank was 'prioritizing the revenues which Mr Lescaudron generated for Credit Suisse over the interests of its clients.'[4] BI was awarded more than $600 million in damages. A few months later, a court in Singapore also sided with BI.[5] During the trial, Credit Suisse's Singapore unit acknowledged that its senior managers had known about potentially fraudulent transactions and unauthorized payments by Lescaudron in relation to BI's accounts but had done nothing to stop the misconduct. The court again slammed the bank, initially awarding BI $926 million, reduced to a still-staggering $743 million a few months later.

The affair was not just another mark against Credit Suisse. It was yet another indication that the bank put its own profits ahead of the interests of its clients, even incredibly wealthy, powerful clients like the former prime minister of Georgia, who happened to be one of the richest people in the world. It was a terrible signal to other super-rich clients who put their money with the Swiss bank precisely because it was safe, because they'd generate a decent return and because the bank could be trusted. If none of this was true, then it would be totally rational for clients to move their money elsewhere, especially those who were no ordinary customers but highly coveted UHNWIs.

The scandal was more than that, though. It also showed once again the bank's tendency to cover up and deny the bad behaviour of some of its well-paid staff. That was true throughout Lescaudron's fraud; the bank had hundreds of warnings, each one an opportunity to right the wrongs perpetrated on its own customers. It was also true once the market – in the form of a sudden sell-off in shares of Raptor Pharmaceutical – had revealed the fraud for all to see.

There were echoes of the Lescaudron affair at other banks. There were rogue staff across the industry and clients losing out over and over again. Yet, somehow, Credit Suisse often managed to have a bigger, more spectacular, more public blow-up than most. Who was to blame? Clearly, individuals like Lescaudron – or Andrew Pearse, in the tuna-bonds case. Beyond that, was it the bank's lackadaisical compliance function? Or perhaps it was the board that failed to hold senior executives to account, or Brady Dougan, the CEO during much of Lescaudron's career at Credit Suisse? Some critics also blamed Rohner, the lawyer who sat atop a bank that always fought against accusations of bad behaviour instead of settling and admitting its guilt. Like so much of what went wrong at Credit Suisse, it's hard to pinpoint a single person. The failures were widespread.

One further aspect of the Lescaudron scandal is that it shone a light on the bank's eagerness to forge connections with clients from former Soviet republics, including Russia. This had been a huge source of profit for some banks in the decades after the collapse of the USSR. However, Credit Suisse scored bigger among wealthy Russians, in part because of the strong connections CSFB had developed in the country in the 1990s. Many of the Russians who Credit Suisse's private bankers worked with were super-wealthy oligarchs, close to President Putin, who made vast fortunes from the privatization of Russian industry in the 1990s and 2000s. The bank helped these oligarchs to invest their money overseas, in gigantic yachts, top-flight soccer clubs and luxurious properties. Often the bank provided loans of hundreds of millions of dollars to help grease the wheels of these transactions. The pay-off was incredibly lucrative. At its peak, Credit Suisse managed more than $60 billion for Russian clients and earned up to $600 million in revenue per year from that business, according to Bloomberg News.[6] But the business was also risky. It brought a raft of compliance issues. Eventually, it would play a part in the broader crisis that engulfed the bank.

The affair also showed the tragic human consequences of financial wrongdoing. Lescaudron was arrested soon after Credit Suisse fired him in 2015. In 2018, he would go to trial in Geneva. In court, Lescaudron wore a grey sweatshirt adorned with the logo of Ferrari, the type of car he had bought with his riches.[7] The once high-flying banker admitted to fraud and forgery and having caused clients to lose more than $150 million while making about $30 million for himself. Lescaudron claimed he had only tried to make money for himself and his clients, and apologized for his actions. He was found guilty and sentenced to five years in jail. After just a few months, he was allowed out, his sentence cut short because he had already served two years of pre-trial detention and because of a series of health issues. The following May, he would write on LinkedIn that he couldn't get a job and would soon lose his Swiss residence permit.[8] It read like a farewell of sorts. His wife had also left him, and he had no money. Weeks later, a few days after his fifty-seventh birthday, Lescaudron was found dead, apparently having killed himself.[9]

# TWENTY

# The Establishment

Back in September 2016, Thiam was flying to Washington to finally negotiate a settlement with US authorities over the toxic mortgage securities from the financial crisis. There, he met with Attorney General Loretta Lynch and her deputy Bill Baer. The Americans had been tough on Wall Street over the mortgage issue. Baer slammed firms that failed to help the government's investigations, prolonging the 'cloud of uncertainty' that hung over them. Banks that delayed ended up paying a lot more than if they'd cooperated early on, Baer warned.[1]

Thiam knew he wouldn't get an easy ride. He explained the vulnerability of his firm and noted that it employed tens of thousands of people whose jobs would be at risk if the punishment were too harsh. Lynch was not easily moved, but clearly nobody wanted to push another firm over the edge and potentially trigger another financial crisis. In December, Credit Suisse finally settled, with a $5.3-billion penalty. This was far worse than Thiam had expected when he became CEO the previous year, but maybe a couple of billion less than he'd feared going into the negotiations.

The punishment contributed to another loss-making year at the bank. In Thiam's first two years at the helm, he'd failed to deliver an annual profit.

Still, Thiam saw reasons to be optimistic. The weight of the mortgage issue was now off his back. The share price was recovering from the lows it had plummeted to earlier in the year. Assets were trickling back into the wealth-management business and the private bank. Costs were way down. There were some indications that the renewed focus on Asia was beginning to bear fruit. The balance of the business was shifting from volatile trading activities – betting on the ups and downs of the markets – to more stable fee-based revenue. At last, there were some reasons for hope. Perhaps, against the odds, Thiam's restructuring would pay off.

Early in the new year, the CEO announced a plan to raise $4 billion in additional capital. Selling the Swiss business was officially off the table. The bank had turned a profit in the first three months of the year and the upward trend continued through 2017. Thiam appeared to be on a roll.

Nevertheless, it felt like he was constantly fighting an uphill battle. A change in US regulations meant the bank had to write off $2 billion in deferred tax assets. It was an obscure, technical matter that affected a lot of firms. But it meant that, despite all the positives, Thiam had to announce yet another loss for the third year in a row.

The background noise of repeated scandals was also making life fraught, even though many of them had nothing to do with Thiam. At a meeting in Bern, a top official from FINMA questioned Thiam about a violation by one of the bank's staff from 2007. Thiam was perplexed. He had been working in the UK at the time, he replied. Why would he know anything about that? On the other hand, the regulator asking the question had been right here in Switzerland when the incident in question took place. 'This happened under your watch,' Thiam pushed back. 'Why don't *you* tell *me* about that?' It was a fair point, but it wasn't the way bankers and the regulator conducted meetings in Switzerland. The official sternly warned Thiam that he needed to be careful, talking to the regulator that way. Thiam stood his ground. He would not be patronized by anyone. But the disagreement reinforced the notion that, whatever happened at Credit Suisse, no matter when it had really occurred, Thiam owned it now. His relationship with FINMA was frosty for the remainder of his time in Switzerland.

Even when things were going well, some investors were sceptical about the improvement in results. The accounts published under longstanding CFO David Mathers were littered with non-standard accounting measures that made it difficult to compare them with those of other banks. Analysts and investors were unimpressed. They criticized the bank for producing overly complex accounts that minimized problems and deployed tricks of financial engineering to make the numbers look better in the short term only. Often, it seemed that Mathers shuffled bits of the bank around so that the results emphasized only the positives, while the negatives were tucked away where they'd be hard to find.

Inside the bank, some executives felt that aggressive revenue and cost targets were putting undue pressure on divisional heads to keep delivering rapidly rising profits. Even as Thiam was preaching a more conservative approach to banking, some bankers felt the targets they'd been set were driving them to take on additional risk, just as in the old days. Among members of the EXB, there were also concerns about how many senior-level staff had left the firm, especially in the investment bank and in risk management. This had helped reduce costs, but the departure of so much experience potentially exposed parts of the business to unexpected and unwanted surprises even more than in the past.

Sometimes it seemed like the entire Swiss establishment was against Thiam. In late 2017, a high-profile Swiss investor began jostling for change at the bank. Rudolf Bohli ran a hedge fund named RBR Capital Advisors. It was based on Zurich's so-called Gold

Coast – an especially prosperous strip along the lake, where the evening summer sun and low taxes are a draw for celebrities and other wealthy homeowners. Bohli was an activist investor. He'd take a stake in a firm and then try to shake it up, to drive the share price higher. He had amassed a chunk of shares in Credit Suisse and had the support of Gaël de Boissard, the experienced investment banker who'd quit not long after Thiam's arrival. It was a clear threat to Thiam's leadership. At a hedge-fund conference in New York, Bohli fired his first broadside. He launched a public attack on Thiam's leadership, called for more aggressive cost-cutting and said the bank should be split into three independent businesses.

Thiam was forced to acknowledge such a public challenge from a big shareholder. He hit back, saying that he had been hired because 'things were not optimal'. He agreed that much change was needed. But his plans needed time to work.[2] Eventually, after several weeks and a private meeting with Thiam, Bohli dropped his campaign. He'd caused a stir, but at that point most other shareholders were still sticking by the CEO.

Outside of the office, Thiam made an effort to win over his adopted home. He met with businesspeople and politicians, and visited branches and offices around the country. He attended conferences and spoke often at public events. He even paraded through Zurich in a traditional cape and bicorn hat as a guest of honour at Zurich's Sechseläuten spring festival. But he was never really accepted by the Swiss.

The media – especially the German-speaking press – ran extensive coverage of his private life. They staked out his home, followed his car and reported on what he wore to visit a nightclub. They said he was acting presidential, flying around in helicopters, staying in expensive hotels and surrounding himself with acolytes. One influential finance-news website even reported that spike-soled winter shoes Thiam had worn at the World Economic Forum meeting in the ski resort of Davos had damaged the parquet floors of a rented apartment he stayed in during the event. The Credit Suisse press room confirmed the story, noting that Thiam had personally paid to repair the wooden floor.[3]

The CEO was particularly irritated when the media wrote about his family. He frequently mentioned an especially annoying story in which a journalist had said he'd forced his wife to convert to Islam, when in fact they'd married in a Baptist church. His relationship with his partner – Thiam separated from his wife before moving to Zurich – was an endless source of gossip too.

Thiam felt the situation had worsened after he openly talked about getting Swiss citizenship in 2019. He told associates that he thought the move would reduce hostility, but it had the opposite effect. Later, after he left the bank, a story in *The New York Times* detailed how the Swiss had 'rejected him as an outsider' and aired allegations of racism. 'In predominantly white Zurich, a city of just 400,000, his powerful role and his skin color made him stand out,' the article said. Thiam was held up at the airport. His sons were singled out by ticket inspectors on public transport. At one of the bank's annual meetings, a shareholder questioned Thiam's strategy of focusing on emerging markets, asking, 'Is that really what we want? That a good, solid, Swiss bank sinks to the level of the third world?'

One incident described in the news article was especially striking. In November 2019, the chairman, Urs Rohner, held a party in a restaurant to celebrate his sixtieth birthday. The festivities had a Studio 54 theme and were arranged by Rohner's wife, who'd invited a few dozen guests, including Thiam and his partner. At one point, a black performer dressed as a janitor danced for the guests. Thiam and his partner left the room. When they returned a little later, they were shocked to find a group of Rohner's friends wearing Afro wigs and dancing on stage to the Sister Sledge song 'We Are Family'. At the time, Thiam didn't say anything, and Rohner was unaware that he'd taken offence. But it understandably rankled.

Thiam downplayed the impact and talk of Swiss racism. He told colleagues that he'd dealt with racism all his life and was unaffected by it. But some colleagues worried the constant stream of negativity was clouding his judgement. They felt that everything was becoming a fight to prove Thiam's detractors wrong. There was certainly a sense that an establishment network of businesspeople, politicians and other powerful forces was out to get him.

Outside of Switzerland, it was a different picture. In 2018, after results had started to improve, the UK-based finance magazine *Euromoney* named him Banker of the Year. Twelve months later, *The Economist* ran a lengthy article under the headline, 'Tidjane Thiam's overhaul of Credit Suisse is paying off'. Credit Suisse was finally back to reporting an annual profit and its capital position looked a lot healthier too. Among Thiam's inner circle, there was even some talk again of launching a bid to merge with UBS on equal terms. Some of the bank's biggest investors were telling the CEO he should start negotiations. UBS's popular CEO, Sergio Ermotti, had announced he was retiring. Perhaps Thiam could combine both banks under his leadership. But, with no compelling reason to pursue such a difficult deal, the merger talk soon petered out.

While Thiam had supporters among investors and backing from his EXB, critics within the bank's upper echelons feared he was becoming more and more insular, closed off to everyone but a tight inner circle of loyalists. Some board members privately talked about him as a 'Louis Quatorze', the Sun King of France who ruled as an absolute monarch. Critics thought his team lacked the heft needed to offer challenging feedback to their charismatic leader. These doubters were concerned that Thiam had lost too many experienced managers; that he'd sold out of wealth management in the US – the richest market in the world; that the vaunted Asian growth strategy hadn't delivered as hoped. Their view, which few aired in public, was that the restructuring had produced some short-term positive momentum, but it had set the bank up for failure in the long term. The chances of a big blow-up seemed even greater than in the past.

In the end, neither Thiam's supporters nor those who were against him would get to prove they were right. Thiam's time was nearly up, and it would end in the most bizarre fashion.

# TWENTY-ONE

# Spygate

In the end, Thiam's downfall had nothing to do with banking. Instead, it was one of the most absurd episodes in Credit Suisse's entire history, one which laid bare the jealousies, egos and betrayals that frequently characterized the bank. The affair came to be known as 'spygate'. It started with a decision the CEO made way back in 2015.

When Thiam joined the bank and asked Rohner for the names of rising executives, Iqbal Khan was top of the list. Khan was ambitious, young, bright and extremely eloquent. He had moved from Pakistan to Switzerland aged twelve, became an apprentice accountant at just fifteen, and, at thirty-one, he was the youngest ever partner at the Swiss arm of the global professional services firm Ernst & Young. He joined Credit Suisse in 2013 and continued his rapid ascent. In 2015, Thiam promoted Khan to head of international wealth management, known as IWM. It was a big step. Even Khan was shocked. He didn't expect to run a whole business so soon. When the experienced head of asset management said he was quitting a short while later, Khan was even more stunned to find that business, too, was rolled into his remit.

For a while, Khan continued to be seen as a rising star. He set ambitious targets and his division delivered strong results. Some staff referred to IWM as 'Iqbal Wants More'. Khan was technically very capable and a vocal proponent of Thiam's strategy. He was smooth with clients and the board and personable with colleagues, including junior staff. He worked the idiosyncrasies of Swiss society while presenting as a truly international executive. His internal town halls were like red-carpet events, slick and glitzy, showcasing the wealth-management business at its best. He was widely seen as the 'crown prince', the CEO-in-waiting. That proved to be an awkward spot.

Within a couple of years, the relationship between Thiam and Khan soured professionally and personally. Thiam didn't like that Khan wore his ambition on his sleeve. Some executives believed the CEO was irritated by the attention his underling seemed to be getting.

In 2018, things took a turn for the worse. Thiam had moved into the second phase of his restructuring plan. He was still driving cost reductions, but he wanted more growth. Results in Khan's division had nearly doubled in the past couple of years, though that was partly thanks to some one-off successes that were not easily repeatable. Yet Thiam's strategy demanded results that kept on improving. At a budget meeting with other executives, Thiam set a growth target for the business that Khan thought was unreasonable. He pushed back, telling the CEO that it couldn't be achieved without more investment. Thiam was visibly angry and demanded that Khan hit the targets. Afterwards, Khan felt that it might have been a misstep to challenge his boss in public. Perhaps he should have talked to Thiam one to one before the meeting. He knew that the CEO prized loyalty and disliked open confrontation.

The two also clashed over a bizarre incident involving one of Khan's direct reports. At a Credit Suisse party in New York, the executive, who was also a friend of Khan's, was gossiping about Thiam's private affairs. He allegedly made lurid comments about Thiam's sex life in London that were overheard by a senior manager in the human-resources department. The indiscretion was later reported to Thiam himself. The CEO called Khan and told him to fire the executive. Khan couldn't defend his employee. He was a high-flyer earmarked for promotion, but if it was true that he'd said what was alleged, then he'd have to go. Khan asked if there would be a full investigation, a proper process to establish what had happened. But he felt the answer was unclear. He had the impression that Thiam did not want him to discuss details of the allegations with the executive. In the end, Khan told his employee that it was in his best interests to leave the firm. He did so shortly afterwards, taking a senior leadership role in a rival European bank.

Khan and Thiam were also neighbours on the Gold Coast. When he emigrated to Zurich in 2015, Thiam had moved into the neighbourhood with his partner – a high-level French investment banker. In December that year, Khan told Thiam he'd bought the house next door a few months earlier and that he and his wife planned extensive renovations. He wanted to give his boss a heads-up. Thiam thought it was an odd choice to live so close to the CEO. The houses were almost on top of one another. But Khan left the meeting believing Thiam was OK with it. The CEO was travelling a lot, so he'd be away for a lot of the heavy construction work Khan and his wife were planning.

As it turned out, there was tension almost immediately. Cranes and other large machinery were operating long hours, even at weekends. The noise and disruption annoyed Thiam and his partner. The CEO was also concerned that Khan's new house literally overlooked his property. Most evenings, Thiam liked to step outside and smoke a cigar. He realized Khan and any guests at his house would be able to watch him from above as he tried to relax. It felt like an invasion of privacy.

The renovation works went on for two years, and Thiam's partner and Khan's wife rowed for months over some trees that had been planted to block the view between the two properties. The neigh-bours pinged emails back and forth over the exact size, species and placement of the trees. Khan's wife alleged Thiam's partner had broken Swiss law, while Thiam's partner said this was not true and that she'd fully consulted her neighbour before anything was planted.

The animosity boiled over in early 2019. Thiam and his partner held a New Year's cocktail party at their home on 11 January. The Khans were invited, along with other Credit Suisse employees. At one point in the evening, Khan said something that upset Thiam's part-ner. What exactly he said is disputed. But the CEO walked Khan downstairs from the party and told him to leave. The discussion became heated, and the two were eventually separated by Khan's wife.

Later, Khan reported the events of the evening to Rohner and asked him to help repair the damage. But the relationship between the CEO and his star executive was broken. The two were barely on speaking terms. People close to Khan believed he felt like the falling-out was holding him back, that his successes were no longer properly recognized. He wanted assurances that he was still destined for the top of the bank, but that discussion was now off the table. Having previously been a big supporter of Thiam's strategy, Khan began to question more and more whether Thiam was the right leader for the job.

In March, a news report said Khan was a candidate to become CEO of a smaller Swiss financial firm named Julius Baer.[1] Executives close to Thiam reported that Khan had told his suitors he would bring clients and staff with him if he was hired. And, though Khan didn't get that role, there were constant rumours he was looking to leave and had been in talks with other firms. Eventually, Khan told Rohner he wanted out. His contract stated that he had a six-month notice period with a non-compete clause of up to a year. Credit Suisse could block him from joining a rival and taking away their clients or his former staff. But Khan asked the chairman to dial back the terms of departure. He wanted to be able to move to a competitor within just three months. All of this was discussed without Thiam's involvement. Rohner agreed to let Khan go as he wished.

On 1 July, Credit Suisse said that Khan was leaving. A month later, cross-town rival UBS announced that Khan would become its new co-head of wealth management, starting in October. The move was a public blow to Thiam's leadership, fuelling gossip about the falling-out. Thiam and his EXB were worried that Khan would repeat his successes from Credit Suisse at their big competitor. It certainly looked like a smart move by UBS to lure away a prized executive from its biggest rival.

What happened next was straight out of a Hollywood movie.

One morning in September 2019, Khan and his wife were heading out for lunch in Zurich. Their kids were busy, and it was rare for the two to spend time alone together when he was working, so they wanted to take advantage of Khan's free time before he started at UBS. The town centre was a short drive from their home in the affluent suburbs. Khan's wife wanted to drop off some dry-cleaning on the way. He went to retrieve it from her car, which was parked across the street from their house, next to some football pitches. As he shut the car door, he noticed another vehicle in the usually empty car park. It struck him as odd because it had unusual number plates, from another canton, and because the driver sitting in it was wearing an earpiece.

Khan didn't think too much of it initially, but when he and his wife set off on their short journey, he noticed the stranger was driving behind them. At first, Khan thought he was being paranoid. When they stopped at the dry-cleaner's, Khan noticed the car was there again. They set off, and the other car set off too. Khan told his wife he thought they were being tailed. 'That's impossible,' she told him. 'You're acting crazy.' He began driving an unusual, twisting route, circling streets to see if the car would follow. Each time he changed direction, the stranger did the same.

When he got to the centre of Zurich, Khan parked near the Swiss

National Bank, not far from the upmarket restaurant where they had a lunch reservation. He looked around. The other car had stopped a little distance away. Khan and his wife began walking when the driver suddenly appeared on the street nearby. Instinct took over. Khan decided quickly to confront the man directly. 'Who the hell are you?' he yelled, and began taking photos of him with his phone. There was a scuffle, and the man eventually hurried away.

Khan, still shaken, called Credit Suisse's head of security. He was looking for advice, but he was also suspicious that Credit Suisse may have ordered the surveillance. 'Do you have something to confess?' he demanded. Khan said he was scared and that he planned to organize personal security for himself.[2] He also made a complaint to the police. He had photos of the suspect, his car and the number plate.

It didn't take long before the police were able to join some dots. The private detective was from Investigo, a Zurich security agency, and was part of a team that had been tracking Khan for the past two weeks. They'd observed him at his home, when he was out jogging, when he was having a coffee with former colleagues. Their mandate was to take photos and record evidence of anyone with whom Khan met. Investigo had been hired by a consultant who was paid to arrange the surveillance operation. This middleman worked for Credit Suisse's chief operating officer, Pierre-Olivier Bouée, one of Thiam's closest lieutenants. When the middleman found out that Khan had blown the cover of the private detectives, he got in touch with his lawyer and went to Credit Suisse and to the police. He offered to help with any investigation, so long as he was given immunity from prosecution.

The story soon burst into the press. Credit Suisse executives gave private briefings to journalists, explaining that they'd been concerned Khan planned to poach the strongest performers from their staff and take them with him to UBS. The identity of the consultant and Investigo also made it into the hands of the news reporters.

Within days, events took an even darker turn. The consultant hired by Bouée was found dead, apparently having killed himself.

Rohner called an emergency meeting of the board. Usually, they met in person, but, in a hurry, several board members dialled in on a video conference. The chairman gave an outline of events. The meeting seemed to be about to pass quickly until the American board member Michael Klein pointed out similarities with an earlier case at the US computing firm Hewlett-Packard. In 2006, HP's general counsel, on the instruction of its chairwoman, had hired private security to track down the source of internal leaks. The investigators spied on the firm's own board members and some journalists in a scandal that severely damaged HP's reputation.[3] Klein asked if the bank had any rules on the use of private investigators – it didn't – and insisted the board get confirmation that they were not under observation too.

At this point, Rohner also got Thiam on the call. He asked the CEO what he knew about the case and whether he had been involved in the decision to spy on Khan. Thiam looked astonished. He knew nothing about it, he told the chairman. The board continued questioning. One comment from Thiam went down badly: 'When I was finance minister in the Cote d'Ivoire,' he said, 'secret service agents would come with information. I would tell them, "Bring it to me, but don't ever tell me how you got it."' Some board members believed this was a tacit admission of guilt.

Rohner announced an internal investigation led by a high-powered Swiss law firm. They reported back within days. Khan had been spied on for seven business days by three private detectives, who had mostly worked during daylight hours. Bouée took full responsibility and said he acted alone. The investigation found no evidence of any involvement from Thiam. Privately, the CEO confided in associates that he could understand the rationale for spying on Khan, given the rumours that he was planning on taking business to the competition. What seemed to irritate Thiam the most was that he felt the snoops had been amateurish and those connected to the spying programme had been incompetent.

Rohner hastily arranged a press conference. They had terminated Bouée's contract, he said. Thiam was not involved. He stood by the CEO. He also expressed condolences to the family of the dead consultant and said that spying on executives would not be tolerated. 'It was wrong . . . It's not, obviously, the standard way as to how we conduct business.'

Thiam also took to live television and repeated his denial of any involvement. What Bouée had done, he said, had been disproportionate, but his trusted lieutenant had believed he was acting in the best interests of the firm. Thiam insisted he personally hadn't known about the decision to snoop on his former employee, saying the action was unprecedented and there was no policy for it. The CEO also expressed regret for the death of the contractor and read out a letter from the dead man's family that seemed to exonerate the bank of any blame. The letter read: 'We do not know with absolute certainty what led him to believe he had no option but to take his own life. There are no guilty parties. He was an honest individual with a sense of integrity, and he is being mourned by those who loved him.'[4]

Any attempt to draw a line under the issue had completely failed. The Swiss media ran daily updates, bashing Thiam and Rohner. The chairman and CEO were desperate to move on. But the salacious story just wouldn't go away.

In December, another allegation of spying emerged. A former Credit Suisse executive told the bank and US and Swiss authorities that she had been followed for three days in July 2017. Colleen Graham had worked for Credit Suisse for twenty years. According to a complaint Graham filed with the US Department of Labor, she believed she was fired from a joint venture half-owned by the bank because she refused to present misleading information to external auditors. Graham believed that, after she was dismissed, she was put under surveillance.[5] A Credit Suisse spokesperson said at the time that the allegations were baseless.

But, around the same time, a detailed exposé in the Swiss press proved the Khan case was no isolated incident. Journalists from the *Neue Zürcher Zeitung*, Zurich's paper of record, had gained access to Investigo's files. They described the minute-by-minute pursuit of Khan. They also confirmed the existence of a second case. According to documents leaked to the reporters, Credit Suisse had hired Investigo in February 2019 to monitor Peter Goerke, the bank's former chief of human resources. Goerke had worked with Thiam at Prudential and followed him to Zurich. The exclusive *NZZ* story included photos of Goerke taken at Zurich airport and copies of notes the spies had written down about what he was wearing. Four cars were made available to follow the executive. It was unclear why he was being followed. Days after the observation, he had been pushed off the EXB.

Rohner quickly announced another internal investigation. Again, this concluded that Thiam didn't know anything about it. The blame was attached to Bouée.

Coverage in the Swiss press seemed relentless. It was starting to pull Rohner and Thiam apart. There were rumours that the board wanted the CEO fired. Thiam took to Instagram to post personal messages of defiance, insisting that another spying story in the Zurich press was 'false and defamatory'. One post read, 'I am a believer in freedom of expression and the importance of free media. Therefore, I regret having to write this message, but the level of misrepresentation that I have had to deal with in the past few months means that staying silent is no longer a viable strategy.' Major investors also weighed in. Several of them offered their support for the CEO. One big shareholder said the spying was 'a little issue', irrelevant outside of the close-knit world of Swiss banking. Thiam, the investor said, was the victim of envy or racism.[6]

For Rohner, the soap opera emanating from the spygate scandal had become too much. He decided that changing the CEO was the only way to change the narrative. It was a discomfiting realization given Rohner had staked his own career on hiring Thiam in the first place. He called the board to a meeting in London on a Saturday afternoon, away from the prying eyes of Switzerland's press and anyone else who might be watching. 'We cannot continue with Tidjane,' he told the other board members. 'He has become a liability, not an asset.'

The board agreed. A day or two later, they met again in Zurich to ratify the decision to oust Thiam. The CEO was summoned. He was told he could resign, or they'd fire him. Thiam chose to quit. He was given five days to clear his desk, although Rohner allowed him to present the annual results a few days later. Profits had jumped 69 per cent from the previous year. Thiam touted his restructuring programme and said the bank was poised to grow even more. 'I am proud of what Credit Suisse has achieved during my tenure. We have turned Credit Suisse around, and our 2019 results show we can be sustainably profitable,' he declared.

By the time of Thiam's downfall, his legacy at the bank looked mixed. He could point to some successes, especially around costs and capital. But there were also plenty of critics. Perhaps his biggest problem was that the Swiss establishment alienated him. Some board members and media commentators grumbled that he used the company's private jet too much and that he was too often accompanied around town by a group of burly security guards. Whether these were legitimate complaints was neither here nor there. Thiam was gone.

The spygate saga wasn't done yet, though. Within months, the law firm hired by Credit Suisse's board to investigate the use of surveillance found two more instances of employees being followed by private detectives.[7] In 2017, investigators had followed a New York-based employee at the request of senior executives. They believed the employee might have been working with the former executive Gaël de Boissard when he was helping the Zurich hedge fund RBR Capital in its campaign against Tidjane's leadership. In another incident – in Asia, in 2018 – a former employee had been put under observation after he'd threatened colleagues who became worried he might turn violent.

FINMA launched its own investigation into the affair, which was completed in 2021.[8] The regulator found that Credit Suisse's spying activities were much broader than previously reported. Khan's children had been photographed. Thiam's partner's ex had been followed. The regulator found evidence of seven separate spying programmes. Several members of the executive board had known about each of these. Nothing was officially documented. Executives covered their tracks. They communicated about the spying programmes on personal WhatsApp accounts or in text messages that were out of reach of the regulators. In one case, an invoice was altered to conceal that it related to the cost of hiring spies. The regulator said the episode was evidence of an inappropriate corporate culture from the top of the bank. FINMA said it had reprimanded two individuals in writing and opened further enforcement proceedings against three others. No one was mentioned by name.

Two months after resigning, Thiam was hit by personal tragedy. His eldest son died of non-Hodgkin lymphoma at the age of twenty-six. He'd been diagnosed about two years earlier and had been sick throughout the toughest period of Thiam's time as CEO.

Thiam continued to deny any involvement in spying. He went on to run his own financial investment vehicle for a while. After the publication of the damning *New York Times* article that aired allegations of racism, the bank apologized to its former CEO. 'People who are prejudiced say, oh, he is playing the race card,' Thiam told a conference later. 'Certain segments of the German-speaking press in Zurich... waged a very toxic and very effective campaign against me.'[9]

In late 2023, Thiam announced his candidacy to become the leader of one of the Ivory Coast's main opposition parties. It was the first step towards a possible run at the presidency. In his home country, many hailed Thiam as a financial genius. In Zurich, he was widely blamed, fairly or otherwise, for hastening Credit Suisse's decline. Thiam always said he needed ten years to turn the bank around. Spygate meant he didn't get it. The firm he left behind was tumbling further into turmoil.

# PART FOUR
## The Last Gasp

# TWENTY-TWO

# A Glimpse of the End

In the spring of 2020, as Credit Suisse grappled with the ludicrous spying scandal, the rest of the world was gripped by the early days of the Covid-19 pandemic. The virus and the lockdowns that followed threatened to stall the global economy.

In Zurich, the spygate scandal had clouded all judgement of Thiam during his time in charge. Some board members felt that hiring the charismatic, egotistical outsider had been a total failure. It was time to try something different. Rohner, who had somehow survived yet another scandal that exposed the bank's dreadful culture and widespread governance issues, was determined that the next CEO would continue the approach he'd laid out years earlier, one which Thiam had broadly followed.

An external candidate made no sense. Good applicants weren't lining up to lead Credit Suisse at this point. The bank's reputation was dire. Besides, another outsider would take months to understand the bank. Internally, the bench was weak. Lara Warner was still relatively inexperienced and had only been the bank's chief risk officer for a short time. The same was even truer for investment-banking chief

Brian Chin. Iqbal Khan, Thiam's one-time heir apparent, was long gone. Most of Brady's top lieutenants had departed years ago.

Rohner turned to Thomas Gottstein, the man Thiam had entrusted with the Swiss business. Gottstein was quiet, likeable, a twenty-year Credit Suisse veteran with experience in both the investment and private banks. He was no superstar, like Thiam or Mack or the big personalities running other global banks, such as Sergio Ermotti at UBS, or Jamie Dimon, the long-time CEO of JPMorgan. Gottstein didn't have a huge ego, he was a steady pair of hands and he was Swiss. He became the first Zurich-born CEO in decades. On Swiss radio, Rohner dismissed suggestions that Gottstein's appointment reflected a kind of xenophobia. 'One thing that was not a factor was the colour of his passport,' he said. But, after all the foreigners that had run the bank in the past, there was certainly an appeal to having a Swiss banker in charge at last.

For Gottstein, the promotion was the culmination of a long, twisting path. He had started out as a tech and media specialist in the investment bank at UBS, before joining Credit Suisse in 1999. There, he'd worked on deals for just about every major Swiss corporation, including Novartis, Roche and Nestlé. In late 2013, Gottstein was shunted sideways and asked to run the Swiss wealth-management business. He wasn't sure about it. He enjoyed the thrill of closing a big deal, whereas the role he'd been offered was more sedate.

Gottstein approached his then boss, Brady Dougan, for advice. Dougan told him it was a great idea. They didn't have enough investment bankers who understood wealth management and vice versa. Gottstein would gain broad experience that would help him climb the ladder, should he want to. 'If you do well enough,' Dougan said, 'maybe one day you'll take my job. But, I have to warn you, it's a shit job.'

Seven years later, Dougan's warning may have been ringing in Gottstein's ears as the world plunged into the Covid crisis just weeks after he'd taken over. He suddenly found himself at the helm during the worst global health catastrophe in a century, which had also sent the world's economy into a tailspin. The stock market sank and global trade dried up. Demand for some banking services fell sharply amid the uncertainty. Banks braced for a wave of defaults from clients who could no longer pay back loans.

Lockdowns and travel restrictions meant Gottstein couldn't even meet with staff around the world. He hardly knew his role and his staff before he was conducting critical meetings via Zoom.

One of the most pressing issues for many banks in the US and Europe was a sudden liquidity crunch. Clients, especially big corporations, feared the impact of the virus on their businesses and rushed to grab as much cash as they could get their hands on. For Credit Suisse, the problem was most acute in the US. The bank had lending commitments of about $70 billion there. Normally, about 10 per cent of this was drawn down by their clients at any given time. Times were clearly no longer normal and everyone worried they would run out of cash. Suddenly, the bank's clients were grabbing dollars fast, drawing down about $1 billion a day as the pandemic began to take hold. A widening hole was tearing through Credit Suisse's liquidity buffers.

Gottstein, barely a month in charge, faced a potentially lethal crisis. He urgently called meetings with the Swiss National Bank and the US Federal Reserve. There was no ready-made solution. As a foreign bank, Credit Suisse didn't have access to the so-called Fed window – a pool of liquidity from the Federal Reserve that banks in the US and some other global banks could tap in an emergency. And though Credit Suisse had plenty of cash in Switzerland, regulations barred it from transferring money outside the country in these circumstances.

The only way out was for Credit Suisse to sell assets in a kind of fire sale to plug the gap. That would generate much needed cash, but at a significant cost. The bank would lose sources of revenue, and it would have to sell the best assets first, given the amount of fear in the markets. Even then, if the drawdowns continued, eventually the bank would run out of liquidity in the US.

It was really a last-ditch attempt to stem the bleeding. And it would not have been sustainable. Fortunately for Gottstein and for Credit Suisse, though, the crisis passed. As governments around the world, including in the US, once again bailed out the system with massive injections of cash, the pressure on markets globally began to ease. Almost as quickly as clients of the bank had started to pull their money out, the potential banking crisis subsided and the bank stabilized. Gottstein breathed a sigh of relief.

In Switzerland, the near-terminal incident led to a brief inquest among the country's top bankers, including Gottstein, and the regulators, especially at the SNB. The sudden liquidity crunch had threatened one of the country's biggest institutions, and it was understandable that vested interests would want to come up with a plan to make sure they were better prepared in the event of a similar crisis in the future. The Swiss authorities considered introducing their own version of the Fed funding window, to provide a safety net for their own banks. It would have been easy enough to make this happen during a period of relative calm after the Covid-induced turbulence. But, with the pressure off, there was no impetus to implement the proposal. Instead, it was shelved.

With the immediate financial crisis over, Gottstein tried to bring some focus to his tenure. He earned plaudits in Swiss political and financial circles early in the pandemic as Credit Suisse rolled out measures to help employees and small businesses too. He seemed to have brought a measure of order to the bank after the drama of spygate. Quiet, cautious, sensitive to Swiss cultural mores – perhaps he was just the leader the bank needed to get on a stable footing.

But this was Credit Suisse. Another scandal (or three) was always lurking in the background. The first of Gottstein's reign had already emerged that spring, when shares in a Chinese Starbucks clone backed by Credit Suisse sank after the company admitted it had fabricated half of its sales for the previous year. Luckin Coffee had been one of the fastest-growing businesses in China over the past couple of years, and its rise had been fuelled by support from Credit Suisse. The Swiss bank had helped Luckin launch an IPO and raise money at a multibillion-dollar valuation. When Thiam was CEO, he had lauded the firm's founder as a dream client. But, in early 2020, a San Francisco-based hedge fund named Muddy Waters circulated a document that alleged widespread accounting fraud at the company. Luckin initially denied the allegations, but mounting evidence forced the company's chairman to acknowledge that staff had been making up revenue numbers. The stock tanked. It was delisted from the US market, and Luckin was hit with a fine by the SEC. Credit Suisse, which had loaned Luckin's chairman $100 million, was left nursing another loss and yet another bruise to its reputation.

Around the same time, the Swiss bank became embroiled in another huge scandal at German payments business Wirecard. The company was one of Europe's few promising technology-sector businesses and it was backed by much of the German financial establishment. It had also been the focus of controversy for years. The *Financial Times* had published a series of articles questioning the accuracy of Wirecard's accounts and the sustainability of its business. Several hedge funds were also betting heavily against its shares. Wirecard had fought back with legal action against the hedge funds and the journalists too.

Typically, Credit Suisse blundered into the fray. One of the bank's treasured clients was SoftBank, a giant Japanese technology investor that threw money around on fast-growing tech companies. SoftBank was a lucrative client, with fees aplenty for banks that worked with it. In 2019, Credit Suisse advised SoftBank on a deal to buy $1 billion in Wirecard bonds. The Swiss bank packaged up the bonds, which were sold on to other investors. But, within months of that deal, an audit of Wirecard's accounts backed up the *FT* 's claims of wrongdoing. The stock plummeted, and the bonds followed suit, quickly falling to about 12 per cent of their face value.[1] Credit Suisse itself avoided major losses. Most of the bonds had been passed on to clients. But the bank was shamed, nonetheless. Wirecard ended up being the biggest fraud case in German history. Recriminations, lawsuits and criminal inquires ran for years after the company collapsed into insolvency. Credit Suisse's name was inevitably dragged through the mud by its association with the ongoing affair.

Then, in December 2020, the reputation of Gottstein's firm took yet another hit when Swiss prosecutors indicted Credit Suisse and one of its former staff for laundering tens of millions of dollars on behalf of Bulgarian drug smugglers.[2] The details of the affair exposed yet again the bank's lax attitude to risk and its capacity for getting into the most ludicrously shady business dealings.

Evelin Banev had been a former wrestler with the Bulgarian national team in the 1980s. When his funding dried up following the end of communism, Banev's sporting career ended. To maintain his income, he became entangled with an organized-crime gang and started trafficking cocaine. For years, he organized the import of tons of illegal drugs into Europe from South America by boat and plane. Pretty soon, he was dubbed Bulgaria's 'cocaine king'. Banev was also connected to Elena Pampoulova, a former Bulgarian tennis star who'd competed in the Olympics and made it into the top one hundred players in the world. In 2006, her career long since over, she married her boyfriend, a Swiss banker. The couple moved to his homeland, where she began a new career with Credit Suisse. Over the next few years, Banev used Pampoulova to launder drug money through Credit Suisse and into the Swiss financial system. His associates would meet with the former tennis star to hand over suitcases full of cash, which she would then deposit in an account. According to Swiss prosecutors, Pampoulova had helped to mask the illicit origins of transactions worth more than $150 million. There was evidence, too, that at least one of Banev's associates had been murdered, shot dead outside a restaurant in Sofia.

The charges brought against Credit Suisse by the Swiss attorney general were focused on activity between 2004 and 2008. Credit Suisse expressed 'astonishment' that prosecutors were pursuing alleged crimes that took place more than a decade ago and pushed for the file to be dropped. But the attorney general was not dissuaded. The case dragged on for years – throughout Gottstein's tenure and beyond – and, when Credit Suisse lost, it was the first domestic bank to be convicted of a crime in a Swiss court.

In her testimony, Pampoulova slammed her employer's compliance procedures. There were practically no safeguards as her colleagues rushed to capture business from wealthy Eastern Europeans. The judges said the bank had ignored glaring warning signs of connections to criminal activity.[3] Pampoulova was convicted of money laundering and given a twenty-month suspended jail sentence. She died the following year, after an illness. Banev had gone on the run. He was given a twenty-year prison sentence in Italy and convicted in absentia by courts in Romania and Bulgaria. In 2021, he was arrested in Ukraine, then released when it turned out he had Ukrainian citizenship, which meant he couldn't be extradited.

For its part in the affair, Credit Suisse was handed a $22-million fine. It was a relatively small financial penalty. But, like each of these scandals, it was a reminder that Credit Suisse's cultural problems had deep roots. They reached back through the reigns of Thiam, Dougan, Grübel and beyond. Gottstein could change nothing about the past, though it was impossible to believe the bank had turned over a new leaf.

Even as the bank blew up again and again, Rohner was working on a plan that was even more explosive. The chairman had met with his opposite number at UBS to discuss the possibility of merging Switzerland's two biggest banks. This idea rolled around every couple of years. It was like the solution to every problem, but one that no one was ever willing to fully embrace. This time, Rohner and Axel Weber, UBS's chairman, were of the same mind. They thought the combined forces of the two big Swiss banks would be better able to compete with the Americans, who were dominating global banking. A merger would produce a truly giant bank in Europe, and it would be the culmination of a long career for both chairmen.

Their idea was that Weber would become chairman of the new combined bank. Rohner was due to retire in 2021 and he would stick to that timeline, but he'd get to pick the new CEO of the combined bank before he left. Gottstein believed he was top of the list, as UBS's CEO Sergio Ermotti had already announced his own plans to retire. Still, although he stood to benefit, Gottstein wasn't in favour of the idea. He thought it would be too difficult to pull it off, especially during the pandemic. There were still travel restrictions that would make it impossible to meet with regulators and shareholders to get their support. The economy was still very uncertain too. There was no guarantee they could get the deal past antitrust regulators. In Switzerland, big companies would be overwhelmingly against a merger that left them with only one option as a banking partner.

Despite Gottstein's concerns, the chairmen ploughed ahead. They hired consultants McKinsey & Co. to advise on the merger proposal and dig into the details: Where did the two banks overlap? Where could they cut duplicate costs? Who was stronger in this region or that type of banking activity?

If Rohner and Weber could pull it off, they would have a genuine merger of equals, with a team of Credit Suisse executives in charge under a chairman from UBS. They took the plan to the Swiss National Bank, FINMA and the Finance Ministry. So far, everyone was on board. But Rohner knew it was still tentative – if the transaction dragged out in public, there'd be a period of uncertainty when other banks would have a chance to pick off their best employees and most lucrative clients. So, in September, when the story leaked into the Swiss media, the whole merger was suddenly at risk. For Rohner, this was too soon to go public. They didn't yet have everything in place, and there was now a chance that politicians and investors would stall progress. Rohner and Weber ended the talks.

Within just a couple of years, this would look like a real sliding-doors moment, when the future of the bank could have gone in another direction and a different history would have been written. But it wasn't to be.

Against the background of all this noise and potential upheaval, Gottstein was still trying to run a bank. Not long after he'd taken over, the board encouraged him to clean up some outstanding legacy issues. This was similar to what happened when Thiam took over with the DLJ write-down. The idea was that a new CEO had a kind of honeymoon period with investors. It would be OK to take a hit from old mistakes that could be portrayed as problems hung over from a previous regime. Gottstein followed orders. He wrote down $450 million related to a stake in a hedge fund called York Capital Management that Dougan had acquired in 2010. He also settled civil litigation in the US, dating from the financial crisis, related to residential mortgage-backed securities, costing another $600 million. These two items took a huge bite out of the results in Gottstein's first year, but, with Covid hitting businesses everywhere, and because they were pre-existing problems, the new CEO hoped investors would cut him some slack.

Indeed, there were reasons to be cautiously optimistic. The banking industry was bouncing back, with pent-up demand for deals and investment driving revenues higher. Credit Suisse was also buoyed by the relative strength of Switzerland, whose economy never hit the depths of some other countries. In the first six months of 2020, despite everything, Gottstein reported that the bank had made about $2.9 billion in profit, its best result in a decade.[4] He heaped praise on staff and used the positive momentum to roll out his own strategic plan. In truth, this amounted to little more than some tinkering and promotions for Thiam's former lead lieutenants. Lara Warner grabbed a new title, becoming the chief risk and compliance officer. Gottstein merged the different parts of the investment bank into one and put Brian Chin in charge.

Towards the end of the year, Gottstein said he wanted to 'start 2021 with as clean a slate as possible.'[5] He believed the worst scandals were out in the open and the bank was headed for even stronger results. Wealth management and Asia-Pacific were growing fast as the world returned to something like normal. Investment-banking revenue had almost doubled from the same period a year earlier.

In February, Gottstein was so optimistic – and clear-headed after the merger talks ended – that he planned to bulk up the bank with a significant acquisition. His target was a Swiss private bank called EFG. It was only about twenty years old, but EFG was growing fast, and it was strong in wealth management and private banking, the areas where Credit Suisse was perennially trying to get bigger. The deal would rebalance the bank away from investment banking, something that had eluded previous CEOs for a decade. Gottstein's plan was approved by FINMA and the bank's biggest shareholder. A better future for the bank was within his grasp.

Against the odds, a year into Gottstein's leadership of the bank, everything looked great. He was anticipating the first quarter's results would be the bank's best ever and that they would even outperform UBS. It would be a moment of genuine triumph.

Then, one day in late February 2021, Lara Warner came to Gottstein's office. She wore a grave look. Warner stood in the doorway and told him, 'Thomas, we've got an issue.'

# TWENTY-THREE

# Greensill

Warner looked shocked as she brought Gottstein the grim news. Forget about the Bulgarian wrestler, Wirecard and the Chinese coffee company. The bank had a much bigger scandal on its hands.

Lex Greensill was an Australian businessman on the move. He said he was going to democratize finance. He was going to screw the banks. He was going to be a multibillionaire, and everyone around him would get rich. In the end, his business was a house of cards. Its collapse shook Credit Suisse and left Gottstein's plans in tatters.

Greensill had a compelling origin story. He had grown up in the Australian bush, in a town called Bundaberg. His parents and their parents were farmers. Greensill was a bookish child in a rough-and-tumble community. He won at debating class when sporting prowess was more highly prized. However, what annoyed young Greensill was the unfair way farms like the one his parents owned were treated by the big grocery chains that bought their produce. The big chains always paid late, and the farmers had to take it on the chin. Years later, Greensill would say it was his mission to solve this problem.

After school, he moved to Sydney, then London, and became a banker at Morgan Stanley and then Citigroup in the early 2000s. He specialized in 'supply-chain finance' – an ancient type of banking service turbocharged for the twenty-first century. Banks provide short-term loans to smooth the payments between buyers and sellers of goods: sellers are paid promptly; buyers pay back the loan later. The bank takes a cut of the deal, and modern technology makes the process run smoothly.

Greensill was hard-working, ultra-ambitious and impatient. In 2011, he set up his own firm, Greensill Capital. For a while, the firm was going nowhere. Unlike a big bank, Greensill Capital didn't have a hefty balance sheet to fund its loans. Nor were clients keen to borrow from a company they'd never heard of.

But Lex Greensill was an arch salesman with a big vision. He eventually managed to get some influential investors to take a stake in the firm. One of them was a nerdy American banker named David Solo, who was well-connected in Swiss financial circles. Solo had been a trading whizz at UBS, and he'd been CEO at a Swiss asset-management company called GAM. He was also chairman of something called Simag, a joint venture between Credit Suisse and a Swiss university, which applied machine learning and complex physics to investments. Solo had introduced Greensill to one of GAM's top portfolio managers, who ran billions of dollars on behalf of pension funds and other big institutions. Greensill and the portfolio manager hit it off. Pretty soon, GAM was investing significant amounts of money with Greensill Capital.

But there was a problem. In 2017, a whistle-blower at GAM alleged that the Greensill investments were difficult to value and hard to sell. Often, they had nothing to do with supply-chain finance. Hundreds of millions of dollars had been poured into investments tied to a Russian cargo plane, to lease payments from a Norwegian airline and to a property developer's disputed claim to a Manhattan skyscraper. The GAM portfolio manager had even invested several hundred million dollars in Greensill itself. A huge proportion of the loans Greensill made were tied to one controversial borrower – a British-Indian steel magnate named Sanjeev Gupta, who was blackballed by most big banks because of problems with his accounts.[1]

GAM launched an investigation. The portfolio manager was suspended and then fired. The value of the funds he'd managed plummeted. GAM's share price cratered. The CEO and several other executives quit. The company survived, but only just.

The episode could have been the end for Greensill. However, the firm had an exit strategy. Solo introduced Lex Greensill to executives at Credit Suisse, including Michel Degen, the head of asset management for Europe, the Middle East and Africa. Lex made his pitch. With interest rates persistently low – they were negative in Switzerland – it was hard for investors to make a return. Supply-chain finance was safe and reliable, according to Greensill, like keeping your money in cash, but it offered a small yield, too. Buying insurance to cover any potential loan defaults added an extra level of protection.

It was a dull but potent investment opportunity. Degen and others bought in. In Lex Greensill, they also saw another dream client, an entrepreneur who'd need personal and business advice for years. He'd need to raise debt and equity. He'd need a private banker to manage his wealth. He was a source of fees and long-term revenue. Pretty soon, Credit Suisse had set up four separate funds that invested in Greensill's supply-chain finance loans.

Even at this early stage, there were already alarm bells that the bank should have heard ringing. GAM's collapse and Greensill's role in it were the subject of widespread media coverage. Authorities in the UK and Switzerland had both launched high-profile investigations. The sketchy nature of some of Greensill's loans was also widely known. There was a discussion of the GAM affair at senior levels of the bank. Credit Suisse bankers who worked in the insurance sector had also raised concerns with senior executives. Lex Greensill was infamous in the insurance industry. Several deals his firm had been involved with had ended in messy legal disputes. Some large insurance companies refused to work with him.

Some staff in Credit Suisse's asset-management division actively avoided anything to do with the Greensill funds. They were growing too fast and the investments were too opaque. Above all, the bank appeared to be earning millions of dollars for managing client money, but all of the work was outsourced to Greensill itself.

In the summer of 2019, the bank launched a review of the governance of the funds, though that appeared to have relied mostly on answers provided by Greensill. When the review came back clean, an email to the entire executive team said there was nothing to worry about, despite the concerns among some staff. Degen and other senior leaders pushed ahead. The bank was aggressively marketing the supply-chain finance funds to clients. Fact sheets gave them a risk score of one or two out of seven, where one was the safest investment the bank offered. Sometimes clients were even encouraged to borrow more from the bank to invest in the funds. Money poured in. At the start of 2019, there was about $2 billion invested with Greensill. By the end of that year, the figure had ballooned to more than $9 billion.[2]

Greensill itself appeared to be booming, too. A US private-equity firm, General Atlantic, took a $250-million stake in the company. The giant Japanese tech investor SoftBank invested about $1.5 billion. Flush with cash, Lex Greensill hired hundreds of staff, opened new offices around the world and bought a fleet of private aircraft. He even hired the former UK prime minister David Cameron as a senior adviser and door-opener, who could introduce the firm to world leaders and business titans.

When Gottstein became CEO of Credit Suisse, Lex Greensill's name was on a list of the bank's one hundred most important clients he should contact during his first hundred days in charge. Because of Covid, their meeting ended up being a brief Zoom call. But Gottstein was soon in touch again. Greensill was planning an IPO that could potentially value the firm at $40 billion. Credit Suisse was among seven banks that pitched to run the process. When Lex Greensill picked the Swiss bank, Gottstein sent an email expressing his gratitude. The message, crafted by an Australian private banker who managed Greensill's personal money, said, 'We will not let you down.'

But the relationship started to unravel in early 2020. First, the pandemic had roiled the markets and investors started to pull money out of the supply-chain funds. Credit Suisse spokespeople wrote this off as a broader market issue, not unique to the Greensill funds. But there was another problem – a string of companies that Greensill had loaned money to defaulted on their debts. In a couple of cases, the borrowers were accused of financial irregularities and fraud. In public and to clients, Credit Suisse still said the funds were fine.

In the spring and early summer, press reports pointed out that there was a strange circularity about the funds. Several hundred million dollars had been loaned to start-up businesses that counted SoftBank as a major investor, just like Greensill. Each of these companies was struggling financially. What's more, SoftBank had invested $1.5 billion into the supply-chain finance funds. The money seemed to be going round in circles.[3]

Gottstein demanded another review and hired an external law firm. He asked Lara Warner to investigate and told the bank's head of asset management, a jockish American named Eric Varvel, to fly over to Europe too. Varvel had been at Credit Suisse for thirty years. He was a renowned salesman, with close ties to the bank's Qatari clients and biggest shareholders. He was also a champion of the supply-chain funds, touting them at investor meetings as a huge opportunity.

The investigation started out as wide-ranging. But in time it became more focused, looking only at the relationship between Greensill and SoftBank. Earlier in 2020, Lex Greensill had been concerned when investors were withdrawing their support. He had called in a favour from SoftBank's chief, the Japanese businessman Masayoshi Son, who agreed to pump money in to stem the bleeding. But there was a condition attached to the bailout. Lex drew up a side letter to the fund documentation. This said that the supply-chain funds run by Credit Suisse would only ever source assets from Greensill. The bankers agreed to it. After all, the bankers who ran the funds outsourced everything to Greensill anyway, so this just felt like a formalization of the existing practice.

When the investigators were done, they reported their findings to an internal disciplinary committee. The side letter was in breach of the rules governing the funds. It would have to be unwound. The bankers who ran the funds were given a warning. At that point, the committee could have escalated matters to the CEO, but chose not to.

Warner reported back to Gottstein. She had met with Lex Greensill twice in person. It turned out that Warner – an Australian-American – had family connections to the same outback town where Greensill grew up. Gottstein was left with the impression that there was no deeper problem to investigate.

No one at the bank seemed to know the dark reality. Despite the apparent success of the funds, Greensill Capital was facing problems that threatened its survival. A bank Greensill owned in Germany was under pressure from regulators concerned it had loaned too much money to Sanjeev Gupta. A small Australian insurer that Greensill relied on had been taken over by a much larger Japanese company that said it wouldn't renew coverage. And, although Greensill now counted some blue-chip companies among its clients, many of its loans were made to much more obscure firms that would have difficulty ever paying them back. Each of these challenges was potentially critical. Taken together, Greensill could not survive.

In late 2020, equity markets had weakened again and the prospect of a Greensill IPO looked distant. Credit Suisse began pitching institutional investors the idea of taking a direct stake in the business. In the meantime, Greensill also asked Credit Suisse for a $140-million loan. A London-based risk manager responsible for reviewing the loan request identified several risks in Greensill's business model. He recommended rejecting the loan. But bankers in Asia and Switzerland who'd courted Lex Greensill for years disagreed. There were big fees on the line if the relationship with Greensill soured. These bankers appealed to Warner, who overruled their colleague in London. The loan was approved.

By then, Greensill was in a tailspin. The insurance issue was especially problematic. Without insurance coverage, many of the biggest investors in the Credit Suisse funds would demand their money back. That would force Greensill and Credit Suisse to recall the loans, which would quickly reveal that many of the borrowers were not able to repay what they owed. In turn, that would trigger a run on the funds, as no one would want to be the last investor out, sitting on enormous losses.

The German financial regulator was also relentless, piling pressure on Greensill to cut exposure to Gupta. By the end of 2020, Greensill was in a full-blown crisis. The company was leaking money all over and Lex was desperately trying to plug holes in the business with whatever cash he could get his hands on. In December, the Greensill board called in restructuring experts to plan for a potential bankruptcy or sale. SoftBank had already decided there was nothing left worth selling and wrote down the value of its stake to zero. Some Greensill directors had already handed in their notice. It seemed a matter of time before the company went bust.

Yet, at Credit Suisse, bankers were somehow still marketing the Greensill funds to clients just days before the inevitable collapse.

That was when Warner walked into Gottstein's office, in late February 2021, with the bad news. Greensill's insurer had refused to renew coverage. The supply-chain funds, which had grown to $10 billion, were finished.

A few days later, Greensill declared insolvency. The truth about its business was that supply-chain finance just wasn't very profitable. Greensill hadn't made much money from short-term loans to blue-chip companies. Instead, Lex had covered this up by making much riskier loans to much riskier companies. When some of those businesses had defaulted on their loans, or just didn't want to pay back what they'd borrowed, Greensill had simply rolled the loan on for another few months, and then rolled it on again, and again.

For Gottstein, the world turned upside down. The excellent performance he'd been looking forward to was blown apart by the Greensill scandal. Instead of delivering record-setting results, he was trying to explain why clients weren't getting back billions of dollars that the Australian huckster had squandered.

In the following months, Credit Suisse was able to recover about two-thirds of the money where the borrowers were blue-chip companies like Nestlé or General Motors. But several billion dollars proved much more difficult to collect. This included loans to Sanjeev Gupta, to a coal mine owned by the governor of West Virginia, to a motor-sports insurance firm owned by the cousin of a Greensill director. It turned out money had been used to buy bad assets out of the GAM funds, to invest in a business run by Lex Greensill's neighbour, to prop up smaller supply-chain finance companies that were themselves making much riskier loans. There were dozens of speculative investments in companies that appeared to have little chance of paying anything back. Many of the loans had nothing to do with supply-chain finance. Greensill had even provided loans to Gupta and to the US coal-mining business backed by made-up invoices related to transactions that hadn't yet happened. Often, Greensill had taken a significant slice of the loan straight out as a fee, meaning borrowers were on the hook for much more than they ever received.

Credit Suisse hired an investigating team of lawyers and auditors to look into what went wrong. It became clear the bankers who ran the supply-chain funds had delegated almost all their responsibility to Greensill. They knew very little about the loans. They knew nothing about most of the borrowers. They had little direct contact with the insurance providers. Senior staff in the asset-management business, including Varvel, were focused on selling the investment to clients and neglected the detailed work of digging into the specific transactions in the funds. Up and down the bank, executives had recklessly entrusted their clients' money to Greensill Capital without proper safeguards in place.

Why had that happened? At the senior levels, Credit Suisse executives had been wooed by Lex Greensill, impressed by his fleet of private jets, smart suits, big vision and political connections. These top-level bankers hadn't looked into the detail. The lower-level bankers had turned a blind eye too. They were steamrolled by Lex's smooth talking and sharp intellect. Lex had the backing of their bosses. And besides, while the funds kept growing, their bonuses ballooned too.

Following the collapse of the funds, Varvel, Warner and Michel Degen were all pushed out of Credit Suisse. Lower-level executives who managed the funds were fired too.

David Cameron's role at Greensill made it a mainstream news story in the UK. The ex-prime minister was heavily criticized for lobbying former government colleagues with dozens of text messages on behalf of Greensill Capital. Cameron had tried desperately to bypass normal channels to get Greensill special access to government Covid bailout loans. He and Lex Greensill were hauled in front of parliamentary inquiries and grilled by MPs. At one point, a parliamentarian asked Greensill if he was a fraud and if his company was a Ponzi scheme (which he categorically denied).

In the years that followed, there were several multibillion-dollar lawsuits related to the company's collapse. Insurance companies, Credit Suisse, SoftBank, angry investors and others sued and countersued to try to recover the lost money or to avoid having to pay out.

FINMA also criticized the bank. The regulator said Credit Suisse seriously breached its obligations. It pointed out that there was plenty of opportunity to investigate the Greensill business properly when GAM collapsed, especially given that journalists were asking difficult questions. Instead of an independent review, Credit Suisse relied on information from the bankers who ran the fund, and, repeatedly, from Lex Greensill himself. As a result, the bank ended up making statements that were 'partly false and overly positive' about the supply-chain funds it managed.[4]

There were criminal investigations related to the company's collapse in Germany, Switzerland and the UK. In September 2021, Swiss police raided Credit Suisse's offices and the homes of four former executives, seizing documents related to Greensill. In 2023, Swiss authorities told four former Credit Suisse bankers that they were suspects in a criminal case. Gottstein himself was under investigation. They told Lex Greensill he was a suspect, too.

But that was all in the future. For the bank, the immediate cost was minimal. Of the $140-million loan to Greensill, $50 million was recovered quickly. The share price had also taken a hit in anticipation of years of costly litigation. But the effect of the Greensill scandal didn't end there. The Greensill failure had burned some of Credit Suisse's biggest clients, including Middle Eastern sovereign wealth funds. Clients like these needed to be handled with care. The wealthiest investors needed to see that Credit Suisse could be trusted with their money. Scandal after scandal proved that they couldn't. This was of far greater importance than losing the bank's own money on a loan to Lex Greensill himself. Losing the trust of clients, losing yet more credibility with investors and the authorities – this was the true, enormous cost of Greensill, and it was yet to be counted.

# TWENTY-FOUR

# Rohner's Last Stand

The appointment of Thomas Gottstein as CEO had been Rohner's final roll of the dice, his last chance to implement the strategy he'd laid out years earlier, in 2012. There had been moments when it looked like Rohner's plan was working. But there were far too many scandals, far too many hiccups that marred any chance of greater success.

Rohner's time was nearly up and, as with almost every doomed leader of Credit Suisse, his departure was marked by yet another scandal.

In late March 2021, the bank was still reeling from the collapse of Greensill Capital when Gottstein and Rohner learned that a hedge-fund client in New York had also imploded.

Bill Hwang, a sharp-suited trader, ran Archegos Capital Management. In the 1990s, he worked for Tiger Management, a pioneer of the hedge-fund industry. Hwang was one of several wunderkinds, dubbed 'Tiger Cubs' by the finance press, who branched out and set up on their own. He made a name for himself with some successful bets on shares in Asia, but his fortunes took a dip in the 2008 financial crisis. Hwang lost money following the collapse of Lehman Brothers, and he became a target of the regulators. In 2012, he settled insider-trading allegations with the SEC and his firm pled guilty to wire fraud with the DOJ.[1]

Hwang concentrated on managing his own wealth through a hedge fund named Archegos, for the Greek word meaning 'one who takes the lead'. Despite his damaged reputation, several banks, including Credit Suisse, continued to provide Hwang with 'prime services' – processing trades and lending money to supercharge his stock picking.

At Credit Suisse, from time to time, there were concerns about working with Hwang. In 2015, a routine internal client review examined the risk of doing business with Archegos. Bankers who worked with the hedge fund pointed to its strong performance and Hwang's self-proclaimed 'best in class' infrastructure. The review pretty much ended there. Three years later, the prime-services group expanded its trade with Archegos, prompting another light-touch review that didn't lead to any significant restrictions. Over the years, the hedge fund frequently pushed up against and even breached trading limits. Each time, the bank found mitigating reasons to bend the rules.

Under Tidjane Thiam, the prime-services division as a whole had been scrutinized as part of the overhaul of the entire investment bank. But the unit was left in place. It was useful when working with wealthy clients who wanted to trade stocks. Thiam wanted the unit to be more focused and take fewer risks, though some executives felt it was one of the areas left exposed by the departure of senior staff during his tenure.

In February 2020, the bank had been struck by a tragedy that led to a potentially crucial change in the chain of command. The key risk manager monitoring prime-services clients was an experienced former currency trader named Jason Varnish. That month, while on a ski holiday in Vail, Colorado, Varnish's jacket had become tangled in a chairlift. He was hauled into the air and, by the time his friends and lift attendants got him down, Varnish had died of asphyxiation. At Credit Suisse, his replacement was a New York-based sales executive named Parshu Shah. In his previous role, Shah's job was to bring in lots of business, including pitching to Archegos, which had been one of his biggest clients. In this new position, his job was almost the opposite. He was the main gatekeeper whose task was to make sure the bank didn't become overexposed to the same hedge funds he'd recently been courting. For anyone, that would be a challenging change of gear.[2]

A month after the tragedy, in March 2020, Credit Suisse casually lost $214 million following the collapse of another hedge fund, Malachite Capital. It was a warning sign that the bank failed to act upon. An investigation into what went wrong listed numerous fixes to prevent it from happening again, though these were implemented slowly and in a piecemeal fashion.

A few months later, a risk manager warned senior executives that key parts of prime services were lacking enough people and sufficient experience. There was no one left he would 'trust to have a backbone', the manager wrote to colleagues. Nothing was done about his warnings. In September 2020, Shah raised his own concerns about Archegos with a high-level executive committee that looked at all the bank's counterparties. Again, there was no action to limit the relationship.

By early 2021, Credit Suisse's exposure to Archegos had ballooned. As of March, Credit Suisse's notional exposure to Archegos – the value of the stocks it had bet on – was more than $20 billion. These bets were concentrated in a handful of stocks, including those of US media company Viacom and Tencent Music Entertainment, a Chinese online music business. The shares had surged in recent months. But, on 22 March, Viacom's stock started to fall sharply after a planned sale of new shares in the company generated less interest than hoped. Shares in Tencent and some others were also falling fast.

At that week's EXB meeting, top billing was Greensill – it had blown up only days earlier. Most of the senior executives had never heard of Archegos at this point. Gottstein asked Brian Chin, the head of the investment bank, why some stocks in the US were suddenly selling off. They discussed whether Chinese companies listed in the US were hurting because of comments from President Joe Biden. No one seemed overly worried.

But, in the meantime, Archegos was imploding. Its bets were getting worse. By Wednesday, 24 March, the hedge fund was collapsing. One of Hwang's key lieutenants called Credit Suisse to say it was running out of funds. That evening, Lara Warner and Brian Chin were told of the crisis. Later, both said it was their first time hearing of Archegos.

Chin called Gottstein with the devastating details. They could be looking at a loss of between $2 billion and $3 billion, he said. A day later, it rose to $4 billion.

Gottstein and his executive team spent the weekend in calls with Archegos and other banks, desperately trying to conjure a solution. UBS, Credit Suisse and some others looked for a collective deal. The Americans wouldn't participate. The banks were racing to get their money back before it ran out. Credit Suisse was left exposed, its safety nets were less effective and it was slower to react.

When the dust settled, Archegos was finished. Japanese bank Nomura lost about $3 billion. UBS had lost a few hundred million dollars. Most of the others took similar damage or dodged it altogether. Credit Suisse had lost an astounding $5.5 billion.

The impact was immediate. Within days, Gottstein had announced plans for a share sale to raise $2 billion in capital to plug the hole left by Archegos. Brian Chin joined Lara Warner and headed for the exit. Shah also left.

The twin Greensill and Archegos scandals had turned the CEO's 'best ever quarter' into one of the most disheartening, destructive periods in the bank's history. It was an utter disaster. In an interview with a Swiss news outlet, Gottstein, a keen skier, likened his position to that of a downhill racer who had fought through injuries and delivered excellent practice runs only to end up tearing a ligament.[3] The headline on the story, tellingly, was, 'What happened in the US?' The Swiss media was still clinging to the view that the bank's problems were all overseas.

Gottstein launched yet another internal investigation. Its conclusions were familiar to anyone tracking the litany of failures at the bank. 'Our key observations revolve around a central point,' wrote the authors from an outside law firm. 'No one at Credit Suisse – not the traders, not the in-business risk managers, not the senior business executives, not the credit risk analysts, and not the senior risk officers – appeared to fully appreciate the serious risks that Archegos' portfolio posed to Credit Suisse. These risks were not hidden. They were in plain sight from at least September 2020.'[4]

It was the same old story: failings lay out in the open; warnings were ignored; chances to avoid a blow-up were missed time and again. These were issues for many big banks – perhaps all of them. But Credit Suisse was the poster child for banking screw-ups. One of the most damning findings was that the bank earned just $16 million from Archegos in 2020. It was a tiny pay-off, given the risks it was taking. The bank fired nine employees and said twenty-three staff had been penalized, forfeiting as much as $70 million in compensation. Rohner gave up the annual fee he was paid as chairman entirely.

The bank was fined almost $400 million by the US and UK – a far larger penalty than the board had expected. The authorities noted that there had been no board oversight of Archegos, yet, at one point, Credit Suisse's exposure to the hedge fund was equivalent to half its equity capital. They pointed out, too, that concerns and red flags raised by employees had not had any effect.

In the US, prosecutors arrested Hwang and one of his top lieutenants. They alleged the pair had deliberately misled Credit Suisse and other banks to get access to loans they'd used to drive up the price of a few shares. In just one year, Hwang's fund had rocketed from

$1.5 billion to $35 billion. Hwang was charged with racketeering conspiracy, securities fraud and wire fraud. He was released on a $100-million bond, secured by $5 million in cash and two properties.[5] Hwang's lawyer said he was 'entirely innocent'.

Gottstein and Rohner were faced with yet more angry shareholders, including staff whose compensation was heavily linked to the company's battered stock price. The quiet CEO, the unlikely CEO, was in the crosshairs. The chairman whose reign had been blighted by a long list of missteps and wrongdoing was also the subject of derision and anger.

Investors, regulators, staff – everyone seemed to want Gottstein out. Swiss media reported his departure pretty much as a fact. He offered his resignation to Rohner. There were persuasive reasons not to accept. For starters, churning through another CEO so soon after Thiam could have deepened the turmoil at the bank. A new chief would want a new strategy and a new executive team. They'd need time to bed in. It was safer to keep Gottstein in place for now.

Instead, it was Rohner who was on the way out. His term as chairman ended in April. After a decade, he was leaving at a brutal low point. Inside and outside the bank, many people pointed to Rohner as the thread that ran through the years of turbulence. The bank's share price had fallen by more than 70 per cent while he was in charge. Naturally, Rohner saw things differently. He repeatedly pointed out that, in his view, the restructured bank was on a surer footing, its capital position was healthier than it had been in years, and it was poised for growth.

After Greensill and after Archegos, the next chairman would take a very different view.

# TWENTY-FIVE

# António

At Rohner's final annual meeting as chairman of the bank, in April 2021, he apologized for Archegos and Greensill: 'We've disappointed not just our clients but also our shareholders, and not for the first time unfortunately.' The chairman said both the recent incidents were inexcusable, cast a shadow over all his previous work and had angered and disappointed staff and investors alike.

It was a chastening end to his leadership. Instead of setting the bank on the path to stability and long-term profitability, Rohner's tenure had left Credit Suisse accelerating from crisis to crisis. From here on out, the bank was like a runaway train without a driver at the controls.

Rohner's final duty was to pick a successor. Back in the middle of 2020 – before Archegos and Greensill blew up – he had led a search that turned out to be yet another disaster. The board hired Egon Zehnder, a large executive headhunting firm with offices around the globe. There were several candidates on their shortlist, including the Dutch businessman Alexander Wynaendts, who was chairman of insurer Aegon; John Thornton, an American who'd worked at

Goldman Sachs and been on the boards of half a dozen global companies; and Jean-Pierre Mustier, who'd been the CEO of the Italian bank UniCredit. The list also included Colm Kelleher, the long-time Morgan Stanley banker. Kelleher was a favourite of several Credit Suisse board members. He was charismatic, incredibly smart, well connected and respected by global banking regulators. There was just one problem – he didn't want to move to Zurich.

Rohner narrowed in on his own top pick, António Horta-Osório, a Portuguese executive who had become a banking celebrity in the UK, just like Tidjane Thiam. Horta-Osório had worked at Citigroup, Goldman Sachs and the Spanish bank Santander. After the 2008 financial crisis, he became the CEO of Lloyds Bank, which had been partially nationalized by the UK government to stop it from going under. Over the next few years, Horta-Osório reduced costs and rebuilt the bank's profits, and the UK government was able to sell down its stake. It was a successful run, for which Horta-Osório was widely lauded.

But his tenure had not been without bumps. From the outset, the workload at Lloyds was enormous and Horta-Osório attacked it relentlessly. He didn't sleep for days at a time and, just a few months in, he had checked out of the bank and into the Priory, a private mental health and rehab clinic famous for treating celebrities. The bank said he was exhausted. His sudden, temporary departure, which lasted for six weeks, shook the board, staff and investors.

Then, in 2016, a tabloid newspaper wrote that the married Horta-Osório was having an affair. The story pictured the CEO and his lover on a business trip in Singapore, which led to questions about his use of corporate expenses. Horta-Osório admitted the affair but denied all allegations the bank had paid for any of it. He apologized in a letter to staff, writing, 'Having the highest professional standards raises the bar against which we are judged and as I have always said, we must recognise that mistakes will be made . . . The important point being how we learn from those mistakes and the decisions and actions we take afterwards.'[1]

As much as these past hiccups were a mark against him, his record of transforming Lloyds had put Horta-Osório in the frame. When Rohner sought references from contacts at Lloyds and at the UK financial regulators, they came back glowing with praise. Because of Covid travel restrictions, interviews were mostly held by video conference. But Horta-Osório and Rohner had met several times previously through a European banking association. Gottstein and other board members had met him too on a handful of occasions. Some board members did question whether he could handle the transition to chairman, but, overall, they were in agreement he was the best candidate.

The position appealed to Horta-Osório, too. He'd already told colleagues at Lloyds that he felt his task there was complete after ten years. He said he didn't want to be a CEO again and was looking for a role that was less hands-on.

In December 2020, Rohner announced Horta-Osório would join the bank the following spring. At that time, Gottstein and Rohner were still upbeat about the prospects for the new year. By the time the new chairman landed, the mood had darkened as Archegos and Greensill plunged the bank back into crisis.

When Horta-Osório arrived, officials from FINMA had stepped up their oversight of the bank. Under the regulator's guidance, executive power was taken away from the EXB and handed to a group of board members known as the tactical crisis committee, or TCC, led by the chairman. Gottstein was invited as an observer only. Horta-Osório might have been looking for a less hands-on role, but that wasn't what he got. Still, though the landscape had shifted significantly, the new chairman felt that he could yet turn things around, as he had done at Lloyds.

At the shareholder meeting in April, he laid out his plans for an overhaul. 'A series of setbacks has been holding us back and we need to reflect on what led us to the issues we face today,' he told shareholders.

Horta-Osório believed the bank lacked a robust risk-management culture, that too many staff were too focused on their bonuses, that clients were ignored and that the board and senior managers didn't understand the urgency of the crisis they were facing. He planned another strategic review of the business, with a new plan that would be announced in November. This was the third new plan in just a few years, and it wouldn't be the last.

Horta-Osório began diving into the balance sheet with gusto. It was the only way he knew. He demanded more and more information. Line by line, he searched for more hidden issues, another Greensill or Archegos. His investigation was more thorough and detailed than anyone could remember and dug up several suspect clients, as well as a handful of overly risky investment strategies. Horta-Osório demanded several senior managers be forced out of the bank and he slammed the quality of the information provided to the board, which seemed swamped with unnecessary data while missing more pertinent information. He pushed Romeo Cerutti – still the chief legal counsel – to settle outstanding litigation, some of which had dragged on for years.

It was a rapid and exhausting tempo. Horta-Osório wanted to change the board, too, though he stalled for a breather. That was a fatal decision. For starters, there were some early points of disagreement among board members. Horta-Osório pushed for the reports on Archegos and Greensill to be published in full. The board agreed in the case of Archegos, but voted down the release of the Greensill review. Those opposed said that, because Greensill was the subject of ongoing litigation, too much transparency could hamper efforts to recover the missing billions. In the end, only a handful of senior executives saw the report and even fewer got their own copy. The causes and lessons of the scandal were mostly buried.

Horta-Osório's strategic plan, when it was announced that

November, picked up many of the threads left behind by Rohner. Some cuts here and there. More resources into risk management. He would unwind some of the changes made by Gottstein, Rohner and Thiam to regionalize the bank. Some functions would be focused at the centre once again.

More important than any of that, though, was that the relationship between Horta-Osório and Gottstein was strained almost from the start. The dynamic chairman thought Gottstein was well intentioned but out of his depth as a CEO. Gottstein thought Horta-Osório was undermining him, upsetting too many senior executives and cutting back in the wrong areas. They clashed over compensation. Horta-Osório wanted to slash way back, even if that upset the investment bankers. The chairman thought he'd deal with Gottstein for a year, and then likely replace him with someone else.

But Horta-Osório was losing allies everywhere. Some staff felt the new chairman was blaming everyone for the failure of a few of their colleagues. Only a handful of the bank's tens of thousands of employees were involved in Greensill and Archegos, for instance. In New York, Horta-Osório told a roomful of investment bankers that they needed to focus more closely on what clients wanted and that they must work more closely with colleagues in wealth management. It seemed like a straightforward request, but some of the investment bankers were upset. They believed the chairman had scolded everyone for mistakes made by a few rogues and careless executives, most of whom – Warner and Chin, for example – had long since gone from the bank. The bankers left the meeting disgruntled, believing the chairman had unfairly tarred them as overpaid, easily replaceable and lower down the pecking order than bankers in other divisions.

It was a sign of the rising resentment that Horta-Osório's enemies inside the bank and in the Swiss establishment were only too willing to share negative stories with journalists and with each other. They said he was self-centred, arrogant and vain. They criticized the number of staff in his office, which had risen from seven under

Rohner to twenty-five now. They said he had the chauffeur-driven company car pick him up to drive fifty metres across the street for lunch. They said he asked to be called 'Sir António' after he was knighted in the UK for services to finance and mental-health awareness.

There was a ring of truth to some of this, but the gossiping revealed as much about the bank's culture as it did about Horta-Osório's conduct. And there was another side to the stories. The chairman's office expanded because of his role in leading the TCC. The chauffeur was taking him on to another destination after lunch at the hotel. Nonetheless, in Switzerland, Horta-Osório was portrayed as a flashy foreigner, a hypocrite who clamped down on costs while living like a celebrity. There were echoes of the treatment meted out to other high-profile outsiders, such as John Mack and Tidjane Thiam. When Horta-Osório inevitably stumbled, there were few inside or outside the bank that had his back.

He had been with the bank just a few months when a particularly damaging story was leaked to the Swiss newspaper *Blick*.[2] In late November 2021, Horta-Osório had flown to Switzerland from the UK. Under Swiss Covid rules, he was required to quarantine for ten days. Instead, three days after arriving in Zurich, he flew out again. When the story was published, Horta-Osório told board members the breach was inadvertent, and that the flights were for business purposes. When it later emerged that he'd sought but failed to get exemptions from the Covid rules from the local and federal government, that seemed to indicate the breach couldn't have been inadvertent. Some board members felt they'd been misled.

It got worse. An internal investigation found a second breach of Covid rules. In July, Horta-Osório had flown from Switzerland to the UK. Instead of isolating in line with the rules then in place, he had attended the Wimbledon tennis tournament. Again, the chairman said he thought he had an exemption, which turned out not to be the case.

The second case sparked more anger and more scrutiny of the chairman's behaviour. His use of the private jets now also became an issue with the board. On one occasion, on the way back from Asia, he'd had the corporate plane drop him off in the Maldives. He seemed to be frequently flying back and forth between his homes in London and Zurich too. Horta-Osório believed each of these flights was done in the interests of efficiency.

In the meantime, he faced possible fines from Swiss and UK authorities for breaking Covid rules. The domestic media had a field day as more gossipy commentary emerged. The chairman was portrayed as a hypocrite who demanded the highest standards from others while his own conduct fell short. The stories were badly received by the orderly Swiss, who frowned on rule breakers, especially those in such a public role.

Having preached personal responsibility to his staff, the chairman was increasingly under pressure. In January 2022, less than a year after his arrival, the board held a meeting to discuss his future. The deputy chairman was Severin Schwan, who was also CEO of Roche, the world's largest pharmaceutical company and a key supplier of Covid tests. Schwan, who didn't get along with Horta-Osório, told others that his position in the drug industry made him particularly attuned to the importance of Covid regulations. The majority of the board was now against the chairman, and Horta-Osório realized it didn't make any sense to stay. Just nine months after he took the job, Horta-Osório resigned.

It had been a turbulent, painful period for Credit Suisse. For all the problems that occurred under Rohner, he had at least provided a symbolic sense of continuity. Now, even that was shattered.

Before leaving, Horta-Osório gave the board members a brutal final message. The bank needed more capital, a clearer focus on improving performance and a cultural overhaul. These issues were urgent. They could not be complacent. If they failed, so too would Credit Suisse.

# TWENTY-SIX

# The Crisis Escalates

Everyone associated with the bank – staff, shareholders, Swiss authorities – was buffeted by the barrage of scandals and the shuffling of senior management, each era coming with a new strategy. With every change in CEO or chairman, time was wasted as the bank edged closer to the precipice.

Axel Lehmann was announced as the new chairman in January 2022. He had spent twenty years at Zurich Insurance, more than a decade at UBS, and he was an adjunct professor at St Gallen, the alma mater of many Swiss financial executives. He was charming, cerebral, rather dry. Lehmann's appointment was a Swiss rejection of the idea that the bank needed a global superstar like Thiam or Horta-Osório or Mack.

He'd only been on the board a few months before stepping into the void left by Horta-Osório, but Lehmann, too, felt the bank's model was broken and its culture needed fixing.

The bank was also struck by another downturn in the markets. The trigger this time was Russia's military invasion of Ukraine, which contributed to rising interest rates and soaring inflation that dampened the global economy. The uncertain political outlook killed the appetite for mergers or acquisitions among corporate clients, while demand for borrowing dried up too.

For Credit Suisse, the war had a direct financial impact. More than a thousand wealthy, politically connected Russians were put on a sanctions list by US authorities. Banking rich Russians had been a huge business for Credit Suisse, but this was now off the table. The problem went beyond the loss of revenue; the renewed focus of regulators and authorities added costly and complex compliance procedures. (Later, in September 2023, Bloomberg News reported that the US Department of Justice was in the early stages of an investigation into possible breaches of Russia sanctions at Credit Suisse.)

At the same time, many of the ailing bank's dirtiest secrets were aired in public. A consortium of international journalists working with reporters from *The Guardian*, *The New York Times*, *Le Monde* and Germany's *Süddeutsche Zeitung* published dozens of stories linked to a trove of leaked information from the Swiss bank. The stories, dubbed 'Suisse Secrets' and coordinated by a group called the Organized Crime and Corruption Reporting Project, were linked to 18,000 accounts at Credit Suisse's private bank.[1] The documents showed that, over the years, Credit Suisse had banked dozens of unsavoury characters, including 'the family of an Egyptian intelligence chief who oversaw the torture of terrorism suspects for the CIA; an Italian accused of laundering criminal funds; and a German executive who bribed Nigerian officials for telecoms contracts.' The leak of information linked the bank to clients involved in human trafficking, bribery and corruption writ large.[2]

Credit Suisse, which was more or less leaderless, responded with a corporate statement that said the stories were mostly based on historical information, some of which dated from decades ago. Laws and regulations and the bank's own processes had all changed. The information was partial and selective, the bank's statement said.

The immediate impact of the stories was limited, in part because investors and staff and anyone paying attention to Credit Suisse had scandal fatigue by this point. But the leaks further eroded the bank's crumbling reputation. The episode was a distraction for senior managers and sapped their will. It was another black mark against the bank for its weary regulators and the Swiss establishment, who were beginning to see Credit Suisse as an embarrassment to the whole country.

At this point, Gottstein was still in the CEO hot seat, though not for long. The strain of running the bank was beginning to show. Three weeks after the change in chairman, Gottstein fell ill. His vision was blurred. His wife, a doctor, insisted he see a specialist. He'd developed stress-related diabetes and was at an elevated risk of a heart attack. Gottstein told the board that it felt almost impossible to step down, given the chairman had only just taken over. He was persuaded to keep going, for now.

By this time, the bank was struggling in all of its core businesses. Officials at FINMA were concerned that Credit Suisse was structurally loss-making and devoid of appropriate governance procedures. The regulators demanded the bank come up with a list of emergency measures they would take should the situation deteriorate. But they were repeatedly underwhelmed by the response from the bank – Credit Suisse executives said they could sell off some bits and pieces or ask for the authorities to cut them some slack – and they continued to pressure the board for a better plan, including measures to right the sinking ship.

Meanwhile, Lehmann had already launched yet another deep dive into the business, involving a group of board members, senior managers and a handful of external advisers from a small investment bank, Centerview. They delivered their findings at an annual off-site board meeting in Bad Ragaz, a spa town in the Swiss countryside. The presentation was sobering. Most board members had long believed that Credit Suisse was competing with the biggest Wall Street banks. The presentation ended that idea for good. In terms of headcount and costs, Credit Suisse's investment bank was similar to the likes of Goldman Sachs. But in revenue terms, it was a fifth of the size. It was far less productive than its rivals, too – each employee generated about 80 per cent less revenue than those at Goldman Sachs and just half of the figure at UBS.

In summary, the investment bank was smaller, more expensive and less productive than its rivals. This was news to many on the board. Whose fault was that? Some on the board maybe lacked the right banking expertise or hadn't been paying attention, but, over the years, they'd also been given poor information, and the permanent restructuring of the bank had made it difficult to follow the numbers. From here on out, however, it was impossible to hide from the truth.

In the summer, Gottstein finally stood down. Lehmann replaced him with Ueli Körner, another former UBS executive who had recently joined Credit Suisse – he had been running the post-mortem on Greensill, desperately trying to recover the missing billions. Like Lehmann, Körner was intelligent, serious, cautious by nature and quite understated. He already felt the bank might not survive and agreed to become CEO as a call of duty. At this moment, the bank suddenly had two very sober leaders, though neither of them was the kind of charismatic figurehead who could rally the troops when things got really tough.

Through the summer of 2022, neither Lehmann nor Körner communicated much with the media or their employees. Körner referred to the media calls and interviews dismissively as the 'blah, blah, blah'. It was noise, when there was more sophisticated work to be done. Instead of promoting a sense that the bank was in safe hands, they locked themselves away and worked on the next strategic plan. In the meantime, the bank's performance continued to slide, with one loss-making quarter after another. The big credit-rating agencies that evaluated the bank's debt said the outlook was grim. Major Swiss corporations that could usually be counted on for business began to call other banks. It sometimes seemed like the bank's latest leaders still didn't fully grasp the urgency of their situation. It seemed like they had their heads in the sand.

The bank was in dire straits, reflected in the carousel of senior leaders. Körner was the fourth CEO in just seven years. There had been four chief risk officers in the same period. The head of the investment bank had changed several times. The net result of all of this was an absence of convincing leadership throughout the firm. In the emptiness, self-fulfilling rumours about the bank's poor health could easily fester. There was a growing danger that, by the time Körner and Lehmann unveiled their new plan, it would already be far too late.

# TWENTY-SEVEN

# The X Factor

On Saturday, 1 October 2022, an Australian journalist composed a short tweet. David Taylor, a business reporter at the Australian Broadcasting Corporation, had been chatting with an analyst who covered the share prices of major global banks. The analyst said that one big institution was looking pretty shaky.

Taylor had posted thousands of times on Twitter under the handle @DaveTaylorNews and had a few thousand followers. His Twitter bio said he was a news junkie, 'In pursuit of the truth and a good yarn.' He typically tweeted about Australian politics, house prices and domestic business stories.

Shortly after seven o'clock that evening, he typed: 'Credible source tells me a major international bank is on the brink'.

Within minutes of Taylor hitting *post*, his message had been retweeted, over and over. The markets at that time were jittery. The UK pound had recently collapsed after the government unveiled a disastrous budget. The Bank of Japan had intervened to bolster the yen for the first time in decades. The US dollar was surging against other currencies, including the Swiss franc. These wild swings were rippling through stocks and bonds, too.

Many of those who retweeted Taylor's line added an extra detail: Credit Suisse was supposedly the bank on the brink. Taylor's original post was being distorted and embellished as it flew around the globe. Some people added charts that purported to show problems with the bank's capital. Others rewrote the tweet in headline format, giving the message an air of authority: 'ABC Journalist: Credit Suisse on the brink.' The rumour resurfaced on the message board Reddit – a platform favoured by armchair investors trading shares from home. It was translated and reposted on WeChat and other Chinese social-media sites that dominated in parts of Asia. Mocking social-media memes proliferated. One image showed the Swiss flag, a white cross on a red background, redrawn as a giant minus sign. Others dubbed the bank 'Debit Suisse'.

Credit Suisse was a compelling target. Its shares had been sliding all year. Its reputation was in the gutter. Körner and Lehmann had been silent for weeks, tinkering away at their new strategic plan. There were already various rumours – that they planned a radical overhaul, that they needed to raise capital, that they might get out of the US market altogether, that they might sell off bits of the bank.

Ironically, a day before the tweet, Ueli Körner had sent a memo meant to rally staff morale, in which he compared Credit Suisse to a phoenix, ready to rise. He said the planned restructuring was at a 'critical moment' and urged employees not to confuse the day-to-day movement in its share price with the underlying strength of the business. In light of the Twitter storm, what had been intended as a reassuring message to staff now looked like a panicked last-minute attempt to steady the ship.

By Monday morning, the scale of the problem was terrifyingly clear. Clients had withdrawn billions of dollars over the weekend. The share price was down 11 per cent. In Australia, Taylor deleted the original tweet and his employers put out a statement denying they had published a story. It was far too late: the rumours of Credit Suisse's demise were feeding on themselves in a kind of doom loop.

Körner and his team were frozen. The bank's brand-new CFO, Dixit Joshi, was scrambling to get a handle on the rapidly worsening numbers. There was a new chief legal officer, too – Markus Diethelm had joined from UBS a few weeks earlier. The chief risk officer, David Wildermuth, had been at the bank just over a year. The entire executive team had just a year or two of experience at the bank between them, and suddenly they were facing a crisis they'd never envisaged. Some in the team felt they could do nothing to stop the social-media-driven rout. Others wondered if they were the victim of a scam, or a coordinated attempt by a hedge fund to drive down the share price. Mostly, they all stalled.

In the communications department, no one had seen anything like it either. The normal crisis playbook was to put out a press release and call financial journalists and equity analysts to get a rational, calmer message out into the market. But this disaster wasn't playing out the normal way. No one knew how you put an end to rumours on Reddit. They urged Körner to make a public appearance to try to calm nerves, but he declined, citing legal advice. The bank's legal team warned that he was not supposed to talk about company data ahead of the strategy announcement planned for later in the month. Yet, it wasn't clear they'd even make it that far. In conversations outside their adjoining offices, some of the bank's EXB team discussed whether Credit Suisse would survive the weekend. They considered whether the bank could find a merger partner, or, more likely, a friendly rival to take over completely.

Over the next week, the bank was bleeding as much as $10 billion a day. Soon, almost $100 billion had been withdrawn.[1] It was a staggering amount. Around a third of all client deposits had been withdrawn.[2] The wealth-management business was decimated. The Swiss business had taken a beating. The bank had come close enough to disaster that the communications team had already written its obituary.

As money continued to bleed from the bank, Körner marshalled executives to call clients directly. Some of them were sympathetic but unmoved. Facts and figures could prove the bank was safe, but why risk it, the clients said, when you could transfer your funds elsewhere easily enough?

Along with Lehmann and several members of the EXB, Körner flew to Singapore, ostensibly for a celebration of the bank's presence in the city for fifty years – in reality, a chance to persuade some of the bank's enormously wealthy Asian clients to come back. The event started out at Credit Suisse's offices and then moved to a glitzy restaurant on Sentosa, the resort island off Singapore's coast. The guest list included some of the richest people in Asia, really big-ticket names, whose wealth ran to billions of dollars. Körner gave a speech imploring clients to stick with the bank. Drinks and conversation ran long into the evening, but most of the potential clients were not biting.

Towards the end of October, the flows of money finally slowed, leaving the bank in a serious but stable condition. Lehmann, Körner and others had managed to persuade enough big clients – often in person – that their money was safe. But the incident had lasting effects. It exposed the desperate state of Credit Suisse's affairs in a most public way. The bank had been utterly powerless in the face of the run, and lacked the kind of charismatic leader who could stand up to the markets. The outflows of client cash had left parts of the bank weakened – if it had been tough to make a profit before the Twitter meltdown, it would be so much harder now.

Twittergate had been a banking-industry first. Sure, social media had played a role in the markets before – there were plenty of examples of Twitter accounts manipulating a company's share price by posting fake news on drug breakthroughs or made-up criminal probes. Campaigners had organized boycotts against this or that brand on social media too. In early 2021, ordinary investors had banded together on Reddit to drive up the share price of unloved stocks in companies including GameStop, Blackberry and AMC Entertainment, costing billions of dollars to hedge funds that were betting the stocks would fall.

But the Credit Suisse fiasco was different. It was the first major digital bank run. In the past, runs had started when bank customers saw others lining up outside bricks-and-mortar branches and joined in. In the digital era, the equivalent of a large queue out in the open was a flutter of retweets, likes, or replies on Reddit. With customers able to move money at the push of a button, banks were especially vulnerable. Credit Suisse was fragile. Social media had stripped away the hubris and layers of protection that had guarded the firm in the past. Social media showed that there was no longer anywhere to hide.

On 27 October, Körner and Lehmann unveiled their long-awaited strategic plan.[3] They would cut costs and planned to raise about $4 billion in capital by selling new shares. More than a third – $1.5 billion – was coming from the Saudi National Bank. The Saudis would instantly become one of the biggest investors, with an approximate 10 per cent stake. With the share price so low, it was a painful, costly way to raise much-needed money.

The biggest changes were in the investment bank. Körner and Lehmann planned to offload the profitable but capital-intensive securitized-products business. They would transfer it to Apollo Global Management, a giant asset-management company. They'd also set up a 'non-core unit' and throw all other unwanted business into that, aiming to run these down or sell them off. The most eye-catching move was a 1990s revival: the CS First Boston brand was back. It would be launched as an independent firm, with Credit Suisse holding most of the shares. Michael Klein, a veteran investment banker who sat on Credit Suisse's board, would step down from his existing role to run the new CS First Boston. The idea was a hit with employees in the New York office, many of whom were still loyal to the First Boston brand. Elsewhere, critics questioned whether bringing back the tainted brand was such a good idea and whether Klein's role represented a conflict of interest.

Overall, the plan was underwhelming. Körner and Lehmann set unambitious targets for their turnaround. Return on tangible equity – a key industry measure of profitability – would hit 6 per cent by 2025. Most big banks aimed for more than 10 per cent. The plan looked like a drawn-out downsizing that would be hard to pull off. At the end of it, investors would be left with shares in a bank that was a shadow of its former self. There was little there to get behind.

The dour mood was compounded by the quarterly results, which were announced on the same day. In the prior three months, the bank had recorded a loss of about $4 billion. In the same period a year before that, it had made a profit of about $470 million. The share price fell 19 per cent in one day – in total, it had halved in under a year.

A week later, Standard & Poor's rating agency downgraded Credit Suisse, giving it a lower credit rating than any of its rivals. It would make Credit Suisse even less profitable than other similar banks. For potential clients, it would make working with Credit Suisse far less appealing too.

The new regime had been in place for just a few months. They'd been dealt a most difficult hand. Yet already the bank was in a much worse position than before. Its decline was gathering speed. When the board met to survey the wreckage of the past few weeks, Körner was brutal and direct. If another scandal or event triggered a run like they'd just seen, Credit Suisse could not survive.

# TWENTY-EIGHT

# The Regulators

Credit Suisse was down on its knees when the regulators showed up. Had they come to save the bank or to close it down? The bank's fate was not solely in the hands of Körner and Lehmann. Maybe it was no longer in their hands at all.

The Swiss regulators had for too long been supine in the unfolding drama. FINMA was toothless, with limited tools for punishing misconduct. The regulator had pressured Credit Suisse to clean up its act, come up with an emergency plan, develop a convincing long-term strategy, but it was largely powerless in enforcing these demands. All FINMA could do was nudge the bank to act responsibly.

In the late summer of 2022, even before Twittergate, FINMA joined a financial crisis management committee that included staff from the Swiss National Bank and the Finance Ministry. This group also contacted authorities overseas, including the SEC in the US. Dozens of staff from different regulators were involved.

The situation was extremely precarious. The crisis committee planned for a worst-case scenario – the outright collapse of Credit Suisse – and explored three possible solutions. First, the bank could merge with a rival. This involved minimal state interference and was everyone's preferred outcome, though they knew that finding a bidder would be tough. Second, the bank could fail completely. It would be wound down in a process called 'resolution'. It's what would happen to companies in most other industries. But, for a systemically important bank, resolution would be dangerous, with unpredictable knock-on effects. The third option was for the Swiss government to nationalize the bank fully or partly, as it had done with UBS during the financial crisis. This was politically tough; government bailouts for bankers were hugely unpopular with voters.

In early November, the seven members of Switzerland's Federal Council – which acts as both the cabinet and the executive office in the Swiss system – were joined in Bern by Thomas Jordan, chairman of the Swiss National Bank, and Marlene Amstad, who ran FINMA. Ueli Maurer, the finance minister, opened the meeting with an unwelcome surprise: 'Guys, we have a problem with Credit Suisse,' he said. The other council members had read the front-page stories about Archegos, Greensill, Twitter, spygate. Everyone in Switzerland knew about these scandals. But the politicians were only just coming to understand that Credit Suisse itself was in serious danger.

Jordan said the SNB was ready to deploy emergency measures if needed. The central bank had 50 billion Swiss francs in liquidity available immediately – about $56 billion – in case the bank ran out of cash. It was an enormous sum, though Jordan said even more might be needed. The SNB could come up with another 100 billion francs, though it could only be given to the bank if the federal government would provide a guarantee. He proposed the government introduce a public liquidity backstop, or PLB – essentially a state guarantee that it would stand behind the bank, aimed at preventing a run. The PLB would require an emergency law. And all of this had to be kept tightly under wraps. If any of it leaked out, it would almost certainly spread panic.

The meeting exploded as the councillors realized the impact of

Jordan's suggestion and demanded answers to a flurry of questions. Why had they not been told earlier? What did Credit Suisse's position mean for the Swiss economy? What did it mean for the global banking industry? They'd need answers to all of these questions before introducing a new law to, ostensibly, bail out Credit Suisse. Maurer, the SNB and FINMA were told to do more work on the plan, ahead of another meeting scheduled for a few days later.

The councillors were shell-shocked. How could this have seemingly come out of nowhere? But, ahead of the second meeting, Maurer called off the panic. He told his colleagues that the situation had calmed down. The emergency was over. And that was pretty much that.

In the following weeks, there was no reason to doubt that everything had stabilized. Credit Suisse had raised the $4 billion in additional capital it had announced in October, and Lehmann appeared on Bloomberg TV saying that the outflows had 'essentially stopped'.

In January 2023, Maurer stepped aside at the Finance Ministry, part of the regular process by which Switzerland's Federal Council effectively rotates through cabinet-level roles. His replacement was the former justice minister, Karin Keller-Sutter, sometimes known as KKS. Keller-Sutter was a pragmatic and level-headed politician who hailed from outside the Zurich financial establishment. Her parents had run a restaurant and she had trained as a teacher and interpreter before moving into local, and then national, politics.

Keller-Sutter had broadly pro-business leanings. She had been on the board of Baloise, a Swiss insurance company, for many years. Like other members of the council, she had been stunned by Maurer's warnings about Credit Suisse in the autumn, but then assumed that everything was OK when the issue was dropped almost as quickly as it had reared up. When she moved into the new role, KKS's predecessor had left no special files or warning about the bank.

On Wednesday, 11 January, she hosted a meet-and-greet with key members of the Swiss finance industry, including Axel Lehmann. Keller-Sutter asked him for an update on the state of the problems she'd been told about the previous year, and the chairman duly obliged. But there was no sense of urgency, no indication that it was anything more than business as usual.

Colm Kelleher, the chairman of UBS, also spoke up at the meeting. He was a big personality, direct and to the point. He told Keller-Sutter that Swiss banks were seeing significant outflows of cash from the country. Investors and depositors were taking their money elsewhere. It could become a problem.

As the meeting ended, Keller-Sutter was concerned. Why wasn't Lehmann more worried? What did the outflows mean for Switzerland? Had the problems at Credit Suisse infected the broader banking ecosystem, and could that spill over into the economy as a whole? Something was off, she told her staff. Credit Suisse's senior managers didn't seem to be really on top of the issues they were facing. It was a hunch. But it turned out the finance minister was right to be nervous.

Later the same day, Keller-Sutter was at a meeting of the financial crisis committee set up to monitor Credit Suisse. This group had been gathering regularly for the prior few months. She asked a simple question: At what point would the government need to intervene to support Credit Suisse? After some discussion, the regulators at the meeting agreed that it would be dangerous to move too early. If details of any government assistance leaked out into the media, then it could lead to a further downturn in the bank's fortunes. Investors and customers would be spooked by the notion that Credit Suisse needed help, and they'd pull their money out, sending the bank deeper into crisis. For now, Keller-Sutter put any measures on hold.

Meanwhile, the bank's executives continued to act as though everything was normal. In late January, Credit Suisse was a big presence at the annual gathering of global elites at the World Economic Forum in the Swiss ski resort of Davos. The bank's name was plastered throughout the town and its senior executives schmoozed with world leaders, business people and media. In a television interview during the forum, Körner issued a calming message: money was coming into the bank and they were making progress on the new strategy, he said.

Behind the scenes, the bank was rocking and the new strategic plan was coming off the rails fast. The CS First Boston revival – a core element of the plan – had run into trouble. Körner and Lehmann had been negotiating to buy an investment bank, owned by board member Michael Klein, for $175 million.[1] They planned to roll it into CS First Boston, which Klein was slated to run. When this came out in the media, shareholders, governance experts and some board members slammed the deal.[2] Körner was forced onto the defensive, saying that the transaction and its price had been cleared by an independent review, while Klein had recused himself from the board.

In February, the bank's stock sank to a new low after it emerged that Lehmann was under investigation by FINMA. The regulator had questioned comments he'd made the previous year. Lehmann had twice stated that clients had stopped taking their money out of the bank and that some money was even coming back in. It turned out this wasn't true. An investigation into the chairman's misleading statements went on for weeks.

At the end of February, there was another blow. FINMA released its report into the Greensill scandal. The regulator said the bank had breached its obligations and said its risk-control processes were 'deficient'.

In the Finance Ministry, all of this was starting to add up to a much greater level of concern. Keller-Sutter was beginning to realize that the emergency Maurer had briefly raised in the autumn was very real. When she looked to the bank's leaders, Körner and Lehmann, Keller-Sutter was hardly convinced they were able to solve the crisis. As the bank crumbled, it was increasingly clear that Credit Suisse could not be trusted to save itself.

# TWENTY-NINE

# Silicon Valley Bank

On the other side of the world, six months after the Twitter storm had engulfed Credit Suisse, social media struck again. This time, the victim was a bank in California with no connection to Zurich. When it collapsed, the domino effect reached all the way to the Alps.

Silicon Valley Bank was founded in the 1980s to support Southern California's nascent tech industry. It had grown on the back of the US technology boom and, by 2023, it was the sixteenth largest bank in the US. By comparison to Credit Suisse, SVB was a newbie and relatively small, though it was a significant player in the regional US banking system, and that meant it was a vital cog in the global banking system too. The modern financial world is interconnected, so the health of even a relatively small US bank can have an outsized impact on the rest of the global sector.

SVB's clients were a close-knit collection of some of the savviest West Coast technology-company investors. They often moved as a pack, piling their millions into the next hot investment trend – social media, AI, the sharing economy, wearable tech, renewable energy and so on. Over the previous couple of decades, many of them had also deposited their cash into SVB; it was marketed as the go-to bank for this forward-thinking cohort. These clients were ambitious and entrepreneurial. They demanded a bank with similar attributes. SVB appealed to them because it would make loans that others wouldn't and it understood the needs of its unusual clients.

But this pooling of money and clients with similar characteristics had a downside. Clients who knew each other and chatted frequently, online or in real life, were not diverse at all. They were clustered geographically, socially and culturally. They all had the same interests. They acted as one. This was a problem few (if any) in SVB or in the wider banking industry had thought much about, until it was too late.

The seeds of SVB's failure were sown in the Covid pandemic. Lockdowns were paradoxically a boon for technology companies, their owners and many of the people who worked for them. Remote working benefited these businesses, while government largesse, intended to get the economy rolling, poured cash into their coffers too. SVB's customer deposits doubled. But that created a problem. Banks don't hold much of the money clients deposit with them. They usually keep a little back and park the rest elsewhere, either lending it out or investing it to generate a return that's greater than the interest they have to pay on the deposits. With so much money flooding into SVB, it was difficult to find a spot in which to put it all. And so, the bank massively increased its holdings of US government Treasury bonds – the next best thing to cash.

This strategy hit a snag. In 2022, the US Federal Reserve started to increase interest rates to tamp down inflation. That hurt SVB in two ways. Depositors wanted to take their money out because they could get a better return elsewhere. At the same time, SVB's holdings of Treasury bonds and similar investments began losing value quickly. The bank was forced to sell its investments at a significant loss.

On 8 March 2023, another California-based lender, an even smaller firm named Silvergate that focused on cryptocurrencies, said it was winding down operations because of problems in the digital-currency market. The announcement sent ripples through California's finance community. When, that same day, SVB announced plans to raise more than $2 billion to stabilize its balance sheet, investors immediately understood that the bank had big problems. SVB's share price plummeted.

A downside of the digital world, which many of SVB's clients thrived on, was that depositors could move their money elsewhere fast. There were resounding echoes of Credit Suisse's near-death experience from the previous October. SVB's wealthy customers just pressed a couple of buttons and collectively syphoned off billions of dollars. By the close of business on 9 March, clients had pulled $42 billion from their SVB accounts. It was the biggest, quickest bank run in US history.[1]

On 10 March, the US government took control of the bank. The stakes were incredibly high. This was the first major test on US soil of the post-financial-crisis rule book. American politicians were well aware of the lasting effects of the 2008 crash. Back then, millions of ordinary citizens had lost their homes. There was a feeling that the aftermath had enriched the wealthiest Americans at the expense of those least well off, fostering a political division that changed the course of US political history.

The regulations that authorities had created after the crisis were supposed to ensure such a catastrophe never happened again. But politicians and bankers – and voters, too – had become complacent. The rules had been bent and then waived, and the banking sector was vulnerable once more. It wasn't just SVB that was in trouble; a couple of other firms were also teetering on the edge. Within days, Silvergate Bank and Signature Bank were both gone as well.

US authorities – led by Treasury Secretary Janet Yellen and Federal Reserve chair Jay Powell – were scrambling just to contain the fallout. SVB was not exactly a household name, but its demise was still the second-biggest banking collapse in US history. Yellen and Powell were both cautious, professorial, smart and methodical. The real danger of SVB's collapse was contagion.

The risk was that depositors at other lesser-known, regional or smaller banks in the US would panic and pull their money out, in the hope of depositing it somewhere safer, such as the bigger Wall Street banks. That process, and the fear that accompanied it, could create chaos that would destabilize the entire global-banking architecture. Banks would be afraid to lend to each other or to clients. That would lead to a sharp downturn in the US and global economies. Stock and bond markets would take a beating. The price of other assets and financial instruments would fall too. The chance of a major investor like a hedge fund or insurance company collapsing would rise. Banks that had nothing to do with SVB could be facing massive losses. Maybe one or more would collapse too, turning the cycle of fear back on itself. This is what happened during the financial crisis of 2008, and it scarred a generation of bank leaders and regulators, who would do anything to avoid a repeat.

By the weekend of 11 March, the possibility of a broader banking crisis had gripped the markets. Shares in many banks were falling, in the US and beyond. First Republic, another large regional US bank, came under pressure. It was saved only after a bailout organized by Wall Street banks that were desperately trying to stop the bleeding. Investors everywhere began looking for weak links in the banking chain. Which would be the next bank to fall?

In the following days, President Biden and other members of the administration moved to calm markets. Treasury Secretary Yellen told Congress, 'our banking is sound and . . . Americans can feel confident that their deposits will be there when they need them.'

It was a clear message: *Don't worry about the banks. We've got their back.* If the entire US government stood behind their banks, then it was hoped that investors and depositors would calm down.

While the Americans were focused round the clock on saving the US financial system, they also had an eye on Zurich. Credit Suisse remained fragile. It was six months since Ueli Körner had warned his colleagues that it wouldn't survive another blow. In California, SVB had pulled the trigger and, suddenly, Credit Suisse was in the crosshairs.

# THIRTY

# The Takeover

In early March 2023, the future of Credit Suisse looked grim. In a climate of fear and near-collapse, the bank had everything to lose, and every hour of every day mattered.

*Wednesday, 8 March*
It was evening in Zurich. The biggest business story of the day was the collapse of American cryptocurrency firm Silvergate. Several time zones away from Switzerland, the full extent of SVB's problems were yet to unravel.

At Credit Suisse, CFO Dixit Joshi was preparing for the release of the bank's annual report, due the following morning. It was Joshi's first full set of accounts, a noteworthy moment in his career for sure. He and the other executives were preparing at an off-site meeting in Bocken, a conference centre and hotel that the bank owned, half an hour from Zurich's city centre. There were nerves, but everything was going as smoothly as possible under the circumstances. Until the phone call.

The US Securities and Exchange Commission was on the line. An official from the US's top financial regulator shocked Joshi. They had questions about the accounts. Worse still, the SEC official said their concerns had been raised as long ago as the previous summer, before Joshi had even arrived.[1] It would be up to Credit Suisse whether to go ahead and publish their annual numbers, but the SEC wanted answers fast.

The timing was brutal. One minute, the senior management team was planning how to put a positive spin on the state of the bank. The next minute, it had been hit by yet another potential scandal, possibly one that was more damning than all the others. It turned out that the SEC's initial contact, in July 2022, had been correspondence with former CFO David Mathers.[2] The Americans had asked about adjustments Mathers had made to accounts from previous years. They were concerned these changes reflected broader problems that needed correcting. Mathers had replied in intricate detail, though the tenor of his message was blunt: it was, in essence, *There is nothing to see here.*[3] The SEC didn't agree and had continued pushing for more answers, but none had been forthcoming. The issue was simply left hanging when Mathers walked out the door.

### Thursday, 9 March

In the early hours of the morning, Körner, Joshi and others frantically assessed their options. All of them were bad. If they published the report and later had to change the accounts, it would send the share price tumbling, as whatever trust was left evaporated. Not publishing the accounts was just as disastrous, as it would send a signal that there was something seriously wrong.

The EXB and the company's outside auditors worked through the night. Twice in the early hours, the audit committee of board and senior management met to discuss what to do –once at 4 a.m. and again an hour later. Körner was quiet, studious. But the energy had been sapped from the entire team by yet another blow. Finally, at around 6 a.m., they decided to withdraw the accounts. When the market opened, Credit Suisse's stock plummeted to an all-time low.

*Friday, 10 March*

SVB was no more. The US bank had collapsed, sending bank shares around the world into turmoil. Credit Suisse was among the worst hit. Its stock price, already beaten down, lost another 30 per cent in a day. If investors were nervous, clients were equally so. Money was bleeding from the bank once more.

A rare piece of positive news: FINMA said it did not see sufficient grounds for proceeding against the bank or Lehmann for his comments about outflows the previous December.

*Saturday, 11 March and Sunday, 12 March*

Over the weekend, Joshi and others at the EXB scrambled to fix the company's accounts and deal with the concerns of the SEC. Körner and Lehmann were still of the view that the bank would be fine, if only they could get enough time to implement their plan. They just needed some calm. The problem was, there was very little calmness around.

*Monday, 13 March*

The front page of the *Neue Zürcher Zeitung* carried a story about the collapse of SVB. After a bank failure, there is a risk of a chain reaction, the headline warned. The story was focused on the US. Washington was on high alert. SVB had a subsidiary in the UK, so there might be problems there too, *NZZ* wrote.[4] But the newspaper made no mention of the calamity unfolding in its own backyard.

Credit Suisse's share price was falling again. It had dropped more than 70 per cent since the beginning of the year. Bankers continued desperately to try to stem the flood of money out of the bank.

In Bern, Karin Keller-Sutter met again with the financial crisis committee that had been monitoring the bank since the previous summer. The finance minister was told that the mood was glum. Fear had taken hold of the banking sector, and investors and clients were desperate to steer clear of anything that could be a problem. For now, though, Credit Suisse was able to fulfil all its regulatory obligations. The strict capital and liquidity requirements introduced after the financial crisis weren't a problem. The bank was struggling, but it was still alive.

*Tuesday, 14 March*
Credit Suisse finally published its delayed annual report. The outcome was not good. The bank warned that it had found 'material weaknesses' in the systems that managed its financial reporting process. For a major global business, such a statement was incredibly rare. It was a dreadful admission at the worst possible time. The bank's shares continued to fall.

By now, Keller-Sutter realized Credit Suisse was in a full-blown crisis. Terrifyingly, neither of its top two leaders were in Switzerland. Körner had headed to a banking conference in London, where he gave interviews suggesting Credit Suisse would soon get back on track. Lehmann had headed to another conference in Saudi Arabia. The bank was in desperate need of a saviour, but neither Lehmann nor Körner appeared to have grasped the severity of the situation. If anyone was going to come to the bank's rescue, it would have to be someone from outside of Credit Suisse.

*Wednesday, 15 March*
Lehmann was in Riyadh, where many of the prime movers in global finance had gathered for a two-day conference hosted by the Saudi central bank and the Ministry of Finance. The chairman knew it was a risky time to leave Zurich, but he felt it was important to nurse critical relationships with Middle Eastern investors whose enormous wealth had rescued the bank before, during the financial crisis.

In the morning, Lehmann met with the chairman of the Saudi National Bank, Ammar Al Khudairy. The SNB was Credit Suisse's largest shareholder after the most recent capital raise, and Lehmann planned to meet again with Al Khudairy, for lunch, later that day.

Before that, though, the SNB chairman had promised a live television interview to Bloomberg News. It was not a big deal, a simple on-air conversation on the sideline of the conference. The SNB chairman talked about markets and the global sell-off in bank stocks. Then the reporter asked if the SNB planned to put more money into Credit Suisse. 'Absolutely not,' Al Khudairy replied.

It was a fateful response. No matter that Al Khudairy went on to explain that the Saudis couldn't technically buy more of the bank's stock without hitting regulatory blockages. His choice of words was catastrophic. Within moments, Bloomberg's online news department ran a headline that said Credit Suisse's top shareholder was refusing to put more money into the bank. Worse, versions of the story appeared on social media that shortened Saudi National Bank to 'SNB'. Saudi National Bank. Swiss National Bank. The two were easily confused, but critically different. It was one thing for the Saudis to say they wouldn't support Credit Suisse, quite another if Switzerland's central bank had said it.

The bank's death spiral accelerated. By the time Lehmann and Al Khudairy finally met for lunch, the Saudi chairman acknowledged his part in the problem.

In Zurich, the effects were felt almost immediately. Clients were pulling money out faster than ever.

Keller-Sutter, the finance minister, was kept appraised of what was happening. She called Credit Suisse, where the absence of its two most senior executives was very alarming. They were quickly summoned for a conference call. Lehmann said the bank just needed some additional liquidity to support it through a tough few days. If they could battle through, the strategic plan would deliver. He seemed sure the bank could get out of the mess. Investors from the Middle East would bail it out once more, he said.

Keller-Sutter was stunned again. The chairman's focus on a long-term plan seemed blind to the immediate crisis. The Credit Suisse executives seemed to her to be on another planet. She told them that, in her view, they didn't have a couple of years. In her view, the bank might not be viable in two days. You're out of time, Keller-Sutter told the two bankers. Credit Suisse would either be wound down or be absorbed by another bank – one way or another, this crisis must end by Sunday evening, she said.

That morning, UBS chairman Colm Kelleher had been in an internal meeting with a couple of senior colleagues. Kelleher, a sharp-witted Irishman and veteran banker, knew how quickly a crisis could develop. In 2007, he became Morgan Stanley's chief financial officer just as the first wave of the sub-prime mortgage disaster began to wash up on Wall Street. Within weeks, he'd had to announce the bank's first-ever quarterly loss. Clients pulled tens of billions of dollars out every single day. The firm only narrowly survived after taking a $9-billion bailout from a Japanese bank.

From the day he landed in Switzerland, a few months earlier, Kelleher had been preparing for a repeat of the scenes he'd witnessed fifteen years before. He thought Credit Suisse was a basket case, doomed to failure. For months, he'd been telling UBS's senior management that, one day, they'd get an emergency phone call, and they'd better be ready.

At that Wednesday meeting, the very meeting during which he was urging colleagues to ramp up their planning, the phone rang. It was FINMA. Kelleher was wanted at a meeting later that day with a delegation of Swiss authorities led by Keller-Sutter and Thomas Jordan, the chair of the Swiss National Bank.

As he put down the phone, the events of a decade-and-a-half ago, when the world's economy hung in the balance, flashed through his mind. The financial crisis was supposed to have been a one-off. Yet, here was Kelleher, thrust into chaos once again.

Two hours later, at FINMA's office in Zurich, Keller-Sutter took the lead. Just four months into her new role, the finance minister was about to start a conversation her predecessors couldn't have imagined.

'We have made a decision that Credit Suisse is not viable. We have a choice, and it's your choice.' She looked straight at Kelleher. 'We are going to put them into resolution, or you're going to step in and buy them.'

The words were almost surreal. Resolution – a government-led wind-down – could cause widespread panic in the markets. The bankruptcy of a giant Swiss bank would certainly hit Switzerland's reputation and its economy. The alternative was UBS swallowing its rival whole. This was clearly the preferred route for the authorities. A private solution was more acceptable politically, and, Keller-Sutter hoped, it would be more likely to instil desperately needed confidence in the financial system.

Either way, though, it was the end of Credit Suisse. The bank had stuttered along for years. Its problems were no secret. But its total demise was still hard to get your head around, even for those in the room who now knew the bank's collapse was unavoidable.

Kelleher put a slip of paper on the table. On it were listed the key conditions for a takeover. Kelleher wanted total flexibility on the closure of any overlapping businesses and on laying off staff. He wanted the government to guarantee UBS would be protected from the cost of Credit Suisse's legal issues. As they read through the document, the Swiss delegation was flustered. The terms were tough. But, as chairman of UBS, Kelleher's duty was to get the best deal for his shareholders. He was in a strong position, although he also knew that, if UBS didn't take over its rival, it could be caught up in the ensuing mess too.

Everyone in the room knew there was still a long way to go, and time was running out.

*Thursday, 16 March*

Around 2 a.m., Credit Suisse announced the Swiss National Bank was providing a backstop of up to 50 billion Swiss francs. It was an extraordinary sum, announced at an extraordinary hour. Nothing about the deal suggested that things were under control. Körner said that it was 'decisive action' and talked about 'moving forward rapidly' on a 'strategic transformation'. In reality, the bank was being put on life support. Prior to taking the emergency funding, Körner's team had confirmed to the SNB that it was under extreme pressure, with money now pouring out of the bank and no prospect of tapping global capital markets to raise more funds.

In the morning, the bank's share price fell yet again.

*Friday, 17 March*

By now, Lehmann and Körner had returned from overseas. Lehmann was resistant to the proposed merger. He felt they could still turn the bank around. Maybe they could sell off some businesses to raise funds or find another potential bidder for the bank, an alternative to UBS. Credit Suisse's top executives were in touch with their peers at the giant US asset-management firm BlackRock, who flew into Zurich like they were on a rescue mission. BlackRock's CEO, Larry Fink, whose career started at First Boston, was open to buying pieces of the bank. But the Swiss authorities were not in favour of an overseas bidder. There was some discussion of a rival bid from Swiss investors engineered by the bank's board. But Lehmann and others felt locked out of talks about the bank's future. In truth, the authorities didn't trust Credit Suisse to save itself.

Meanwhile, the crisis was getting ever worse. Clients had pulled about $30 billion out of Credit Suisse accounts over the prior forty-eight hours. Insolvency was merely hours away – it could potentially have happened as soon as midday on Friday. The bank urgently pleaded for another $20 billion in liquidity support from the SNB, which was granted. But the global financial infrastructure was now shutting Credit Suisse out. By mid-afternoon, the main clearing house for European currencies even cut Credit Suisse out of the trade in Swiss francs.

*Saturday, 18 March*

At UBS, the senior management team and its external advisers were digging deeper into Credit Suisse's numbers. This kind of due-diligence work ahead of a deal usually took place over days or even weeks. UBS had hours. They worked through the night. A deal had to be struck before the weekend was over, before Credit Suisse collapsed.

On Saturday evening, Kelleher and the Swiss authorities met by video conference to discuss the terms of the deal in more detail. The UBS chairman was in Zurich, in one of his bank's conference rooms, a giant photo of the cliffs in Cornwall looming on the wall behind him.

The number on the table, the price for Credit Suisse, was $1 billion. It was a staggeringly small sum, lower even than UBS had envisaged. Kelleher had thought he would have to pay more to get approval from Credit Suisse's investors, who theoretically had a say in what happened next. But the government planned an emergency law to bypass shareholders. The authorities would make available more than $250 billion in additional emergency liquidity, plus another $10 billion to cover the potential losses that UBS might incur from legacy issues it would inherit from the takeover. They also planned to write off more than $16 billion worth of the so-called AT1 bonds – a move that proved controversial later, when thousands of bondholders filed complaints alleging the government had ridden roughshod over their rights.

With the details more or less nailed down, Kelleher called Lehmann around 7 p.m. to make a formal offer to buy his bank. The Irishman had been on the receiving end of a similar call all those years ago when he was at Morgan Stanley. He knew it would be difficult. The call didn't go through. Lehmann didn't pick up.

Kelleher decided to head for dinner with his wife and another board member at an Italian restaurant opposite the office. They had hardly eaten in days. It was time for a breather and for some sustenance. But, just as Kelleher's pasta arrived, Lehmann returned the call.

The UBS chairman stepped outside the restaurant, into the cobbled street. 'We're bidding a billion dollars,' he said.

Lehmann was silent. He seemed stunned. The call was brief. Lehmann said he would take the offer to his board.

Meanwhile, Keller-Sutter was clearing the path for the takeover, knocking down any hurdles inside Switzerland and abroad.

She called her counterparts in Germany, the UK and France. In each case, she gave assurances the Swiss had a plan, and asked in turn that the national regulators would not stand in the way of the proposed combination of the two largest Swiss banks. She also spoke with Janet Yellen, the US Treasury secretary. Yellen quickly grasped the urgent need for an orderly outcome. She was still grappling with the unfolding crisis in the US banking sector. The last thing the Americans needed was more chaos damaging fragile confidence in the financial markets. Besides, Credit Suisse still had a multibillion-dollar US business. It was in everyone's interests for Yellen to ensure American regulators didn't oppose Keller-Sutter's plan.

That evening, Keller-Sutter spoke with one of the bank's Middle Eastern investors. The senior financier said his organization was willing to put another $3.5 billion into Credit Suisse to help stabilize the situation. Keller-Sutter was astonished. It was far too late for that. The sums involved were now many multiples higher. It was clear that no one at Credit Suisse had been in touch with this important shareholder. No one had told him – his shares were worthless.

*Sunday, 19 March*

Kelleher and Lehmann travelled separately to Bern, to meet with the Swiss Federal Council. Teams of executives from each bank waited in separate rooms. They barely said hello.

Credit Suisse went first. Outside, Kelleher and his small team waited. And waited. And waited.

Finally, Kelleher was summoned to meet with the authorities. The mood was sombre. Credit Suisse was already dead. It was just a case of reading the will.

It was clear that the meeting with Lehmann had been tense. UBS was told to increase its price and to drop some of the demands Kelleher had made a few days earlier. The chairman stared back across the table. 'I've seen this all before,' he warned. 'I've seen a bank run in action, how it can get out of control.' Kelleher warned the politicians of the dire consequences of not getting the deal over the line. In time, he would be willing to drop the guarantees he'd asked for, if they weren't needed. 'But if there is no agreement tomorrow morning,' he said, 'you won't just have a Credit Suisse problem; you'll have a Switzerland problem, with UBS and all the other Swiss banks pulled in too.'

Kelleher agreed to pay about $3 billion for Credit Suisse, though most of the rest of his terms stayed more or less intact. He sent the revised terms to Lehmann at Credit Suisse. And waited again.

Time ticked by, late into the afternoon and early evening. They needed a deal that day, before markets opened in Asia for Monday morning.

Eventually, just before 7 p.m. on Sunday evening, Lehmann got back to them. It was done. The deal was on.

It was raining in Bern that Sunday evening. Outside the greenish-grey sandstone of the Department of Finance building, bankers, politicians and reporters began pulling up ahead of an emergency press conference to announce the takeover of Credit Suisse by its oldest rival. After 167 years, the death of the bank was to be televised on a prime-time Sunday-evening news show.

Kelleher was in a dark blue suit and green tie. With him were Keller-Sutter and the Swiss president, Alain Berset, as well as Thomas Jordan from the central bank and Marlene Amstad, chair of FINMA. The mood was serious, dour, too early yet for a sense of relief. There had been some discussion of excluding anyone from Credit Suisse, whose failure was a painful, embarrassing event for the whole country. But Keller-Sutter insisted Lehmann join them, to show some leadership and some respect to the bank's employees, customers and history.

At the press conference, Lehmann, the bank's last-ever chairman, looked stricken. He had simply been the last to hold office – in the wrong place at the wrong time.

Before they headed into the media room to face the press, Kelleher thanked Lehmann and Keller-Sutter for getting the deal done.

Lehmann replied: 'It's good to finally have a solution.'

# Epilogue

The end of Credit Suisse seemed to have happened overnight. It was a victim of the frenzied pace of modern finance, yet it had been decades in the making. The whole of the bank's troubled history was a prelude to this humbling, humiliating meltdown.

And yet, though Credit Suisse was finished, the scandals kept on coming.

In April 2023, American senators accused the bank of blocking further investigations into its links to Nazis. Their digging revealed the bank didn't close an account belonging to a former Nazi commander sentenced at Nuremberg until 2002; another account for a Nazi-linked official in Argentina wasn't closed until 2020.

A few months later, reports emerged that the Department of Justice was ramping up an inquiry into Credit Suisse's work for wealthy Russian clients. According to several press reports, the DOJ was investigating potential compliance failures that allowed Russians to use the bank to evade sanctions imposed following the invasion of Ukraine.[1]

The takeover itself was also controversial. Switzerland's own brand of democracy gives the population a say on just about everything. Critics were irritated the government had enacted an emergency law to push through the deal and bypass shareholders. Thousands of jobs were lost, and corporate Switzerland was alarmed that there was only one big domestic bank to service the country's businesses.

Holders of Credit Suisse's AT1 – or CoCo – bonds were also angry. Around 2,500 bondholders filed complaints. They said the government-led process unfairly short-changed them and benefited shareholders instead (though shareholders, too, saw their holdings more or less wiped out). The legal cases around this issue are set to run for years and the outcome is expected to have a profound impact on the market for AT1 bonds and similar financial instruments across Europe.

UBS, meanwhile, seemed to have hit the jackpot. For years, the bank had balanced the pros and cons of a merger and decided against it. In the end, UBS picked up its rival for a song. Following the deal, Kelleher squeezed out his CEO, Ralph Hamers, and brought back Sergio Ermotti, the bank's popular, charismatic and capable former chief. In August, Ermotti announced the bank's second-quarter results – a profit of $29 billion, twice the previous record for the global banking industry. The numbers were inflated by an enormous accounting gain that reflected the huge difference between the price UBS paid for Credit Suisse and the value of the assets it had bought.

The scale of Credit Suisse's collapse was such that the dust is still only just settling at the time of writing, a year or so after the deal with UBS was struck. But there is already plenty of analysis of what went wrong. A lengthy report produced by FINMA – the regulator that oversaw and failed to prevent the bank's long descent – pointed to several important factors.

First, the bank never succeeded in fixing on a sustainable, profitable business model. For years, CEOs and chairmen had wrestled with the oversized and volatile investment bank. In the good times, it could produce bumper profits. But these periods were far too irregular. Instead, the bank's leaders tried, and failed, to wean themselves off investment banking, each taking a slightly different approach, making cuts here and there, but without ever fully disengaging from this business. The result was that Credit Suisse was using fewer and fewer resources to compete against larger, better investment banks. It became impossible to succeed. This was an even bigger failure considering the period after the financial crisis was one of relatively strong markets and benign economic conditions. If Credit Suisse couldn't turn a profit in such circumstances, then it surely never would.

There were clear and disturbing deficiencies in the bank's approach to corporate governance, too. FINMA said successive CEOs and chairmen failed to set a strong 'tone at the top'. The behaviour of the bank's leaders hardly inspired other staff to be the best versions of themselves. Spygate and Horta-Osório's Covid breaches were clear examples of this weakness. The absence of effective leadership was exacerbated in the bank's final couple of years, by the rapid turnover in senior executives.

FINMA also cited a too-generous approach to compensation that failed to provide incentives for the right kind of behaviour. Credit Suisse bankers got paid well, whatever happened. When the bank was making a profit, staff made a bundle, regardless of whether the results were driven by strong markets or great management. When the bank made a loss – because of misconduct, fines, bad behaviour or poor strategic decisions – the bonuses were good then too. FINMA noted that the bank made a cumulative net loss of more than $2 billion in the ten years before it collapsed, yet paid out bonuses of about $35 billion in the same period. With such rewards available for failure, who needs success?

Clearly, Credit Suisse was also harmed by repeated scandals. From 2010 onwards, the bank paid fines of more than $15 billion in relation to misconduct by its own employees. But the damage was much greater than these financial penalties. There were also massive losses, as in the Archegos scandal, and huge settlements with wronged clients, as in the Lescaudron affair. Top executives were bogged down in litigation and crisis management when they should have been running day-to-day operations. Eventually, clients had had enough and the authorities ran out of patience. FINMA said in its report that it repeatedly imposed measures on the bank to fix serious shortcomings. Eventually, the regulator said, it had 'exhausted the tools available to it to influence the bank.'

Two more technical areas are also worth considering: capital and liquidity. Credit Suisse, like its peer group of global banks, had to meet specific capital ratios which were set by international and national regulators. Over the years, the bank's capital position had become contentious. In 2021, for instance, an analyst at the research company Autonomous wrote a detailed report indicating the bank had a capital problem. The report was headed 'Credit Suisse Group: Less than meets the eye'. It was an issue that dogged the bank's leaders for years, and it was linked closely to other concerns about strategy and conduct. The flawed business model led to losses that ate away at capital. Poor governance and scandals cost the bank billions in lost capital too. Frequent changes in leadership meant the bank could never get on top of this issue.

After the bank collapsed, a new narrative emerged that critiqued FINMA for its role in the long-running capital saga. This view, expressed most clearly in a *Wall Street Journal* article, said that FINMA had cut the bank too much slack, allowing it to exploit loopholes and run with a capital position that was weaker than that of its rivals.[2]

The problem with this view, though, is that capital wasn't what killed Credit Suisse. It was certainly an issue that bedevilled the bank's leaders for years. But, at the end of 2022 and even into the bank's final days, Credit Suisse more than met all the requirements of the global capital rules. What's more, though the regulator did allow the bank some leeway on capital at the level of its Swiss parent company, this was not entirely unusual. Nor was it unusual for banks to have problems with maintaining capital at the right level. Since the financial crisis, many banks had run close to the limits without going out of business. Capital was an issue at Credit Suisse, but it wasn't the primary cause of death.

Liquidity was a different problem. Again, the bank maintained all the liquidity ratios required by global and national rule books, almost until the end. But this wasn't enough. The Twitter affair in October 2022 had shown clearly that clients were willing and able to withdraw funds rapidly. No liquidity buffers were sufficient if tens of billions of dollars flooded out for days on end. Under those circumstances, the bank could not survive without external help. The only solution would have been for the government to intervene with a clear, decisive and early message to depositors that their money was safe.

FINMA's analysis only gets us so far. It doesn't answer two fundamental questions. The first is, who caused Credit Suisse to collapse?

One idea that gained traction in Zurich was that the bank was doomed from the appointment of Tidjane Thiam as CEO. The non-banker, the outsider, restructured the bank in a way that undermined good risk management and left the bank heading for failure, according to his critics. This analysis is problematic. For starters, Thiam's restructuring did not happen in a vacuum. He was hired to change the bank, and it seems fundamentally unfair to criticize him for doing that. Also, his time in charge was marred by scandals that were seeded in the past – this was the same for CEOs who went before and after him, which suggests that, if risk management was a problem, it wasn't entirely Thiam's fault. Of course, Thiam's exit was ultimately prompted by spygate, a scandal that was entirely conceived during his own tenure. But it's impossible to think that the criticism he has faced in light of the collapse of the bank doesn't also reflect the xenophobia, racism and snobbery that Thiam encountered while in charge.

Who else played a role? It's possible that every one of Credit Suisse's leaders –especially over its last four or five decades – shares some of the blame. Rainer Gut's ambitious, expansive approach set up the clash of US and Swiss values that no leader ever reconciled. Allen Wheat allowed star bankers to run free, which encouraged a high tolerance for risky behaviour and aggressive pay packets. Under Brady Dougan, the bank failed to capitalize on its winning position coming out of the financial crisis and, crucially, never got to grips with its problematic investment bank. Thomas Gottstein was ineffective, hobbled by scandals that he didn't see coming. Ueli Körner and Axel Lehmann arrived too late to make much of a difference, though they largely ignored the onrushing tsunami and refused to show the kind of inspirational leadership the crisis demanded. Across much of this period, at the top of the bank stood Urs Rohner, who made the wrong appointments at the wrong time. As chairman, Rohner could have demanded a pivotal change in the culture of the bank. But that never happened.

All of these men led the bank through decades of overexpansion, expensive acquisitions, scandal after scandal. Many of them considered a merger with UBS on equal terms or better – a more favourable outcome than the end result – before calling it off. None of them fixed the bank's broken business model and its discreditable culture. Who is to blame for Credit Suisse's demise? The bank's failure was a group effort.

The other big question posed by Credit Suisse's collapse is what it means for the global banking system and whether any new rules are needed.

The global banking industry often instinctively rejects any notion of greater regulation. In the US, Wall Street came out in force during a debate over capital rules following the collapse of Silicon Valley Bank. A proposal to toughen the rules was thoroughly quashed. But

Credit Suisse should be a warning against any sense of hubris. Banks are not like other businesses. They are, as journalist Jonathan Guthrie wrote in the *Financial Times*, 'massively regulated, state-guaranteed, quasi-public franchises financed with private capital. Their job is to create and distribute money for their franchisers, governments, and central banks.'[3] When one of them fails, there must be a proper reckoning.

In November 2023, Sergio Ermotti spoke at a banking awards ceremony at the University of Zurich. He gave a frank assessment of Credit Suisse, the bank his firm had swallowed whole. 'First and foremost,' he said, 'Credit Suisse was an entirely idiosyncratic banking failure.'

This is true, though only to a certain extent.

Yes, all banks are unique, each with a different business model, different regulators, shareholders and customers. But they all suffer from the same structural problems, especially the trade-off between risk and reward, safety and profitability. And yes, banks each have their own scandals. But no institution is immune from scandal in an industry that too often promotes greed as a career plan and encourages an unhealthy obsession with money. At Credit Suisse, management was perhaps worse than elsewhere. But, in different circumstances, it's not hard to imagine a similar fate at another big global bank – indeed, there are plenty of examples of Credit Suisse's peers falling into peril, only to be rescued by taxpayers or foreign investors.

Ermotti's speech also pointed to possible concerns and solutions that are useful. (Many of his suggestions foreshadowed proposals from the Swiss government a few months later in its own response to the collapse of Credit Suisse. There was one exception. The government suggested a more stringent capital regime, something Swiss bank executives were dead against.)

For instance, Ermotti noted the need to 'evolve the liquidity framework for the era of digital banking'. This seems critical. The demise of Credit Suisse revealed how quickly a bank – even a massive 167-year-old bank – can be brought down by internet rumours, and the speed with which money can move through the modern financial system. This ought to have scared bankers and the authorities equally. A new era demands a new set of rules.

Ermotti also expressed support for a stronger regime to ensure individuals are held accountable for their actions. This seems sensible, and much needed too. In the past few decades, pay in the financial sector has exploded, with soaring compensation only slightly weighted down after the financial crisis. The system too frequently incentivizes short-term thinking at the expense of clients and other stakeholders. Skirting the rules is still too often handsomely rewarded. Those who cross the line are too rarely punished. The authorities need greater power to go after individuals who are downright negligent or worse.

The story of Credit Suisse is above all a reminder of the fickle nature of banking as a whole. Here was an enormous global institution that processed trillions of dollars and had tens of thousands of employees, brought to its knees by an errant tweet and finished off by confusion over whether the S in the acronym SNB meant 'Swiss' or 'Saudi'. So fragile was the entire edifice that, in the final few months, some in the bank feared having chairman Axel Lehmann speak in public because his surname was an echo of the collapse of Lehmann Brothers more than a decade earlier. This fragility, blended with the fact that banks underpin so much of our modern capitalist economy, is a toxic mess, made even worse by the handsome pay packets that reward excessive risk-taking.

Yet, there's no risk at all if the government is waiting in the wings for when things go wrong. Somehow, within Switzerland, there are still bankers who cling to the idea that Credit Suisse could have survived if only the authorities had stood by the bank. The decision to let the bank fail, proponents of this idea say, was a political one. If

Karin Keller-Sutter had more forcefully stood behind the bank, the crisis could have been averted, these people insist.

Of course, it's impossible to say what *might* have happened had things been different. But it is hardly surprising that KKS and the other Swiss authorities chose an alternative path. Trust in Credit Suisse had evaporated. Its leaders were not credible. When KKS looked around the room for a plausible solution to the crisis foisted upon her and found nothing, she wisely looked elsewhere. Perhaps it would have been possible to save Credit Suisse, but after so many chances, so many lapses, embarrassments and farcical missteps, why should anyone have bothered?

Certain authorities, notably in the US, criticized KKS and the Swiss authorities for engineering a takeover by UBS instead of simply letting Credit Suisse fall into bankruptcy. This view is expressed with the full benefit of hindsight and ignores the sense of emergency that gripped 2023. It will only be truly tested when a Goldman Sachs or JP Morgan or Morgan Stanley teeters on the brink – then we shall see whether American regulators find it helpful to let one of those major banks collapse.

Still, there is a valid point to be made about bank failures. That is, there ought to be consequences for misconduct and mismanagement. Bankers and economists talk about moral hazard – the idea that people engage in riskier behaviour if they think someone else bears the consequences when things go wrong. Executives at Credit Suisse had decades to reform the bank, but they never could.

Eventually, it just had to end.

# Glossary

**Additional Tier 1 (AT1) Bonds:** After the financial crisis, banks sometimes issued AT1 bonds to help bolster their balance sheets. These bonds are sometimes known as CoCos, or contingent convertible debt bonds. When the bank that issues the AT1s gets in financial trouble, it can convert the bonds to equity shareholdings or write them off. At Credit Suisse, about $16 billion in AT1s was controversially written off in March 2023.

**AML:** Anti-money-laundering rules require banks to follow certain processes to ensure they're not participating in money laundering. Typically, this involves research into clients and a system of filters that flag potentially illegitimate transactions.

**CSFB:** Credit Suisse First Boston, or CSFB, was the investment-banking unit of Credit Suisse, based in New York, between 1996 and 2006. The business evolved from a joint venture between Credit Suisse and First Boston, launched in 1978. Later, Credit Suisse acquired a direct stake in First Boston itself, which it increased over several years between 1988 and 1996. The CSFB brand was retired in

2006 and the business operated as the Credit Suisse investment-banking division.

**Dot.com Bubble:** From 1995, shares in many technology firms, known as dot.com companies, increased sharply in price. But this bubble burst in mid-2000 as investors became wary of the long-term viability of these new businesses. Investors lost billions of dollars as many dot.com companies went bust, although other new technology firms subsequently went on to be hugely successful.

**Due Diligence:** A review of a business or deal or assets undertaken to ascertain whether the price is right and whether there are any other issues, such as potential fraud, that could scupper the transaction.

**Eurobond Market:** Eurobonds are debts issued by companies in a currency that is different from the one in their home country. For example, a US-dollar bond issued by an Italian company would be considered a Eurobond. The market for this kind of debt took off in the 1970s and 1980s and was centred on the City of London.

**EXB:** Credit Suisse's executive board, known as the EXB, was the inner circle of senior managers closest to the chief executive officer.

**FINMA:** The Swiss Financial Market Supervisory Authority, known as FINMA, is the Swiss body that regulates all banks and other financial institutions in the country. Based in Bern, it is independent of the government, financed by fees and levies charged to the firms it regulates.

**GFC:** From 2007 to 2009, the global financial crisis shook the worldwide economy. The crisis, which was sparked by a downturn in the US mortgage market, led to the collapse of several major banks and the forced mergers of others. Several banks, especially in Europe, survived only after receiving billions of dollars in government bailouts. The crisis was followed by a clampdown from banking regulators around the world.

**G-SIB:** Since the GFC, thirty banks are designated as G-SIBs, or globally systemically important banks, by the Financial Stability Board, a global banking authority. These banks are subject to stricter rules meant to safeguard the global economy against their possible collapse. The G-SIB designation is a reflection of the size and interconnectedness of these institutions.

**Investment Bank:** An investment bank typically acts as an intermediary on financial transactions. These are typically complex deals involving major institutions, such as big corporations, private-equity firms or pension funds. For instance, it can provide services to help clients trade in stocks or bonds, or it can help companies issue shares in an IPO (see below) or assist with merger and acquisition activity.

**IPO:** An initial public offering happens when a private company issues shares to the public for the first time. Investment banks get a fee for helping the company through the process.

**Junk Bonds:** Junk or high-yield bonds are bonds that carry a higher risk of default than investment-grade bonds. Because they are riskier, they also pay a higher yield than bonds issued by investment-grade companies.

**Leveraged Finance:** Leveraged finance is the use of debt, rather than cash or shares, to pay for an asset. Typically, investment banks provide this debt, often to private-equity companies.

**Mortgage-Backed Securities:** A security, or investment, that is backed by home loans. Typically, a broker or bank pools together lots of individual mortgages. This pool of loans is packaged up and sold to investors.

**Prime Brokerage:** This is a set of services offered by investment banks to their institutional clients, such as hedge funds. The prime broker helps clients to trade stocks and bonds, often providing them with loans and cash-management services.

**Private Bank:** Private banking typically involves the provision of highly personalized financial services to wealthy clients, known as high-net-worth or ultra-high-net-worth individuals (HNWIs or UHNWIs). These services can involve providing investment advice, making investment decisions, or setting up trust accounts, for instance. Private bankers also often become closely involved in other aspects of their clients' lives, helping them to find schools for their children, locate homes and vacation properties, securing advice on how to minimize taxes, or helping them get loans for major purchases like yachts or private aircraft.

**SEC:** The Securities and Exchange Commission, or SEC, is the US's top financial regulator responsible for protecting investors.

**Sub-prime Mortgages:** Home loans issued to borrowers with weaker-than-typical credit ratings. These mortgages usually charge a higher rate of interest to reflect the greater risk of the borrower defaulting on payments.

**Supply-Chain Finance (SCF):** This is a financing technique that involves making short-term loans to facilitate trade between buyers and sellers of goods and services. Greensill Capital became one of the biggest suppliers of SCF, using money from Credit Suisse's clients, until it collapsed in March 2021.

**Swiss Bank Secrecy Act:** The Swiss Bank Secrecy Act was introduced into law in 1934. The law made it a criminal offence for banks to reveal client data without permission, even when requested by government agencies. It has been controversial because, in the view of some foreign governments, some Swiss banks have hidden behind the law to avoid revealing information about the nefarious activities of clients.

**Swiss National Bank (SNB):** The SNB is Switzerland's central bank, the equivalent of the Bank of England or the Federal Reserve. It shouldn't be confused with the Saudi National Bank, though the two share the same initials.

# Acknowledgements

This book was only possible because of the generosity of my sources, and their interest in helping me tell an accurate and compelling history of Credit Suisse. To the extent I've succeeded, they deserve the plaudits. Any shortcomings are mine alone.

I first discussed this book with my agent Matthew Cole at Northbank Talent over coffee outside a central London cafe. Matt immediately backed the case for a book on this subject. He has been incredibly supportive, encouraging and helpful in setting out why it needed to be written. His understanding, advice and his dedication to the cause have been invaluable. I also owe enormous gratitude to my publisher Macmillan and their commitment to and support for deeply reported stories. Ause Abdelhaq is a brilliant and thoughtful editor. His guidance on the narrative and structure of this book simplified Credit Suisse's story in my mind and, I believe, made for a much more compelling and impactful retelling.

Readers should know that I leaned on great work by many excellent journalists who've covered Credit Suisse over the years. On many occasions, scandals would have been covered up, and perpetrators of wrongdoing would have been unpunished, had it not been for intrepid reporters who unearthed the truth. Their work has been acknowledged directly in the notes to the text.

I also want to express specific gratitude to former *Wall Street Journal* reporter Randall Smith for writing a rich and thorough biography of Frank Quattrone. Randall's incredible journalism in *The Prince of Silicon Valley* both informed and inspired parts of this book. *Swiss Banks and Jewish Souls*, Gregg Rickman's fascinating account of the efforts to reunite Holocaust victims with money that was rightfully theirs, is a fascinating and important read. We all owe Rickman thanks for shedding light on this troubling episode.

I have been fortunate to work with some fantastic journalists over the years. I've tried to learn from each of them. I'm even luckier that a small group of smart writers kindly agreed to read early drafts of this book. Lionel Laurent provided great guidance, delivered as always with effortless charm. His advice helped me better understand the shape of the bank's story and my role in telling it. I'm also grateful to Jared Bibler, whose tips and pointers were a huge help, especially when it comes to understanding the finer points of Swiss-German. Francesco Guerrera is one of the best financial journalists I know, eminently knowledgeable and a consummate storyteller. His generously given advice improved this book immeasurably. His friendship is invaluable. I am extraordinarily lucky to have worked alongside Sara Abdullah, a hugely talented editor and as thoughtful a friend as anyone could wish for. Sara's suggestions on early drafts were precise, prompt, insightful. They always, always improved my prose and my thinking.

I also want to thank Lucy Woods, who checked the facts in this book. Lucy is incredibly diligent and kept me on the straight and narrow. If anything somehow sneaked through her net, I take sole responsibility.

I owe a debt of gratitude to friends and family who have tolerated my obsession with Swiss banking over the duration of the writing process. Authoring a book like this is hard work, but being around the author is so much more difficult. Thank you for your patience.

Most importantly, I owe enormous gratitude to my wife, Bambi, and to my three boys, who gave me the time and space to get this done. Bambi – thank you for your tolerance, patience and unwavering belief. I quite literally couldn't do this without you. To Duke, Cooper and Robson – you are my inspiration. Whatever anyone says, keep asking the questions.

# Notes

## CHAPTER 1 – A CHILD OF TWO NATIONS

1 Joseph Jung, *Alfred Escher, 1819–1882: Aufstieg, Macht, Tragik* (Basel: NZZ Libro, 2008); Marc Tribelhorn, 'Alfred Escher – der König der Schweiz', *NZZ Magazin*, 7 February 2019, https://www.nzz.ch/geschichte/alfred-escher-der-koenig-der-schweiz-ld.1454617. Specific references to the works of Swiss historian Joseph Jung are cited here, but Jung's body of work broadly has been very informative about the life of Alfred Escher.

2 Tribelhorn, 'Alfred Escher – der König der Schweiz', *NZZ Magazin*, 7 February 2019.

3 Noele Illien, 'Banking and slavery: Switzerland examines its colonial conscience', *The Guardian*, 19 November 2020, https://www.theguardian.com/world/2020/nov/19/banking-slavery-switzerland-examines-its-colonial-conscience.

4 Joseph Jung, *Das Laboratorium des Fortschritts: Die Schweiz im 19. Jahrhundert* (Basel: NZZ Libro, 2020).

5 C. H. Church and R. C. Head, *A Concise History of Switzerland* (Cambridge: Cambridge University Press, 2013).

6 Tribelhorn, 'Alfred Escher – der König der Schweiz', *NZZ Magazin*, 7 February 2019.

7 This is expertly described by historian Joseph Jung in his book, *The Laboratory of Progress: Switzerland in the Nineteenth Century, Volume 2* (New York, NY: Routledge, 2023).

8 Ibid.

9 Ibid.

10 'Alfred Escher: a visionary of modern Switzerland', Federal Department of Foreign Affairs, House of Switzerland (website), 12 May 2020, https://www.houseofswitzerland.org/swissstories/history/alfred-escher-visionary-modern-switzerland.

11 Tribelhorn, 'Alfred Escher – der König der Schweiz', *NZZ Magazin*, 7 February 2019.

## CHAPTER 2 – SECRETS AND LIES

1 Avera Dorsey, 'Shh— It's a Secret! The Evolution of the Swiss Banking System & International Tax Implications', International Program Papers, 125, Chicago Unbound, University of Chicago Law School, 2021, https://chicago unbound.uchicago.edu/international_immersion_program_papers/125.

2 Daniel Dematos, 'Swiss Banks and Secrecy', The Tontine Coffee-House (website), 14 June 2021, https://tontinecoffeehouse.com/2021/06/14/swiss-banks-and-secrecy/.

3 There are various accounts of this raid by French authorities. By far the most detailed modern account is included in Sébastian Guex, 'The Origins of the Swiss Banking Secrecy Law and Its Repercussions for Swiss Federal Policy', *The Business History Review* 74(02), June 2000, pp. 237–66. Guex's version of the story draws on various contemporary documents.

4 Ibid. Also, Robert Vogler, *Swiss Banking Secrecy: Origins, Significance, Myth* (Switzerland and Principality of Liechtenstein: Association for Financial History, 2006). In one famous case, a German, Arthur Pfau, was expelled from Switzerland, having been accused of trying to persuade employees of UBS to hand over information about their German clients.

5 French bank clients withdrawing money from Switzerland: Vogler, *Swiss Banking Secrecy*.

6 Anmol Makhija, 'Switzerland: Schweizerische Volksbank (SVB), 1933- YPFS Case Study' (Yale University: School of Management, Yale Program on Financial Stability, 2023).

7 There are many examples of Credit Suisse acting in this way. In the late 1960s, a Credit Suisse banker opened four accounts for Ferdinand Marcos – the brutal dictator of the Philippines – and his wife Imelda under the false

names William Saunders and Jane Ryan. In 1986, after revolution gripped the Philippines, the new government began efforts to recover billions of dollars from the bank, but it took many years and an international legal battle to get access to even a fraction of the stolen money. See Nick Davies, 'The $10bn question: what happened to the Marcos millions?', *The Guardian*, 7 May 2016, https://www.theguardian.com/world/2016/may/07/10bn-dollar-question-marcos-millions-nick-davies and Pieter J. Hoets and Sara G. Zwart, 'Swiss Bank Secrecy and the Marcos Affair', *New York Law School Journal of International and Competitive Law* 9(1), 1988, https://core.ac.uk/download/pdf/270263765.pdf. A few years later, Credit Suisse was among a group of banks accused by Swiss authorities of handling funds tied to the entourage of the Nigerian dictator, Sani Abacha. Investigators found the bank had accepted $214 million, deposited by two of Abacha's sons, without properly identifying the two customers. See 'Abacha Funds at Swiss Banks', Report of the Swiss Federal Banking Commission, 30 August 2000, https://www.FINMA.ch/FINMAArchiv/ebk/e/archiv/2000/pdf/neu14a-00.pdf and Paul Coudret, 'Abacha affair: the serious faults of Credit Suisse', *Le Temps*, 27 February 2001, https://www.letemps.ch/economie/affaire-abacha-lourdes-fautes-credit-suisse.

8 OCCRP and Süddeutsche Zeitung, 'Historic Leak of Swiss Banking Records Reveals Unsavory Clients', OCCRP, 20 February 2022, https://www.occrp.org/en/suisse-secrets/historic-leak-of-swiss-banking-records-reveals-unsavory-clients. Includes a comment by Frank Vogl, a former World Bank official, that fines seem like 'the cost of doing business.'

## CHAPTER 3 – THE CHIASSO AFFAIR

1 'Chiasso is a dreary little frontier town, almost totally dependent on its role as a repository for capital fleeing from Italy,' wrote Nicholas Faith, a British journalist, in his book, *Safety in Numbers: The Mysterious World of Swiss Banking* (London: Viking, 1982). At that point, the Chiasso affair was fresh in the memory, having broken only five years earlier. This chapter draws heavily on Faith's excellent account of the affair.

2 Michael Getler, 'Credit Suisse Scandal Casts Shadow Over Swiss Banks', *The Washington Post*, 21 May 1977, https://www.washingtonpost.com/archive/business/1977/05/22/credit-suisse-scandal-casts-shadow-over-swiss-banks/3a5e8c74-0ea8-422b-beb1-f0f2e7b59344/

3 'Banking: Suicide in Switzerland', *Time* magazine, 23 May 1977, https://content.time.com/time/subscriber/article/0,33009,911980-1,00.html.

4 Emmanuel Garessus, 'Les grandes affaires économiques de la Suisse. Le scandale de Chiasso, ou l'histoire d'une banque dans la banque', *Le Temps*, 31 July 2008, https://www.letemps.ch/economie/grandes-affaires-economiques-suisse-26-scandale-chiasso-lhistoire-dune-banque-banque.

5 Getler, 'Credit Suisse Scandal Casts Shadow Over Swiss Banks', *The Washington Post*, 21 May 1977.

6 Ibid.

7 Faith's book, *Safety in Numbers*, here quotes extensively from the earlier work, by Max Mabillard and Roger de Weck, *Scandale au Credit Suisse* (Geneva: Tribune, 1977). According to the authors, the auditors' visits to Chiasso could often end in even more scandalous behaviour. They claim, 'it was not rare after a night of festivities that an auditor found upon returning to his room at the Corso an appetizing young woman in his bed.'

8 'Aides Sentenced in Credit Suisse Case', *The New York Times*, 4 July 1979.

9 More recently, the bank still seemed unashamed of such an enormous failure and preferred to see the positives. Credit Suisse's website says the scandal 'prompted the bank to strike out for new shores and transform itself from a traditional Zurich institution into an international financial services provider.' A photo on the website confidently shows the dismissive German-language newspaper headline: see 'Our story in Pictures', Credit Suisse website, https://www.credit-suisse.com/about-us/en/our-company/who-we-are.html#14.-221947533.

10 Getler, 'Credit Suisse Scandal Casts Shadow Over Swiss Banks', *The Washington Post*, 21 May 1977.

### CHAPTER 4 – GUT INSTINCTS

1 Renato Morosoli, 'Emil Gut', Historisches Lexikon der Schweiz HLS (website), 28 June 2004, https://hls-dhs-dss.ch/de/articles/041155/2004-06-28/

2 Claude Baumann, 'Little Known Facts About Rainer E. Gut', finews.com (website), 16 October 2023, https://www.finews.com/news/english-news/59735-rainer-e-gut-ska-credit-suisse-ubs-us-investment-banking-chiasso-scandal.

3 Ibid.

4 Chris Bowlby, 'Why are Swiss Bankers called gnomes?', BBC Magazine (website), 25 February 2010, http://news.bbc.co.uk/1/hi/magazine/8534936.stm.

5 The 'scandal bank' reference is from former Credit Suisse executive Josef Ackermann, speaking on the podcast *A Long Time in Finance*, in the episode 'The Nine Lives of Credit Suisse: Part One', 1 September 2023.

6 Paul Lewis, 'Scandal Could Alter Swiss Banking', *The New York Times*, 30 May 1977, https://www.nytimes.com/1977/05/30/archives/scandal-could-alter-swiss-banking-swiss-banking-facing-changes-in.html.

## CHAPTER 5 – SHIPPING UP TO BOSTON

1 Allen Berger, Rebecca Demsetz and Philip Strahan, 'The Consolidation of the Financial Services Industry: Causes, Consequences, and Implications for the Future', *Journal of Banking and Finance* 23(2–4), February 1999, pp. 135–94.

2 Mitchell Martin, 'Citicorp and Travelers Plan to Merge in Record $70 Billion Deal: A New No. 1: Financial Giants Unite', *The New York Times*, 7 April 1998.

3 'For the first time in the history of international finance, Wall Street firms, and a few US commercial banks, are becoming leaders in markets traditionally dominated by local outfits.' Brett D. Fromson, 'The Golden Years', *The Washington Post*, 3 July 1994.

4 'Investment Bank Deal Discussed', *The New York Times*, 18 July 1978, https://www.nytimes.com/1978/07/18/archives/investment-bank-deal-discussed.html.

5 Suzanna Andrews, 'Larry Fink's $12 Trillion Shadow', *Vanity Fair*, March 2010. The market for mortgage-backed securities eventually played a central role in the 2008 financial crisis. 'But long before it spiraled out of control, it was considered an incredible innovation. Looking back, Fink says, "We were able to narrow the cost of housing." ' Fink was estimated to have added $1 billion to First Boston's profits. He was eventually forced out of the bank after his team lost about $100 million following an incorrect bet on the direction of interest rates.

6 Karen W. Arenson, 'First Boston's Merger Makers', *The New York Times*, 21 April 1981, https://www.nytimes.com/1981/04/21/business/first-boston-s-merger-makers.html.

7 Nickname reference, David Brewerton, 'Bruce Wasserstein Obituary', *The Guardian*, 22 October 2009, https://www.theguardian.com/business/2009/oct/22/bruce-wasserstein-obituary.

8 Peter Petre, 'Merger fees that bend the mind', *Fortune* magazine, 20 January 1986, https://fortune.com/2012/11/21/merger-fees-that-bend-the-mind/

9 Steven Greenhouse, 'Swiss Bank Turns Aggressive', *The New York Times*, 10 April 1989, https://www.nytimes.com/1989/04/10/business/swiss-bank-turns-aggressive.html.

10 James B. Stewart, Bryan Burrough and Steve Swartz, 'Wasserstein and Perella, Stars and Profit Centers, Plan a New Merchant Bank – Can They Do

It Alone?', *The Wall Street Journal*, 3 February 1988, https://www.wsj.com/articles/BL-DLB-15825.

11 Cal Mankowski, 'First Boston Deal Expands Credit Suisse Presence', *The Washington Post*, 11 October 1988, https://www.washingtonpost.com/archive/business/1988/10/11/first-boston-deal-expands-credit-suisse-presence/7d26cbc7-61f0-420f-a57c-dd245d648975/

12 Greenhouse, 'Swiss Bank Turns Aggressive', *The New York Times*, 10 April 1989.

13 Kurt Eichenwald, 'First Boston to Sell Sealy Stake', *The New York Times*, 28 January 1993, https://www.nytimes.com/1993/01/28/business/company-news-first-boston-set-to-sell-sealy-stake.html and Al Lewis, 'The Churning Bed', *The Wall Street Journal*, 29 September 2012, https://www.wsj.com/articles/SB10000872396390443389604578024163612472992.

14 Steven Greenhouse, 'Reviving a Humbled First Boston', *The New York Times*, 11 March 1991, https://www.nytimes.com/1991/03/11/business/reviving-a-humbled-first-boston.html.

15 Greenhouse, 'Swiss Bank Turns Aggressive', *The New York Times*, 10 April 1989.

16 Ibid.

## CHAPTER 6 – A SWISS RECKONING

1 Blaine Harden, 'New York's Veteran "Senator Pothole" Gets Run Over by Schumer', *The Washington Post*, 4 November 1998, https://www.washingtonpost.com/wp-srv/politics/campaigns/keyraces98/stories/ny110498.htm.

2 This entire chapter is largely based on interviews and Gregg Rickman's excellent book, *Swiss Banks and Jewish Souls* (Abingdon and New York, NY: Routledge, 2017, first published 1999). Where there are specific references from other sources, those have been indicated in the notes.

3 Daniel Dancis, 'Miriam and Me: The Beginnings of an Archival Adventure and Friendship in 1996', The Text Message (blog), Textual Records Division, National Archives, 29 March 2016, https://text-message.blogs.archives.gov/2016/03/29/miriam-and-me-the-beginnings-of-an-archival-adventure-and-friendship-in-1996/

4 Many of the details of this scandal can be found in the account published on the website of the Securities and Exchange Commission Historical Society, under the heading 'The Enforcement Division: A History – The Reagan Era and Insider Trading, 1980–1990', https://www.sechistorical.org/museum/galleries/enf/enf05c_winning-battle.php.

5 David A. Vise, 'Bank Leu Accused of Insider Trading', *The Washington Post*, 17 January 1987, https://www.washingtonpost.com/archive/business/1987/01/17/bank-leu-accused-of-insider-trading/a28f9d54-39d9-4e41-bfe8-d51674384a8c/

6 David Shirreff, 'Credit Suisse and UBS: Gut Takes a Tumble', *Euromoney*, 1 May 1996, https://www.euromoney.com/article/b1320b99n1m3nf/credit-suisse-and-ubs-gut-takes-a-tumble.

7 Stephanie Strom, 'Swiss Banks Considering Giant Merger', *The New York Times*, 10 April 1996, https://www.nytimes.com/1996/04/10/business/international-business-swiss-banks-considering-giant-merger.html.

8 Shirreff, 'Credit Suisse and UBS: Gut Takes a Tumble', *Euromoney*, 1 May 1996.

9 Rickman, *Swiss Banks and Jewish Souls*.

10 Itamar Levin, *The Last Deposit: Swiss Banks and Holocaust Victims' Accounts*, Natasha Dornberg (trans.) (New York, NY: Praeger, 1999).

11 Blaine Harden, Saundra Torry, 'N.Y. Law Firm to Advise Swiss Bank Accused of Laundering Nazi Loot', *The Washington Post*, 27 February 1997, https://www.washingtonpost.com/archive/politics/1997/02/28/ny-law-firm-to-advise-swiss-bank-accused-of-laundering-nazi-loot/bb7552a7-2676-428d-9376-572be8f33c47/

12 Levin, *The Last Deposit*.

13 David E. Sanger, 'Under Pressure: Big Swiss Bank Yields to Daughter of Nazi Victim', *The New York Times*, 5 May 1998, https://www.nytimes.com/1998/05/05/nyregion/under-pressure-big-swiss-bank-yields-to-daughter-of-nazi-victim.html.

14 Rickman, *Swiss Banks and Jewish Souls*.

15 Shirreff, 'Credit Suisse and UBS: Gut Takes a Tumble', *Euromoney*, 1 May 1996.

16 Rickman, *Swiss Banks and Jewish Souls*.

17 Tani Freedman, 'Swiss banks reeling from latest business blow in California', Agence France-Presse, 14 October 1997.

18 Transcript of *Morning Edition*, National Public Radio, 13 August 1998.

19 In its final report in 1999, the Volcker Commission said it had found 54,000 accounts worth as much as $1.3 billion that were probably linked to victims of the Nazis. The report also criticized the banks for 'questionable and deceitful actions' and 'a general lack of diligence' in connecting dormant accounts with their true owners. '"They were lackadaisical, to say the least," Volcker

said in an interview. "The banks had no incentive to find out the truth about the assets because they felt they should protect the honor of Switzerland." ' Quote taken from William Drozdiak, 'Panel Finds 54,000 accounts of Nazi Victims', *The Washington Post*, 7 December 1999, https://www.washington-post.com/wp-srv/WPcap/1999-12/07/070r-120799-idx.html?itid=lk_inline_manual_18

20 'U.S. class actions: banks reach settlement', UBS and Credit Suisse joint press release, 12 August 1998.

### CHAPTER 7 – WHEAT'S CROP OF STARS

1 Linda Grant, 'Will CS First Boston Ever Win? Swiss–American Relations', *Fortune* magazine, 19 August 1996, https://web.archive.org/web/201312030 65900/https://money.cnn.com/magazines/fortune/fortune_archive/1996/08/19/215626/

2 'Allen Wheat Just Loves Volatility', Bloomberg, 9 June 1991, https://www.bloomberg.com/news/articles/1991-06-09/allen-wheat-just-loves-volatility.

3 Ian Kerr, 'The Rise and Fall', Financial News (website), 23 July 2001, https://www.fnlondon.com/articles/the-rise-and-fall-20010723.

4 Monica S. Tew, 'The Dark Side of Derivatives: A Book Note on Infectious Greed: How Deceit and Risk Corrupted the Financial Markets by Frank Portnoy', *North Carolina Banking Institute* 8(1), 2004, http://scholarship.law.unc.edu/ncbi/vol8/iss1/14.

5 'Credit Suisse's Mack Buffeted by Wall Street's Perfect Storm', Bloomberg, 27 March 2003, https://www.bloomberg.com/news/articles/2003-03-27/credit-suisse-s-mack-buffeted-by-wall-street-s-perfect-storm.

6 Kirsten Craze and Sonja Koremans, 'Australia's priciest pad at $60m', *The Advertiser*, 12 August 2013, https://www.adelaidenow.com.au/realestate/news/australia8217s-priciest-pad-at-60m/news-story/6a34f4902 2bf5eb57c9da1a411c2b5ea.

7 Stephen Dabkowski, 'Emerging Markets Man', *Australian Financial Review*, 25 May 1998, https://www.afr.com/companies/emerging-markets-man-1998 0525-kb3xu.

8 Devin Leonard, 'Andy Stone's Big Hangover: After Lending Binge, Mogul Fights for C.S. First Boston Bonus', *New York Observer*, 11 August 1999, https://observer.com/1999/11/andy-stones-big-hangover-after-lending-binge-mogul-fights-for-cs-first-boston-bonus/

9 Stephanie Baker-Said, 'Credit Suisse Tightens Up on Fiefdoms Amid IPO Probe', Bloomberg, 29 June 2001, https://www.bloomberg.com/news/arti-

cles/2001-06-29/credit-suisse-tightens-up-on-fiefdoms-amid-ipo-probe-correct.

10 Leonard, 'Andy Stone's Big Hangover', *New York Observer*, 11 August 1999.

11 Randall Smith, 'Andrew Stone Is Likely To Leave First Boston', *The Wall Street Journal*, 28 October 1999, https://www.wsj.com/articles/SB94105837635 2859965.

12 Gavin Lumsden, 'Flaming Ferraris live life in the fast lane', *The Times*, 26 December 1998.

13 Silvia Ascarelli, 'Credit Suisse First Boston Fires Traders in London', *The Wall Street Journal*, 8 March 1999, https://www.wsj.com/articles/SB920837394327 890000.

14 Jonathan Watts and Dan Atkinson, 'Case Leaves Credit Suisse Arm's Reputation in Shreds', *The Guardian*, 30 July 1999, https://www.theguardian.com/business/1999/jul/30/16 and Stephanie Baker-Said, 'Credit Suisse Tightens Up on Fiefdoms Amid IPO Probe', Bloomberg, 29 June 2001.

15 'Credit Suisse unit found guilty in Japan', CNN (website), 8 March 2001, https://edition.cnn.com/2001/BUSINESS/asia/03/08/japan.creditsuisse/

16 Stephanie Baker-Said, 'Credit Suisse Tightens Up on Fiefdoms Amid IPO Probe', Bloomberg, 29 June 2001.

17 Squabbling over bonus: Leonard, 'Andy Stone's Big Hangover', *New York Observer*, 11 August 1999. Bad loans: Christine Haughney, 'Risky Business: Former Deal Maker Looks to Get Back Into Real Estate', *The Wall Street Journal*, October 2005, https://www.wsj.com/articles/SB113037848228 780839.

18 Andrew Garfield, 'CSFB's exposure in Russia put at $2.2bn', *The Independent*, 9 September 1998, https://www.independent.co.uk/news/business/csfb-s-exposure-in-russia-put-at-2-2bn-1197151.html. UBS had already merged with Swiss Bank Corporation earlier in the year, increasing the pressure on Credit Suisse.

19 Ibid.

20 Randall Smith, 'Credit Suisse's Wheat Faces Biggest Challenge in Deal', *The Wall Street Journal*, 31 August 2000, https://www.wsj.com/articles/SB9681 83815932681662.

## CHAPTER 8 – THE BUBBLE

1 Randall Smith, *The Prince of Silicon Valley: Frank Quattrone and the Dot-Com Bubble* (New York, NY: St Martin's Press, 2010).

2 'Paranoia Reigns at CSFB; the Milken Spin for Quattrone', *Barron's*, 23 July 2001, https://www.barrons.com/articles/SB99567059253374258?mod=news_archive.

3 Value of tech IPOs and Quattrone salary: Smith, *The Prince of Silicon Valley.*

4 Ibid.

5 Stephanie Baker-Said, 'Credit Suisse Tightens Up on Fiefdoms Amid IPO Probe', Bloomberg, June 2001, https://www.bloomberg.com/news/articles/2001-06-29/credit-suisse-tightens-up-on-fiefdoms-amid-ipo-probe-correct.

6 Anita Raghavan, 'Credit Suisse Hires Quattrone In Bid to Boost High-Tech Effort', *The Wall Street Journal*, 1 July 1998, https://www.wsj.com/articles/SB899254160603702500.

7 Smith, *The Prince of Silicon Valley.*

8 Baker-Said, 'Credit Suisse Tightens Up on Fiefdoms Amid IPO Probe', Bloomberg, June 2001.

9 Smith, *The Prince of Silicon Valley.*

10 'Quattrone's quandary: How to top 1999', *Forbes*, 27 Dec 1999, https://www.forbes.com/1999/12/27/mu3.html?sh=5746ecad769e.

11 Baker-Said, 'Credit Suisse Tightens Up on Fiefdoms Amid IPO Probe', Bloomberg, June 2001.

12 Smith, *The Prince of Silicon Valley.*

13 'Uno, Dos, Tres, Quattrone', *Forbes*, 13 April 2004, https://www.forbes.com/2004/04/13/cx_da_0413topnews.html.

14 Smith, *The Prince of Silicon Valley.* The whole set-up was an 'intricate, highly evolved system of back-scratching and favor trading', according to Smith.

15 Ibid.

16 Jack Willoughby, 'Burning up', *Barron's* (website), 20 March 2000, https://www.barrons.com/articles/SB953335580704470544. The article greatly enhanced *Barron's* reputation among investors at the time. But enthusiasm for its forecasts were tempered later, given that some of the companies it had pointed to as risky, such as Amazon, went on to become enormously successful global businesses. Nevertheless, its broader point about the sector stood.

17 All the email messages cited here were included in court documents that can be found at *United States v. Quattrone* (2006), https://caselaw.findlaw.com/court/us-2nd-circuit/1386292.html.

18 Ibid.

19 Brooke A. Masters, 'Prosecutors Dispute Quattrone on IPOs', *The Washington Post*, 10 October 2003, https://www.washingtonpost.com/archive/

business/2003/10/11/prosecutors-dispute-quattrone-on-ipos/030d2289-
a72e-4765-863b-56d4c1056534/


## CHAPTER 9 – A DEAL AT THE TOP


1 Brian Mullen, 'I wrote a memo saying junior bankers should work 96-hour
weeks', efinancialcareers (website), 6 January 2022, https://www.efinancial
careers.co.uk/news/finance/dlj-memo-too-busy.

2 Randall Smith and Nikhil Deogun, 'UBS Merger Sends Investors Racing to
Buy Securities Stocks', *The Wall Street Journal*, 13 July 2000, https://www.wsj.
com/articles/SB963444340549791165.

3 Monique Wise, 'DLJ Sale Price: $13.4 Billion', *The Washington Post*, 31 August
2000, https://www.washingtonpost.com/archive/business/2000/08/31/dlj-
sale-price-134-billion/42008bbe-4964-4a7b-9027-45eec2075319/

4 Randall Smith, 'Credit Suisse's Wheat Faces His Biggest Challenge in Deal',
*The Wall Street Journal*, 31 August 2000, https://www.wsj.com/articles/SB9
68183815932681662.

5 Randall Smith and Charles Gasparino, 'Credit Suisse Unit Confirms Agreement to Acquire DLJ in a $11.5 Billion Deal', *The Wall Street Journal*, 30
August 2000, https://www.wsj.com/articles/SB967567494108117264. The sale
was an initial payment of $11.5 billion, rising to $13.4 billion.

6 Beth Piskora, 'DLJ'$ Big Payout – But 5,000 May Go in Swiss Bank Merger',
*New York Post*, 31 August 2000, https://nypost.com/2000/08/31/dlj-big-
payout-but-5000-may-go-in-swiss-bank-merger/

7 James Verini, 'The Last Dance: They Decease for Credit Suisse', *New York
Observer*, 11 December 2000, https://observer.com/2000/12/the-last-dance-
they-decease-for-credit-suisse/


## CHAPTER 10 – MACK THE KNIFE


1 Patricia Sellers, 'The Trials of John Mack', *Fortune* magazine, 1 September
2003, available at https://money.cnn.com/magazines/fortune/fortune_
archive/2003/09/01/348191/

2 William Grimes, 'Four Seasons, Lunch Spot for Manhattan's Prime Movers,
Moves On', *The New York Times*, 10 July 2016, https://www.nytimes.
com/2016/07/10/nyregion/four-seasons-lunch-spot-for-manhattans-prime-
movers-moves-on.html.

3 John Mack details the interaction, which has been corroborated with sources, in his autobiography, *Up Close and All In: Life Lessons from a Wall Street Warrior* (London: Simon & Schuster/Simon Element, 2022).

4 Ian Kerr, 'The rise and fall', Financial News (website), 23 July 2001, https://www.fnlondon.com/articles/the-rise-and-fall-20010723, and Antony Currie, 'A murder on Madison Avenue', *Euromoney*, 1 August 2001, https://www.euromoney.com/article/b1320mtmqkb1np/a-murder-on-madison-avenue.

5 Mack, *Up Close and All In*.

6 Ibid.

7 Ibid.

8 Ibid.

9 'Credit Suisse's Mack Buffeted by Wall Street's "Perfect Storm"', Bloomberg, 27 March 2003, https://www.bloomberg.com/news/articles/2003-03-27/credit-suisse-s-mack-buffeted-by-wall-street-s-perfect-storm.

10 Sellers, 'The Trials of John Mack', *Fortune* magazine, 1 September 2003.

11 Emily Thornton, 'Online Extra: Q&A with CSFB's John Mack', Bloomberg Businessweek, 22 September 2002, https://www.bloomberg.com/news/articles/2002-09-22/online-extra-q-and-a-with-csfbs-john-mack.

12 'Credit Suisse's Mack Buffeted by Wall Street's "Perfect Storm"', Bloomberg, 27 March 2003.

13 Mack, *Up Close and All In*.

14 Sellers, 'The Trials of John Mack', *Fortune* magazine, 1 September 2003.

## CHAPTER 11 – ONE BANK

1 Alice Ratcliffe and Christine Harper, 'Gruebel, Credit Suisse Survivor, Enforces Profit Discipline', Bloomberg, 27 June 2006, https://www.bloomberg.com/news/articles/2006-06-27/gruebel-credit-suisse-survivor-enforces-profit-discipline.

2 For instance, before he became CEO, Grübel had met with the New York financier Bernie Madoff, then one of the most high-profile investors anywhere in the world. Madoff managed billions of dollars for wealthy clients, including celebrities like Steven Spielberg and Kyra Sedgwick. Grübel couldn't understand how Madoff generated the extravagant returns he was promising. He advised Credit Suisse's clients to pull their money from Madoff's funds, years before they collapsed, exposing Madoff as the architect of the world's biggest Ponzi scheme. Some Credit Suisse clients ignored the warnings on Madoff and left their money in the US investor's Ponzi scheme; their losses ran to hundreds of millions of dollars. Elena Logutenkova and

Ben Holland, 'Saint Ossie Resisted Madoff as Credit Suisse Man Savior for UBS', Bloomberg, 27 February 2009, https://www.bloomberg.com/news/articles/2009-02-27/saint-ossie-resisted-madoff-as-credit-suisse-man-savior-for-ubs.

3 'The Thunder of Grubel', *Forbes*, 26 December 2006, https://www.forbes.com/forbes/2005/1226/088.html.

4 Geraldine Lambe, 'Towers of Strength: Part 2, Private Banking', *The Banker*, 6 June 2005, https://www.thebanker.com/Private-banking-1118012400.

5 Heidi N. Moore, 'The Next Jamie Dimon and Sandy Weill: "Saint Ossie" at UBS vs. Dougan at Credit Suisse', *The Wall Street Journal*, 26 February 2009, https://www.wsj.com/articles/BL-DLB-6319.

6 Peter Thal Larsen and Haig Simonian, 'Grübel leaves bank in peak condition', *Financial Times*, 15 February 2007, https://www.ft.com/content/382132f4-bd3f-11db-b5bd-0000779e2340.

7 David Gow, 'US investment banker takes helm at Credit Suisse', *The Guardian*, February 2007, https://www.theguardian.com/business/2007/feb/15/13. Footnote: Julia Werdigier, 'UBS Says Trading Losses Were Closer to $2.3 Billion', *The New York Times*, September 2011, https://www.nytimes.com/2011/09/19/business/global/ubs-says-trading-losses-closer-to-2-3-billion.html.

8 Speech by Oswald J. Grübel, Annual General Meeting of Credit Suisse Group, 4 May 2007, https://www.credit-suisse.com/media/assets/corporate/docs/about-us/investor-relations/events-presentations/agm-2007-speech-ojg-en.pdf.

## CHAPTER 12 – THE FINANCIAL CRISIS

1 Julia K. Dean, 'Credit Suisse CEO Expresses Optimism on Economy', *The Harvard Crimson*, 19 September 2011, https://www.thecrimson.com/article/2011/9/19/harvard-dougan-credit-suisse/

2 Jenny Anderson, 'Stepping Lively at Credit Suisse', *The New York Times*, 16 February 2007, https://www.nytimes.com/2007/02/16/business/16bank.html.

3 Peter Thal Larsen and Haig Simonian, 'Grübel leaves bank in peak condition', *Financial Times*, 15 February 2007, https://www.ft.com/content/382132f4-bd3f-11db-b5bd-0000779e2340.

4 Speech by Brady W. Dougan, Annual General Meeting of Credit Suisse Group, 25 April 2008, https://www.credit-suisse.com/media/assets/corporate/docs/about-us/investor-relations/events-presentations/agm-2008-speech-bd-en.pdf.

5 Eric Dash, '5 days of pressure, fear and ultimately, failure', *The New York Times*, 15 September 2008, https://www.nytimes.com/2008/09/15/business/worldbusiness/15iht-reconstruct.4.16159552.html.

6 Reuters Staff, 'UBS considered merger before turning to state-paper', Reuters, 17 October 2008, https://www.reuters.com/article/ubs-report-idUSLH1 3971220081017.

7 Speech by Brady W. Dougan, Annual General Meeting of Credit Suisse Group, 24 April 2009, https://www.credit-suisse.com/media/assets/corporate/docs/about-us/investor-relations/events-presentations/agm-2009-speech-bd-en.pdf.

8 Kareem Serageldin et al., 'U.S. Securities and Exchange Commission: Litigation Release No. 22247 / February 1, 2012', https://www.sec.gov/litigation/litreleases/lr-22247.

9 Ibid.

10 US Attorney's Office, 'Former Credit Suisse Managing Director Sentenced in Manhattan Federal Court to 30 Months in Prison in Connection with Scheme to Hide Losses in Mortgage-Backed Securities Trading Book', FBI Archive, 22 November 2013, https://archives.fbi.gov/archives/newyork/press-releases/2013/former-credit-suisse-managing-director-sentenced-in-manhattan-federal-court-to-30-months-in-prison-in-connection-with-scheme-to-hide-losses-in-mortgage-backed-securities-trading-book.

11 Jesse Eisinger, 'The Rise of Corporate Impunity', ProPublica (website), 30 April 2014, https://www.propublica.org/article/the-rise-of-corporate-impunity.

12 'Credit Suisse Agrees to Pay $5.28 Billion in Connection with its Sale of Residential Mortgage-Backed Securities', US Department of Justice (press release), 18 January 2017, https://www.justice.gov/opa/pr/credit-suisse-agrees-pay-528-billion-connection-its-sale-residential-mortgage-backed.

13 See, for instance, Gretchen Morgensen, 'Credit Suisse Documents Point to Mortgage Lapses', *The New York Times*, 10 March 2014, https://www.nytimes.com/2014/03/10/business/credit-suisse-documents-point-to-mortgage-lapses.html. In 2017, US Attorney General Loretta Lynch said the bank had 'made false and irresponsible representations about residential mortgage-backed securities, which resulted in the loss of billions of dollars of wealth and took a painful toll on the lives of ordinary Americans'. The bank's settlement with the Department of Justice alone was $5.3 billion, one of the largest penalties paid by any bank in relation to the crisis.

## CHAPTER 13 – SANCTIONS BUSTING

1 The following paragraphs draw on details from the Department of Justice as reported in *US v. Credit Suisse AG* 'Factual Statement', 16 December 2009, https://www.justice.gov/opa/pr/credit-suisse-agrees-forfeit-536-million-connection-violations-international-emergency.

2 Claudio Gatti and John Eligon, 'Iranian Dealings Lead to a Fine for Credit Suisse', *The New York Times*, 15 December 2009, https://www.nytimes.com/2009/12/16/business/16bank.html.

## CHAPTER 14 – TAX DODGING

1 The following paragraphs draw from two Department of Justice press releases: 'Former UBS Banker Sentenced to 40 Months for Aiding Billionaire American Evade Taxes', 21 August 2009, https://www.justice.gov/opa/pr/former-ubs-banker-sentenced-40-months-aiding-billionaire-american-evade-taxes and 'UBS Enters into Deferred Prosecution Agreement', 18 February 2009, https://www.justice.gov/opa/pr/ubs-enters-deferred-prosecution-agreement.

2 James Vicini, 'UBS to identify clients, pay $780 million in tax case', Reuters, 19 February 2009, https://www.reuters.com/article/us-ubs-tax-sb-idUSTRE51H7NI20090219.

3 Michael Bronner, 'Telling Swiss Secrets: A banker's betrayal', GlobalPost via the National Whistleblower Center (website), 6 August 2010, https://www.whistleblowers.org/news/telling-swiss-secrets-a-bankers-betrayal/

4 Ibid.

5 Department of Justice press release, 'UBS Enters into Deferred Prosecution Agreement', 18 February 2009.

6 Tom Brown, 'UBS whistleblower asks why he is going to prison', Reuters, 30 December 2009, https://www.reuters.com/article/idUSTRE5BT4DJ/

7 David Kocieniewski, 'Whistle-Blower Awarded $104 Million by I.R.S.', *The New York Times*, 11 September 2012, https://www.nytimes.com/2012/09/12/business/whistle-blower-awarded-104-million-by-irs.html.

8 Robert D. McFadden, 'Carl Levin, the Senate Scourge of Corporate America, Dies at 87', *The New York Times*, 29 July 2021, https://www.nytimes.com/2021/07/29/us/politics/carl-levin-dead.html.

9 Many of the details in this section are to be found in the following document: United States Senate Permanent Subcommittee on Investigations, 'Offshore Tax Evasion: The Effort to Collect Unpaid Taxes on Billions in Hidden Offshore Accounts', 26 February 2014, https://www.hsgac.senate.gov/

wp-content/uploads/imo/media/doc/REPORT%20-%20OFFSHORE%20
TAX%20EVASION%20(Feb%2026%202014,%208-20-14%20FINAL).pdf.

10 Karin Matussek, 'Credit Suisse's German Offices Raided in Tax Probe', Bloomberg, 14 July 2010, https://www.bloomberg.com/news/articles/2010-07-14/credit-suisse-has-13-german-offices-searched-as-part-of-tax-evasion-probe.

11 Department of Justice press release, 'Four Swiss Bankers Charged with Helping U.S. Taxpayers Use Secret Accounts at Swiss Banks to Evade U.S. Taxes', 23 February 2011, https://www.justice.gov/opa/pr/four-swiss-bankers-charged-helping-us-taxpayers-use-secret-accounts-swiss-banks-evade-us.

12 Ibid.

## CHAPTER 15 – DOUGAN'S DOWNFALL

1 Daniel Schäfer, 'SNB Puts Spotlight on Credit Suisse', *Financial Times*, 17 June 2012 https://www.ft.com/content/5190b404-b720-11e1-bdoe-0014 4feabdco.

2 Simone Foxman, 'Credit Suisse To SNB: Sorry But We're Not Going To Listen To You', Business Insider (website), 17 June 2012, https://www.business insider.com/credit-suisse-to-snb-sorry-but-were-not-going-to-listen-to-you-2012-6?r=US&IR=T.

3 Emma Thomasson, 'C. Suisse CEO – no plans for capital hike after SNB', Reuters, 17 June 2012, https://www.reuters.com/article/creditsuisse-capital-idUKL5E8HH1F720120617.

4 Katharina Bart, 'Credit Suisse boss under pressure despite outsmarting rivals', Reuters, 3 December 2012, https://www.reuters.com/article/uk-creditsuisse-ceo-idUKBRE8B20DU20121203.

5 John Letzing and David Enrich, 'Credit Suisse CEO Brady Dougan Nearly Lost Job During Tax Probe', *The Wall Street Journal*, 20 May 2014, https://www.wsj.com/articles/SB10001424052702304198504579573720899025160.

6 Dirk Schütz, *Too Close to the Wind: Why Credit Suisse had to go down* (Zurich: Beobachter Edition, 2023).

7 Katharina Bart, 'Ex-Credit Suisse chairman calls Dougan's 90 million Swiss francs payout a "mistake"', Reuters, 28 October 2013, https://www.reuters.com/article/us-creditsuisse-idUSBRE99R10D20131028.

8 Senator Carl Levin, Opening Statement: Senate Permanent Subcommittee on Investigations Hearing on 'Offshore Tax Evasion: The Effort to Collect Unpaid Taxes on Billions in Hidden Offshore Accounts', 26 February 2014, https://www.hsgac.senate.gov/wp-content/uploads/imo/media/doc/

OPENING%20STMT%20-%20Senator%20Carl%20Levin%20(Feb%20 26%202014).pdf.

9 Letzing and Enrich, 'Credit Suisse CEO Brady Dougan Nearly Lost Job During Tax Probe', *The Wall Street Journal*, 20 May 2014.

10 Rachel Bade, '$2.6 Billion Penalty for Credit Suisse', *Politico*, 19 May 2014, https://www.politico.com/story/2014/05/credit-suisse-tax-conspiracy-106851.

11 John Letzing and Christopher M. Matthews, 'Credit Suisse Monitor Neil Barofsky Does Job With Gusto', *The Wall Street Journal*, 30 April 2015, https:// www.wsj.com/articles/credit-suisse-monitor-neil-barofsky-does-job-with-gusto-1430384275.

12 Department of Justice press release, 'Credit Suisse Pleads Guilty to Conspiracy to Aid and Assist U.S. Taxpayers in Filing False Returns', 19 May 2014, https://www.justice.gov/opa/pr/credit-suisse-pleads-guilty-conspiracy-aid-and-assist-us-taxpayers-filing-false-returns.

13 Bade, '$2.6 Billion Penalty for Credit Suisse', *Politico*, 19 May 2014.

14 Lynnley Browning, 'How Credit Suisse Got Off Easy', *Newsweek*, 19 June 2014, https://www.newsweek.com/2014/06/27/how-credit-suisse-got-easy-255453.html.

15 Katharina Bart, 'Swiss pressure rises on Credit Suisse boss Dougan after U.S. deal', Reuters, 21 May 2014, https://www.reuters.com/article/uk-creditsuisse-dougan-idUKKBN0E11S420140521.

16 James Shotter, Martin Arnold and Daniel Schäfer, 'Dougan says no plan to quit Credit Suisse after fine', *Financial Times*, 20 May 2014, https://www.ft.com/content/d50f434e-dfe7-11e3-b709-00144feabdc0.

17 Clive Horwood, 'Best global bank 2014: UBS – Model of a modern bank', *Euromoney*, 10 July 2014, https://www.euromoney.com/article/b12kjytzpovt sd/best-global-bank-2014-ubs-model-of-a-modern-bank.

18 Katharina Bart, 'Credit Suisse under pressure, despite outsmarting rival', Reuters, 3 December 2012, https://www.reuters.com/article/uk-creditsuisse-ceo-idUKBRE8B20DU20121203.

## CHAPTER 16 – THE MAN FROM THE PRUDENTIAL

1 John Letzing, 'New Credit Suisse CEO Tidjane Thiam Reins in Hopes for a Quick Fix', *The Wall Street Journal*, 6 July 2015, https://www.wsj.com/articles/ new-credit-suisse-ceo-reins-in-hopes-for-a-quick-fix-1435951423.

2 David Teather, 'Very British Coup for an African Francophone', *The Guardian*, 4 May 2007, https://www.theguardian.com/business/2007/may/04/ insurance.money.

3 Jeffrey Vögeli and Sarah Jones, 'Credit Suisse Names Thiam Chief to Replace Dougan', Bloomberg, 10 March 2015, https://www.bloomberg.com/news/articles/2015-03-10/credit-suisse-names-prudential-s-thiam-as-ceo-to-replace-dougan.

## CHAPTER 17 – CAPITAL LETTERS

1 John Letzing, 'Credit Suisse to Launch $6.3 Billion Capital Increase', *The Wall Street Journal*, 21 October 2015, https://www.wsj.com/articles/credit-suisse-to-launch-6-3-billion-capital-increase-1445402936.

2 Joshua Franklin, 'Credit Suisse faces tough questions after $1 billion write-downs', Reuters, 11 April 2016, https://www.reuters.com/article/us-credit-suisse-writedowns-idUSKCN0X12F9.

3 Donal Griffin and Vogeli Voegeli, 'Credit Suisse Confusion on Costly Trades Adds to CEO's Woes', Tidjane Thiam interview with Bloomberg, 24 March 2016, https://www.bloomberg.com/news/articles/2016-03-24/credit-suisse-confusion-on-costly-trades-casts-pall-on-overhaul.

4 Jenny Strasburg, John Letzing and Max Colchester, 'Inside Credit Suisse, Finger-Pointing and Confusion Over $1 Billion Loss', *The Wall Street Journal*, 28 April 2016, https://www.wsj.com/articles/inside-credit-suisse-finger-pointing-and-confusion-over-1-billion-loss-1461868516.

5 Vogeli Voegeli, 'Pay Is a Battle Ground as Bankers Don't Accept Cuts, Thiam Says', Bloomberg, 12 January 2016, https://www.bloomberg.com/news/articles/2016-01-12/pay-is-a-battle-ground-as-bankers-don-t-accept-cuts-thiam-says.

6 Strasburg, Letzing and Colchester, 'Inside Credit Suisse, Finger-Pointing and Confusion Over $1 Billion Loss', *The Wall Street Journal*, 28 April 2016.

7 Joshua Franklin, 'Credit Suisse's Thiam faces shareholder ire at AGM', Reuters, 29 April 2016, https://www.reuters.com/article/us-credit-suisse-gp-agm-idUSKCN0XQoVX.

8 Francine Lacqua, 'Q&A With Tidjane Thiam: "I Will Never Declare Victory"', Bloomberg, 9 August 2016, https://www.bloomberg.com/features/2016-tidjane-thiam-interview/

## CHAPTER 18 – TUNA BONDS

1 US Securities and Exchange Commission press release, 'Barclays, Credit Suisse Charged With Dark Pool Violations', 31 January 2016, https://www.sec.gov/news/press-release/2016-16.

2 Tom Wright and Bradley Hope, 'The Billion-Dollar Mystery Man and the Wildest Party Vegas Ever Saw', *The Wall Street Journal*, 15 September 2018, https://www.wsj.com/articles/the-billion-dollar-mystery-man-and-the-wildest-party-vegas-ever-saw-1536984061.

3 US Securities and Exchange Commission press release, 'SEC Charges Goldman Sachs with FCPA Violations', 22 October 2020, https://www.sec.gov/news/press-release/2020-265.

4 Many of the details related to this episode can be found in various legal cases related to the events described in this chapter, including testimony in the US District Court of the Eastern District of New York, *USA v. Jean Boustani*, October 2019, and *US v. Credit Suisse Securities (Europe) Limited*, October 2021, and submissions to the UK's High Court of Justice, the Republic of Mozambique, and Credit Suisse International & Ors., and Manuel Chang & Ors., December 2023.

5 Matt Wirz and Julie Wernau, 'Tuna, and Gunships: How $850 Million in Bonds Went Bad in Mozambique', *The Wall Street Journal*, 3 April 2016, https://www.wsj.com/articles/tuna-and-gunships-how-850-million-in-bonds-went-bad-in-mozambique-1459675803.

6 Ibid.

7 Ibid.

8 Aslak Orre et al., 'Costs and consequences of the hidden debt scandal of Mozambique', Chr. Michelsen Institute and Centro de Integridade Pública, May 2021, https://www.cmi.no/publications/7841-costs-and-consequences-of-the-hidden-debt-scandal-of-mozambique.

## CHAPTER 19 – THE LESCAUDRON AFFAIR

1 Bethany McLean, ' "The battle has started": Ex-Credit Suisse banker's fraud victims still want an apology', Yahoo News (website), 15 July 2019, https://finance.yahoo.com/news/credit-suisse-patrice-lescaudron-fraud-130345221.html. This article includes many details about Lescaudron's career, some of them derived from his interviews with police.

2 Project Beta, Investigation at Credit Suisse AG on behalf of the Swiss Financial Market Supervisory Authority (FINMA), April 2017. This report includes many details pertaining to Credit Suisse's actions during this period.

3 Stephanie Nebehay and Brenna Hughes Neghaiwi, 'Former Credit Suisse "star" gets five-year jail term for "clever fraud"', Reuters, 9 February 2018, https://www.reuters.com/article/credit-suisse-gp-crime-idUSKBN1FT1Uo.

4 Court documents from the Supreme Court of Bermuda, *Bidzina Ivanishvili et al. v. Credit Suisse Life (Bermuda) Limited*, 29 March 2022, https://www.gov.bm/sites/default/files/FINAL-Judgment-2017_No_293_civ_2020_No_373_civ_Bidzina_Ivanishvili_et_al_v_Credit_Suisse_Life_Bermuda_Limited_with_citation.pdf.

5 Court documents from the Singapore International Commercial Court of the Republic of Singapore, *Bidzina Ivanishvili et al. v. Credit Suisse Trust Limited*, 26 May 2023, https://www.elitigation.sg/gd/s/2023_SGHCI_9.

6 Hugo Miller and Ava Benny-Morrison, 'DOJ Steps Up Probe of Credit Suisse and UBS Over Sanctions Breaches', Bloomberg, 27 September 2023, https://www.bloomberg.com/news/articles/2023-09-27/ubs-credit-suisse-face-growing-probe-over-alleged-russian-sanctions-evasion.

7 Nebehay and Hughes Neghaiwi, 'Former Credit Suisse "star" gets five-year jail term for "clever fraud"', Reuters, 9 February 2018.

8 'Ex-Credit Suisse Banker Commits Suicide', finews.com, 13 August 2020, https://www.finews.com/news/english-news/42487-ex-credit-suisse-banker-suicide-suicide-bidzina-ivanishvili-patrice-lescaudron-georgia-fraud.

9 Sven Milischer, 'Ex-Starbanker der Credit Suisse begeht Suizid', Handelszeitung, 13 August 2020, https://www.handelszeitung.ch/unternehmen/ex-starbanker-der-credit-suisse-begeht-suizid-308229.

## CHAPTER 20 – THE ESTABLISHMENT

1 David McLaughlin, 'U.S. Faults Foot-Dragging Banks Amid Deutsche Bank Talks', Bloomberg, 27 September 2016, https://www.bloomberg.com/news/articles/2016-09-27/u-s-urges-cooperation-from-banks-to-settle-mortgage-cases.

2 Sam Meredith, 'Credit Suisse CEO responds to calls for bank to break up – and will meet with activist investor', CNBC (website), 2 November 2017, https://www.cnbc.com/2017/11/02/credit-suisse-ceo-responds-to-calls-for-bank-to-break-up.html.

3 Lukas Hässig, 'Thiam zerstörte Parkett in WEF-Nobelloge', 14 May 2019, https://insideparadeplatz.ch/2019/05/14/thiam-zerstoerte-parkett-in-wef-nobelloge/

## CHAPTER 21 – SPYGATE

1 Oliver Hirt and Brenna Hughes Neghaiwi, 'Julius Baer has Credit Suisse wealth manager Khan on list for CEO job – sources', Reuters, 29 March 2019, https://www.reuters.com/article/idUSKCN1RA1S4/

2 Zoé Baches, Ermes Gallarotti, Martin Beglinger, 'Affäre Khan Teil 1 von 3: Ein weiterer Kadermann der Credit Suisse wurde observiert', *NZZ Magazin*, 17 December 2019, https://www.nzz.ch/wirtschaft/affaere-khan-ein-weiterer-kadermann-der-credit-suisse-wurde-observiert-ld.1528911.

3 The Hewlett-Packard spying scandal was first revealed by *Newsweek* magazine: David A. Kaplan, 'Suspicions and Spies in Silicon Valley', *Newsweek*, 17 September 2006, https://www.newsweek.com/suspicions-and-spies-silicon-valley-109827.

4 Elliot Smith, 'Credit Suisse CEO reads out a letter from the family of a contractor who committed suicide', CNBC (website), 30 October 2019, https://www.cnbc.com/2019/10/30/credit-suisse-ceo-letter-from-contractors-family-who-committed-suicide.html.

5 Gretchen Morgensen, 'Ex-Credit Suisse Exec says she was fired and harassed when she wouldn't bend accounting rules', NBC News (website), 11 December 2019, https://www.nbcnews.com/business/corporations/ex-credit-suisse-exec-says-she-was-fired-harassed-when-n1100046.

6 'Herro Says He's 100% Behind Credit Suisse CEO Thiam', Bloomberg Surveillance, 3 February 2020, https://www.bloomberg.com/news/videos/2020-02-03/herro-says-he-s-100-behind-credit-suisse-ceo-thiam-video.

7 Margot Patrick and Patricia Kowsmann, 'Credit Suisse Spied on More Employees Than Previously Disclosed', *The Wall Street Journal*, 30 November 2020, https://www.wsj.com/articles/credit-suisse-spied-on-more-employees-than-previously-disclosed-11606731591?mod=article_inline.

8 FINMA press release, 'Credit Suisse observation activities: FINMA identifies serious breaches of supervisory law', 19 October 2021, https://www.FINMA.ch/en/news/2021/10/20211019---mm---obs/

9 Owen Walker and Stephen Morris, 'Former Credit Suisse Chief Tidjane Thiam Defends His Record', *Financial Times*, 29 November 2022, https://www.ft.com/content/97b5d4c8-e000-4bdd-aaf4-b289397dc753.

## CHAPTER 22 – A GLIMPSE OF THE END

1 Pranav Nair, 'Wirecard Bonds Selling at 12% of Notional Value – Bloomberg', S&P Global Market Intelligence (website), 10 July 2020, https://www.

spglobal.com/marketintelligence/en/news-insights/latest-news-headlines/
wirecard-bonds-selling-at-12-of-notional-worth-8211-bloomberg-59368963.

2 'Bulgarian criminal organisation: indictment filed against organisation
members and Credit Suisse', Office of the Attorney General of Switzerland,
17 December 2020, https://www.admin.ch/gov/en/start/documentation/
media-releases.msg-id-81686.html.

3 Swiss Federal Criminal Court press release, 'Strafsache Bundesanwalts
chaft gegen Credit Suisse AG und wietere Beschuldigte', 27 June 2022,
https://www.bstger.ch/en/media/comunicati-stampa/2022/2022-06-27/
1275.html.

4 Credit Suisse media release, 'Credit Suisse Second Quarter 2020 financial
results', 30 July 2020, https://www.credit-suisse.com/media/assets/corporate/
docs/about-us/media/media-release/2020/07/q2-20-press-release-en.pdf.

5 Owen Walker and Stephen Morris, 'Credit Suisse chief vows a "clean slate"
in 2021', *Financial Times*, 20 December 2020, https://www.ft.com/content/
47471301-2898-4144-9882-475dcf4030ab.

## CHAPTER 23 – GREENSILL

1 Duncan Mavin, 'Inside the Investigation That Brought Down a Star Trader',
*Barron's*, 25 March 2020, https://www.barrons.com/articles/gam-scandal-
inside-the-probe-into-star-traders-conduct-51585084312.

2 Duncan Mavin, 'Yield-hungry investors pile into Credit Suisse supply-chain
funds', Financial News (website), 2 December 2019, https://www.fnlondon.
com/articles/yield-hungry-investors-pile-into-credit-suisse-supply-chain-
funds-20191202.

3 I covered this in detail in my book *Pyramid of Lies: The Prime Minister, the
Banker and the Billion-Pound Scandal* (London: Macmillan, 2022). Press
reports: Duncan Mavin, 'How Credit Suisse's clients finance Softbank's
Vision Fund', Financial News (website), 28 April 2020, https://www.fnlondon.
com/articles/how-credit-suisse-clients-finance-softbanks-vision-fund-
20200428, and Robert Smith and Arash Massoudi, 'SoftBank invests
in Credit Suisse funds that finance its technology bets', *Financial Times*,
14 June 2020, https://www.ft.com/content/6995af3b-5f66-4e1b-9143-1e9dac
cfc9b4.

4 FINMA press release, 'FINMA concludes "Greensill" proceedings against
Credit Suisse', 28 February 2023, https://www.FINMA.ch/en/news/2023/02/
20230228-mm-greensill/

## CHAPTER 24 – ROHNER'S LAST STAND

1 US Securities and Exchange Commission press release, 'Hedge Fund Manager to Pay $44 Million for Illegal Trading in Chinese Bank Stocks', 12 December 2012, https://www.sec.gov/news/press-release/2012-2012-264htm, and Paul, Weiss, Rifkind, Wharton & Garrison LLP, 'Credit Suisse Group Special Committee of the Board of Directors Report on Archegos Capital Management', 29 July 2021, https://www.credit-suisse.com/about-us/en/reports-research/archegos-info-kit.html.

2 Emily Glazer, Maureen Farrell and Margot Patrick, 'Inside Credit Suisse's $5.5 Billion Breakdown', *The Wall Street Journal*, 7 June 2021, https://www.wsj.com/articles/inside-credit-suisses-5-5-billion-breakdown-archegos-11623072713.

3 Ermes Gallarotti, Chanchal Biswas, Andre Muller, 'Credit-Suisse-Chef Thomas Gottstein: "Was in den USA passiert ist, ist absolut inakzeptabel"', *NZZ*, 6 April 2021, https://www.nzz.ch/wirtschaft/was-in-den-usa-passiert-ist-ist-absolut-inakzeptabel-sagt-credit-suisse-chef-thomas-gottstein-ld.1610113.

4 Credit Suisse Group Special Committee of the Board of Directors report on Archegos Capital Management, July 29, 2021, https://www.credit-suisse.com/about-us/en/reports-research/archegos-info-kit.html.

5 Matthew Goldstein and Lananh Nguyen, 'Archegos stock manipulation was "historic", U.S. attorney says', *The New York Times*, 27 April 2021, https://www.nytimes.com/2022/04/27/business/archegos-bill-hwang-patrick-halligan.html.

## CHAPTER 25 – ANTÓNIO

1 Sean Farrell, 'Lloyds chief apologises for damage caused by affair allegations', *The Guardian*, 24 August 2016, https://www.theguardian.com/business/2016/aug/24/lloyds-chief-antonio-horta-osorio-apologises-damage-caused-affair-allegations.

2 Christian Dorer and Guido Schätti, 'Credit-Suisse-Präsident António Horta-Osório zeigt sich selbst an', *Blick*, 8 December 2021, https://www.blick.ch/wirtschaft/nach-einreise-aus-risikoland-credit-suisse-praesident-verstoesst-gegen-quarantaenepflicht-id17052079.html.

## CHAPTER 26 – THE CRISIS ESCALATES

1 Organized Crime and Corruption Reporting Project, 'Suisse Secrets', 20 February 2022, https://www.occrp.org/en/suisse-secrets/
2 Organized Crime and Corruption Reporting Project and *Süddeutsche Zeitung*, 'Historic Leak of Swiss Banking Records Reveals Unsavory Clients', 20 February 2022, https://www.occrp.org/en/suisse-secrets/historic-leak-of-swiss-banking-records-reveals-unsavory-clients.

## CHAPTER 27 – THE X FACTOR

1 Credit Suisse media release, 'Credit Suisse makes strong progress on Group strategic priorities; reports net revenues of CHF 3.1 bn and pre-tax loss of CHF 1.3 bn along with a CET1 ratio of 14.1% in 4Q22', 9 February 2023, https://www.credit-suisse.com/media/assets/corporate/docs/about-us/media/media-release/2023/02/q4-22-press-release-en.pdf.
2 FINMA, 'FINMA Report: Lessons Learned from the CS Crisis', 19 December 2023, https://www.finma.ch/en/~/media/finma/dokumente/dokumentencenter/myfinma/finma-publikationen/cs-bericht/20231219-finma-bericht-cs.pdf?sc_lang=en&hash=3F13A6D9398F2F55B90347A64E269F44.
3 Credit Suisse media release, 'Credit Suisse unveils new strategy and transformation plan', 27 October 2022, https://www.credit-suisse.com/media/assets/corporate/docs/about-us/media/media-release/2022/10/strategy-update-press-release-en.pdf.

## CHAPTER 28 – THE REGULATORS

1 Credit Suisse press release, 'Credit Suisse announces the acquisition of The Klein Group LLC, the appointment of Michael Klein as Chief Executive Officer of Banking and of the Americas as well as CEO designate of CS First Boston', 9 February 2023, https://www.credit-suisse.com/about-us-news/en/articles/media-releases/acquisition-klein-group-llc-appointment-michael-klein-csfb-202302.html.
2 Myriam Belazou, 'Credit Suisse Chief Not Concerned Over Conflicts in Klein Deal', Bloomberg, 18 January 2023, https://www.bloomberg.com/news/articles/2023-01-18/credit-suisse-chief-not-concerned-over-conflicts-in-klein-deal.
3 'FINMA concludes "Greensill" proceedings against Credit Suisse', 28 February 2023, https://www.finma.ch/en/news/2023/02/20230228-mm-greensill/.

## CHAPTER 29 – SILICON VALLEY BANK

1 Felix Salmon, 'The largest bank run in history', Axios (website), 11 March 2023, https://www.axios.com/2023/03/11/the-largest-bank-run-in-history.


## CHAPTER 30 – THE TAKEOVER

1 Credit Suisse press release, 'Credit Suisse announces technical delay of publication of 2022 Annual Report', 9 March 2023, https://www.credit-suisse.com/about-us-news/en/articles/media-releases/csg-announces-delay-publication-2022-annual-report-202303.html.

2 US Securities and Exchange Commission, letter to David Mathers, 15 July 2022, https://www.sec.gov/Archives/edgar/data/1053092/000000000022007501/filename1.pdf.

3 David Mathers, letter to US Securities and Exchange Commission, 22 August 2022, https://www.sec.gov/Archives/edgar/data/1159510/000110465922093402/filename1.htm.

4 Christof Leisinger, 'Das Fed garantiert die Einlagen der Silicon Valley Bank und der Signature-Bank. Die Behörde ist mitschuld an den Turbulenzen der vergangenen Tage', *NZZ*, 13 March 2023, https://www.nzz.ch/wirtschaft/nach-der-bankpleite-die-angst-vor-einer-kettenreaktion-haelt-washington-auf-trab-ld.1730090.


## EPILOGUE

1 Hugo Miller and Ava Benny-Morrison, 'DOJ Steps Up Probe of Credit Suisse and UBS Over Sanctions Breaches', Bloomberg, 27 September 2023, https://www.bloomberg.com/news/articles/2023-09-27/ubs-credit-suisse-face-growing-probe-over-alleged-russian-sanctions-evasion.

2 Margot Patrick, 'How a Banking Capital of the World Botched Its Own Banking Rules', *The Wall Street Journal*, 8 November 2023, https://www.wsj.com/finance/banking/how-a-banking-capital-of-the-world-botched-its-own-banking-rules-ad4dcc2b.

3 Jonathan Guthrie, 'What I have learnt in 37 years in financial journalism', *Financial Times*, 10 December 2023, https://www.ft.com/content/2d92cb41-9381-44f7-b71f-e859131c7c2e.

# Index

## ABOUT THE AUTHOR

Duncan Mavin is a seasoned international financial journalist. He is currently an editor at *Bloomberg News* in London, and has previously been a reporter, editor and columnist for *The Wall Street Journal*, *The Washington Post*, *Barron's* and Canada's *National Post*. He's also the bestselling author of *Pyramid of Lies*, the political and financial exposé about the Greensill scandal that *The Sunday Times* dubbed 'Britain's version of *Bad Blood*'.